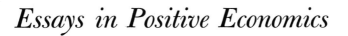

Essays in Positive Economics

Essays in Positive Economics

BY

MILTON FRIEDMAN

THE UNIVERSITY OF CHICAGO PRESS

*Acknowledgment is hereby made to the following publishers
for permission to reprint material which originally
appeared over their imprints:*

AMERICAN ECONOMIC REVIEW

RICHARD D. IRWIN, INC.

HARVARD UNIVERSITY PRESS

THE UNIVERSITY OF CHICAGO PRESS, CHICAGO 37
Cambridge University Press, London, N.W. 1, England

Table of Contents

PART I

Introduction

The Methodology of Positive Economics*

I N HIS admirable book on *The Scope and Method of Political
Economy* John Neville Keynes distinguishes among "a *positive
science* . . . [,] a body of systematized knowledge concerning
what is; a *normative* or *regulative science* . . . [,] a body of systematized knowledge discussing criteria of what ought to be
. . . ; an *art* . . . [,] a system of rules for the attainment of a
given end"; comments that "confusion between them is common and has been the source of many mischievous errors"; and
urges the importance of "recognizing a distinct positive science
of political economy."[1]

This paper is concerned primarily with certain methodological
problems that arise in constructing the "distinct positive science"
Keynes called for—in particular, the problem how to decide
whether a suggested hypothesis or theory should be tentatively
accepted as part of the "body of systematized knowledge concerning what is." But the confusion Keynes laments is still so
rife and so much of a hindrance to the recognition that economics can be, and in part is, a positive science that it seems well
to preface the main body of the paper with a few remarks about
the relation between positive and normative economics.

I. THE RELATION BETWEEN POSITIVE AND NORMATIVE
ECONOMICS

Confusion between positive and normative economics is to
some extent inevitable. The subject matter of economics is regarded by almost everyone as vitally important to himself and
within the range of his own experience and competence; it is

* I have incorporated bodily in this article without special reference most of my
brief "Comment" in *A Survey of Contemporary Economics,* Vol. II (B. F. Haley,
ed.) (Chicago: Richard D. Irwin, Inc., 1952), pp. 455–57.

I am indebted to Dorothy S. Brady, Arthur F. Burns, and George J. Stigler for
helpful comments and criticism.

1. (London: Macmillan & Co., 1891), pp. 34–35 and 46.

the source of continuous and extensive controversy and the occasion for frequent legislation. Self-proclaimed "experts" speak with many voices and can hardly all be regarded as disinterested; in any event, on questions that matter so much, "expert" opinion could hardly be accepted solely on faith even if the "experts" were nearly unanimous and clearly disinterested.[2] The conclusions of positive economics seem to be, and are, immediately relevant to important normative problems, to questions of what ought to be done and how any given goal can be attained. Laymen and experts alike are inevitably tempted to shape positive conclusions to fit strongly held normative preconceptions and to reject positive conclusions if their normative implications—or what are said to be their normative implications—are unpalatable.

Positive economics is in principle independent of any particular ethical position or normative judgments. As Keynes says, it deals with "what is," not with "what ought to be." Its task is to provide a system of generalizations that can be used to make correct predictions about the consequences of any change in circumstances. Its performance is to be judged by the precision, scope, and conformity with experience of the predictions it yields. In short, positive economics is, or can be, an "objective" science, in precisely the same sense as any of the physical sciences. Of course, the fact that economics deals with the interrelations of human beings, and that the investigator is himself part of the subject matter being investigated in a more intimate sense than in the physical sciences, raises special difficulties in achieving objectivity at the same time that it provides the social scientist with a class of data not available to the physical sci-

2. Social science or economics is by no means peculiar in this respect—witness the importance of personal beliefs and of "home" remedies in medicine wherever obviously convincing evidence for "expert" opinion is lacking. The current prestige and acceptance of the views of physical scientists in their fields of specialization—and, all too often, in other fields as well—derives, not from faith alone, but from the evidence of their works, the success of their predictions, and the dramatic achievements from applying their results. When economics seemed to provide such evidence of its worth, in Great Britain in the first half of the nineteenth century, the prestige and acceptance of "scientific economics" rivaled the current prestige of the physical sciences.

entist. But neither the one nor the other is, in my view, a fundamental distinction between the two groups of sciences.[3]

Normative economics and the art of economics, on the other hand, cannot be independent of positive economics. Any policy conclusion necessarily rests on a prediction about the consequences of doing one thing rather than another, a prediction that must be based—implicitly or explicitly—on positive economics. There is not, of course, a one-to-one relation between policy conclusions and the conclusions of positive economics; if there were, there would be no separate normative science. Two individuals may agree on the consequences of a particular piece of legislation. One may regard them as desirable on balance and so favor the legislation; the other, as undesirable and so oppose the legislation.

I venture the judgment, however, that currently in the Western world, and especially in the United States, differences about economic policy among disinterested citizens derive predominantly from different predictions about the economic consequences of taking action—differences that in principle can be eliminated by the progress of positive economics—rather than from fundamental differences in basic values, differences about which men can ultimately only fight. An obvious and not unimportant example is minimum-wage legislation. Underneath the welter of arguments offered for and against such legislation there is an underlying consensus on the objective of achieving a "living wage" for all, to use the ambiguous phrase so common in such discussions. The difference of opinion is largely grounded on an implicit or explicit difference in predictions about the efficacy of this particular means in furthering the agreed-on end. Proponents believe (predict) that legal minimum wages diminish poverty by raising the wages of those receiving less than the minimum wage as well as of some receiving more than the

3. The interaction between the observer and the process observed that is so prominent a feature of the social sciences, besides its more obvious parallel in the physical sciences, has a more subtle counterpart in the indeterminacy principle arising out of the interaction between the process of measurement and the phenomena being measured. And both have a counterpart in pure logic in Gödel's theorem, asserting the impossibility of a comprehensive self-contained logic. It is an open question whether all three can be regarded as different formulations of an even more general principle.

minimum wage without any counterbalancing increase in the number of people entirely unemployed or employed less advantageously than they otherwise would be. Opponents believe (predict) that legal minimum wages increase poverty by increasing the number of people who are unemployed or employed less advantageously and that this more than offsets any favorable effect on the wages of those who remain employed. Agreement about the economic consequences of the legislation might not produce complete agreement about its desirability, for differences might still remain about its political or social consequences; but, given agreement on objectives, it would certainly go a long way toward producing consensus.

Closely related differences in positive analysis underlie divergent views about the appropriate role and place of trade-unions and the desirability of direct price and wage controls and of tariffs. Different predictions about the importance of so-called "economies of scale" account very largely for divergent views about the desirability or necessity of detailed government regulation of industry and even of socialism rather than private enterprise. And this list could be extended indefinitely.[4] Of course, my judgment that the major differences about economic policy in the Western world are of this kind is itself a "positive" statement to be accepted or rejected on the basis of empirical evidence.

If this judgment is valid, it means that a consensus on "correct" economic policy depends much less on the progress of normative economics proper than on the progress of a positive economics yielding conclusions that are, and deserve to be, widely accepted. It means also that a major reason for dis-

4. One rather more complex example is stabilization policy. Superficially, divergent views on this question seem to reflect differences in objectives; but I believe that this impression is misleading and that at bottom the different views reflect primarily different judgments about the source of fluctuations in economic activity and the effect of alternative countercyclical action. For one major positive consideration that accounts for much of the divergence see "The Effects of a Full-Employment Policy on Economic Stability: A Formal Analysis," *infra,* pp. 117–32. For a summary of the present state of professional views on this question see "The Problem of Economic Instability," a report of a subcommittee of the Committee on Public Issues of the American Economic Association, *American Economic Review,* XL (September, 1950), 501–38.

tinguishing positive economics sharply from normative economics is precisely the contribution that can thereby be made to
agreement about policy.

II. Positive Economics

The ultimate goal of a positive science is the development of
a "theory" or "hypothesis" that yields valid and meaningful
(i.e., not truistic) predictions about phenomena not yet observed. Such a theory is, in general, a complex intermixture of
two elements. In part, it is a "language" designed to promote
"systematic and organized methods of reasoning."[5] In part, it
is a body of substantive hypotheses designed to abstract essential features of complex reality.

Viewed as a language, theory has no substantive content; it
is a set of tautologies. Its function is to serve as a filing system
for organizing empirical material and facilitating our understanding of it; and the criteria by which it is to be judged are
those appropriate to a filing system. Are the categories clearly
and precisely defined? Are they exhaustive? Do we know where
to file each individual item, or is there considerable ambiguity?
Is the system of headings and subheadings so designed that we
can quickly find an item we want, or must we hunt from place
to place? Are the items we shall want to consider jointly filed
together? Does the filing system avoid elaborate cross-references?

The answers to these questions depend partly on logical, partly
on factual, considerations. The canons of formal logic alone can
show whether a particular language is complete and consistent,
that is, whether propositions in the language are "right" or
"wrong." Factual evidence alone can show whether the categories of the "analytical filing system" have a meaningful empirical counterpart, that is, whether they are useful in analyzing
a particular class of concrete problems.[6] The simple example of
"supply" and "demand" illustrates both this point and the pre-

5. Final quoted phrase from Alfred Marshall, "The Present Position of Economics" (1885), reprinted in *Memorials of Alfred Marshall*, ed. A. C. Pigou (London: Macmillan & Co., 1925), p. 164. See also "The Marshallian Demand Curve,"
infra, pp. 56–57, 90–91.

6. See "Lange on Price Flexibility and Employment: A Methodological Criticism," *infra*, pp. 282–89.

ceding list of analogical questions. Viewed as elements of the language of economic theory, these are the two major categories into which factors affecting the relative prices of products or factors of production are classified. The usefulness of the dichotomy depends on the "empirical generalization that an enumeration of the forces affecting demand in any problem and of the forces affecting supply will yield two lists that contain few items in common."[7] Now this generalization is valid for markets like the final market for a consumer good. In such a market there is a clear and sharp distinction between the economic units that can be regarded as demanding the product and those that can be regarded as supplying it. There is seldom much doubt whether a particular factor should be classified as affecting supply, on the one hand, or demand, on the other; and there is seldom much necessity for considering cross-effects (cross-references) between the two categories. In these cases the simple and even obvious step of filing the relevant factors under the headings of "supply" and "demand" effects a great simplification of the problem and is an effective safeguard against fallacies that otherwise tend to occur. But the generalization is not always valid. For example, it is not valid for the day-to-day fluctuations of prices in a primarily speculative market. Is a rumor of an increased excess-profits tax, for example, to be regarded as a factor operating primarily on today's supply of corporate equities in the stock market or on today's demand for them? In similar fashion, almost every factor can with about as much justification be classified under the heading "supply" as under the heading "demand." These concepts can still be used and may not be entirely pointless; they are still "right" but clearly less useful than in the first example because they have no meaningful empirical counterpart.

Viewed as a body of substantive hypotheses, theory is to be judged by its predictive power for the class of phenomena which it is intended to "explain." Only factual evidence can show whether it is "right" or "wrong" or, better, tentatively "accepted" as valid or "rejected." As I shall argue at greater length below, the only relevant test of the *validity* of a hypothesis is

7. "The Marshallian Demand Curve," *infra,* p. 57.

comparison of its predictions with experience. The hypothesis is rejected if its predictions are contradicted ("frequently" or more often than predictions from an alternative hypothesis); it is accepted if its predictions are not contradicted; great confidence is attached to it if it has survived many opportunities for contradiction. Factual evidence can never "prove" a hypothesis; it can only fail to disprove it, which is what we generally mean when we say, somewhat inexactly, that the hypothesis has been "confirmed" by experience.

To avoid confusion, it should perhaps be noted explicitly that the "predictions" by which the validity of a hypothesis is tested need not be about phenomena that have not yet occurred, that is, need not be forecasts of future events; they may be about phenomena that have occurred but observations on which have not yet been made or are not known to the person making the prediction. For example, a hypothesis may imply that such and such must have happened in 1906, given some other known circumstances. If a search of the records reveals that such and such did happen, the prediction is confirmed; if it reveals that such and such did not happen, the prediction is contradicted.

The validity of a hypothesis in this sense is not by itself a sufficient criterion for choosing among alternative hypotheses. Observed facts are necessarily finite in number; possible hypotheses, infinite. If there is one hypothesis that is consistant with the available evidence, there are always an infinite number that are.[8] For example, suppose a specific excise tax on a particular commodity produces a rise in price equal to the amount of the tax. This is consistent with competitive conditions, a stable demand curve, and a horizontal and stable supply curve. But it is also consistent with competitive conditions and a positively or negatively sloping supply curve with the required compensating shift in the demand curve or the supply curve; with monopolistic conditions, constant marginal costs, and stable demand curve, of the particular shape required to produce this result; and so on indefinitely. Additional evidence with which the

8. The qualification is necessary because the "evidence" may be internally contradictory, so there may be no hypothesis consistent with it. See also "Lange on Price Flexibility and Employment," *infra*, pp. 282–83.

hypothesis is to be consistent may rule out some of these possibilities; it can never reduce them to a single possibility alone capable of being consistent with the finite evidence. The choice among alternative hypotheses equally consistent with the available evidence must to some extent be arbitrary, though there is general agreement that relevant considerations are suggested by the criteria "simplicity" and "fruitfulness," themselves notions that defy completely objective specification. A theory is "simpler" the less the initial knowledge needed to make a prediction within a given field of phenomena; it is more "fruitful" the more precise the resulting prediction, the wider the area within which the theory yields predictions, and the more additional lines for further research it suggests. Logical completeness and consistency are relevant but play a subsidiary role; their function is to assure that the hypothesis says what it is intended to say and does so alike for all users—they play the same role here as checks for arithmetical accuracy do in statistical computations.

Unfortunately, we can seldom test particular predictions in the social sciences by experiments explicitly designed to eliminate what are judged to be the most important disturbing influences. Generally, we must rely on evidence cast up by the "experiments" that happen to occur. The inability to conduct so-called "controlled experiments" does not, in my view, reflect a basic difference between the social and physical sciences both because it is not peculiar to the social sciences—witness astronomy—and because the distinction between a controlled experiment and uncontrolled experience is at best one of degree. No experiment can be completely controlled, and every experience is partly controlled, in the sense that some disturbing influences are relatively constant in the course of it.

Evidence cast up by experience is abundant and frequently as conclusive as that from contrived experiments; thus the inability to conduct experiments is not a fundamental obstacle to testing hypotheses by the success of their predictions. But such evidence is far more difficult to interpret. It is frequently complex and always indirect and incomplete. Its collection is often arduous, and its interpretation generally requires subtle analysis and involved chains of reasoning, which seldom carry real conviction. The denial to economics of the dramatic and direct evidence of the "crucial" experiment does hinder the adequate testing of hypotheses; but this is much less significant than the difficulty it places in the way of achieving a reasonably prompt and wide consensus on the conclusions justified by the available evidence. It renders the weeding-out of unsuccessful hypotheses slow and difficult. They are seldom downed for good and are always cropping up again.

There is, of course, considerable variation in these respects. Occasionally, experience casts up evidence that is about as direct, dramatic, and convincing as any that could be provided by controlled experiments. Perhaps the most obviously important example is the evidence from inflations on the hypothesis that a substantial increase in the quantity of money within a relatively short period is accompanied by a substantial increase in prices. Here the evidence is dramatic, and the chain of reasoning required to interpret it is relatively short. Yet, despite numerous instances of substantial rises in prices, their essentially one-to-one correspondence with substantial rises in the stock of money, and the wide variation in other circumstances that might appear to be relevant, each new experience of inflation brings forth vigorous contentions, and not only by the lay public, that the rise in the stock of money is either an incidental effect of a rise in prices produced by other factors or a purely fortuitous and unnecessary concomitant of the price rise.

One effect of the difficulty of testing substantive economic hypotheses has been to foster a retreat into purely formal or tautological analysis.[9] As already noted, tautologies have an extremely important place in economics and other sciences as a specialized language or "analytical filing system." Beyond this, formal logic and mathematics, which are both tautologies, are essential aids in checking the correctness of reasoning, discovering the implications of hypotheses, and determining whether supposedly different hypotheses may not really be equivalent or wherein the differences lie.

But economic theory must be more than a structure of tautol-

9. See "Lange on Price Flexibility and Employment," *infra, passim.*

ogies if it is to be able to predict and not merely describe the consequences of action; if it is to be something different from disguised mathematics.[10] And the usefulness of the tautologies themselves ultimately depends, as noted above, on the acceptability of the substantive hypotheses that suggest the particular categories into which they organize the refractory empirical phenomena.

A more serious effect of the difficulty of testing economic hypotheses by their predictions is to foster misunderstanding of the role of empirical evidence in theoretical work. Empirical evidence is vital at two different, though closely related, stages: in constructing hypotheses and in testing their validity. Full and comprehensive evidence on the phenomena to be generalized or "explained" by a hypothesis, besides its obvious value in suggesting new hypotheses, is needed to assure that a hypothesis explains what it sets out to explain—that its implications for such phenomena are not contradicted in advance by experience that has already been observed.[11] Given that the hypothesis is

10. See also Milton Friedman and L. J. Savage, "The Expected-Utility Hypothesis and the Measurability of Utility," *Journal of Political Economy, LX* (December, 1952), 463–74, esp. pp. 465–67.

11. In recent years some economists, particularly a group connected with the Cowles Commission for Research in Economics at the University of Chicago, have placed great emphasis on a division of this step of selecting a hypothesis consistent with known evidence into two substeps: first, the selection of a class of admissible hypotheses from all possible hypotheses (the choice of a "model" in their terminology); second, the selection of one hypothesis from this class (the choice of a "structure"). This subdivision may be heuristically valuable in some kinds of work, particularly in promoting a systematic use of available statistical evidence and theory. From a methodological point of view, however, it is an entirely arbitrary subdivision of the process of deciding on a particular hypothesis that is on a par with many other subdivisions that may be convenient for one purpose or another or that may suit the psychological needs of particular investigators.

One consequence of this particular subdivision has been to give rise to the so-called "identification" problem. As noted above, if one hypothesis is consistent with available evidence, an infinite number are. But, while this is true for the class of hypotheses as a whole, it may not be true of the subclass obtained in the first of the above two steps—the "model." It may be that the evidence to be used to select the final hypothesis from the subclass can be consistent with at most one hypothesis in it, in which case the "model" is said to be "identified"; otherwise it is said to be "unidentified." As is clear from this way of describing the concept of "identification," it is essentially a special case of the more general

consistent with the evidence at hand, its further testing involves deducing from it new facts capable of being observed but not previously known and checking these deduced facts against additional empirical evidence. For this test to be relevant, the deduced facts must be about the class of phenomena the hypothesis is designed to explain; and they must be well enough defined so that observation can show them to be wrong.

The two stages of constructing hypotheses and testing their validity are related in two different respects. In the first place, the particular facts that enter at each stage are partly an accident of the collection of data and the knowledge of the particular investigator. The facts that serve as a test of the implications of a hypothesis might equally well have been among the raw material used to construct it, and conversely. In the second place, the process never begins from scratch; the so-called "initial stage" itself always involves comparison of the implications of an earlier set of hypotheses with observation; the contradiction of these implications is the stimulus to the construction of new

problem of selecting among the alternative hypotheses equally consistent with the evidence—a problem that must be decided by some such arbitrary principle as Occam's razor. The introduction of two substeps in selecting a hypothesis makes this problem arise at the two corresponding stages and gives it a special cast. While the class of all hypotheses is always unidentified, the subclass in a "model" need not be, so the problem arises of conditions that a "model" must satisfy to be identified. However useful the two substeps may be in some contexts, their introduction raises the danger that different criteria will unwittingly be used in making the same kind of choice among alternative hypotheses at two different stages.

On the general methodological approach discussed in this footnote see Tryvge Haavelmo, "The Probability Approach in Econometrics," *Econometrica*, Vol. XII (1944), Supplement; Jacob Marschak, "Economic Structure, Path, Policy, and Prediction," *American Economic Review*, XXXVII, (May, 1947), 81–84, and "Statistical Inference in Economics: An Introduction," in T. C. Koopmans (ed.), *Statistical Inference in Dynamic Economic Models* (New York: John Wiley & Sons, 1950); T. C. Koopmans, "Statistical Estimation of Simultaneous Economic Relations," *Journal of the American Statistical Association*, XL (December, 1945), 448–66; Gershon Cooper, "The Role of Economic Theory in Econometric Models," *Journal of Farm Economics*, XXX (February, 1948), 101–16. On the identification problem see Koopmans, "Identification Problems in Econometric Model Construction," *Econometrica*, XVII (April, 1949), 125–44; Leonid Hurwicz, "Generalization of the Concept of Identification," in Koopmans (ed.), *Statistical Inference in Dynamic Economic Models*.

hypotheses or revision of old ones. So the two methodologically distinct stages are always proceeding jointly.

Misunderstanding about this apparently straightforward process centers on the phrase "the class of phenomena the hypothesis is designed to explain." The difficulty in the social sciences of getting new evidence for this class of phenomena and of judging its conformity with the implications of the hypothesis makes it tempting to suppose that other, more readily available, evidence is equally relevant to the validity of the hypothesis—to suppose that hypotheses have not only "implications" but also "assumptions" and that the conformity of these "assumptions" to "reality" is a test of the validity of the hypothesis *different from* or *additional to* the test by implications. This widely held view is fundamentally wrong and productive of much mischief. Far from providing an easier means for sifting valid from invalid hypotheses, it only confuses the issue, promotes misunderstanding about the significance of empirical evidence for economic theory, produces a misdirection of much intellectual effort devoted to the development of positive economics, and impedes the attainment of consensus on tentative hypotheses in positive economics.

In so far as a theory can be said to have "assumptions" at all, and in so far as their "realism" can be judged independently of the validity of predictions, the relation between the significance of a theory and the "realism" of its "assumptions" is almost the opposite of that suggested by the view under criticism. Truly important and significant hypotheses will be found to have "assumptions" that are wildly inaccurate descriptive representations of reality, and, in general, the more significant the theory, the more unrealistic the assumptions (in this sense).[12] The reason is simple. A hypothesis is important if it "explains" much by little, that is, if it abstracts the common and crucial elements from the mass of complex and detailed circumstances surrounding the phenomena to be explained and permits valid predictions on the basis of them alone. To be important, therefore, a hypothesis must be descriptively false in its assumptions; it

12. The converse of the proposition does not of course hold: assumptions that are unrealistic (in this sense) do not guarantee a significant theory.

takes account of, and accounts for, none of the many other attendant circumstances, since its very success shows them to be irrelevant for the phenomena to be explained.

To put this point less paradoxically, the relevant question to ask about the "assumptions" of a theory is not whether they are descriptively "realistic," for they never are, but whether they are sufficiently good approximations for the purpose in hand. And this question can be answered only by seeing whether the theory works, which means whether it yields sufficiently accurate predictions. The two supposedly independent tests thus reduce to one test.

The theory of monopolistic and imperfect competition is one example of the neglect in economic theory of these propositions. The development of this analysis was explicitly motivated, and its wide acceptance and approval largely explained, by the belief that the assumptions of "perfect competition" or "perfect monopoly" said to underlie neoclassical economic theory are a false image of reality. And this belief was itself based almost entirely on the directly perceived descriptive inaccuracy of the assumptions rather than on any recognized contradiction of predictions derived from neoclassical economic theory. The lengthy discussion on marginal analysis in the *American Economic Review* some years ago is an even clearer, though much less important, example. The articles on both sides of the controversy largely neglect what seems to me clearly the main issue—the conformity to experience of the implications of the marginal analysis—and concentrate on the largely irrelevant question whether businessmen do or do not in fact reach their decisions by consulting schedules, or curves, or multivariable functions showing marginal cost and marginal revenue.[13] Perhaps these

13. See R. A. Lester, "Shortcomings of Marginal Analysis for Wage-Employment Problems," *American Economic Review*, XXXVI (March, 1946), 62–82; Fritz Machlup, "Marginal Analysis and Empirical Research," *American Economic Review*, XXXVI (September, 1946), 519–54; R. A. Lester, "Marginalism, Minimum Wages, and Labor Markets," *American Economic Review*, XXXVII (March, 1947), 135–48; Fritz Machlup, "Rejoinder to an Antimarginalist," *American Economic Review*, XXXVII (March, 1947), 148–54; G. J. Stigler, "Professor Lester and the Marginalists," *American Economic Review*, XXXVII (March, 1947), 154–57; H. M. Oliver, Jr., "Marginal Theory and Business Behavior," *American Economic Review*, XXXVII (June, 1947), 375–83; R. A. Gordon,

two examples, and the many others they readily suggest, will serve to justify a more extensive discussion of the methodological principles involved than might otherwise seem appropriate.

III. Can a Hypothesis Be Tested by the Realism of Its Assumptions?

We may start with a simple physical example, the law of falling bodies. It is an accepted hypothesis that the acceleration of a body dropped in a vacuum is a constant—g, or approximately 32 feet per second per second on the earth—and is independent of the shape of the body, the manner of dropping it, etc. This implies that the distance traveled by a falling body in any specified time is given by the formula $s = \frac{1}{2} gt^2$, where s is the distance traveled in feet and t is time in seconds. The application of this formula to a compact ball dropped from the roof of a building is equivalent to saying that a ball so dropped behaves *as if* it were falling in a vacuum. Testing this hypothesis by its assumptions presumably means measuring the actual air pressure and deciding whether it is close enough to zero. At sea level the air pressure is about 15 pounds per square inch. Is 15 sufficiently close to zero for the difference to be judged insignificant? Apparently it is, since the actual time taken by a compact ball to fall from the roof of a building to the ground is very close to the time given by the formula. Suppose, however, that a feather is

---

"Short-Period Price Determination in Theory and Practice," *American Economic Review*, XXXVIII (June, 1948), 265–88.

It should be noted that, along with much material purportedly bearing on the validity of the "assumptions" of marginal theory, Lester does refer to evidence on the conformity of experience with the implications of the theory, citing the reactions of employment in Germany to the Papen plan and in the United States to changes in minimum-wage legislation as examples of lack of conformity. However, Stigler's brief comment is the only one of the other papers that refers to this evidence. It should also be noted that Machlup's thorough and careful exposition of the logical structure and meaning of marginal analysis is called for by the misunderstandings on this score that mar Lester's paper and almost conceal the evidence he presents that is relevant to the key issue he raises. But, in Machlup's emphasis on the logical structure, he comes perilously close to presenting the theory as a pure tautology, though it is evident at a number of points that he is aware of this danger and anxious to avoid it. The papers by Oliver and Gordon are the most extreme in the exclusive concentration on the conformity of the behavior of businessmen with the "assumptions" of the theory.

dropped instead of a compact ball. The formula then gives wildly inaccurate results. Apparently, 15 pounds per square inch is significantly different from zero for a feather but not for a ball. Or, again, suppose the formula is applied to a ball dropped from an airplane at an altitude of 30,000 feet. The air pressure at this altitude is decidedly less than 15 pounds per square inch. Yet, the actual time of fall from 30,000 feet to 20,000 feet, at which point the air pressure is still much less than at sea level, will differ noticeably from the time predicted by the formula— much more noticeably than the time taken by a compact ball to fall from the roof of a building to the ground. According to the formula, the velocity of the ball should be gt and should therefore increase steadily. In fact, a ball dropped at 30,000 feet will reach its top velocity well before it hits the ground. And similarly with other implications of the formula.

The initial question whether 15 is sufficiently close to zero for the difference to be judged insignificant is clearly a foolish question by itself. Fifteen pounds per square inch is 2,160 pounds per square foot, or 0.0075 ton per square inch. There is no possible basis for calling these numbers "small" or "large" without some external standard of comparison. And the only relevant standard of comparison is the air pressure for which the formula does or does not work under a given set of circumstances. But this raises the same problem at a second level. What is the meaning of "does or does not work"? Even if we could eliminate errors of measurement, the measured time of fall would seldom if ever be precisely equal to the computed time of fall. How large must the difference between the two be to justify saying that the theory "does not work"? Here there are two important external standards of comparison. One is the accuracy achievable by an alternative theory with which this theory is being compared and which is equally acceptable on all other grounds. The other arises when there exists a theory that is known to yield better predictions but only at a greater cost. The gains from greater accuracy, which depend on the purpose in mind, must then be balanced against the costs of achieving it.

This example illustrates both the impossibility of testing a theory by its assumptions and also the ambiguity of the concept "the assumptions of a theory." The formula $s = \frac{1}{2} gt^2$ is valid for bodies falling in a vacuum and can be derived by analyzing the behavior of such bodies. It can therefore be stated: under a wide range of circumstances, bodies that fall in the actual atmosphere behave *as if* they were falling in a vacuum. In the language so common in economics this would be rapidly translated into: the formula assumes a vacuum. Yet it clearly does no such thing. What it does say is that in many cases the existence of air pressure, the shape of the body, the name of the person dropping the body, the kind of mechanism used to drop the body, and a host of other attendant circumstances have no appreciable effect on the distance the body falls in a specified time. The hypothesis can readily be rephrased to omit all mention of a vacuum: under a wide range of circumstances, the distance a body falls in a specified time is given by the formula $s = \frac{1}{2} gt^2$. The history of this formula and its associated physical theory aside, is it meaningful to say that it assumes a vacuum? For all I know there may be other sets of assumptions that would yield the same formula. The formula is accepted because it works, not because we live in an approximate vacuum—whatever that means.

The important problem in connection with the hypothesis is to specify the circumstances under which the formula works or, more precisely, the general magnitude of the error in its predictions under various circumstances. Indeed, as is implicit in the above rephrasing of the hypothesis, such a specification is not one thing and the hypothesis another. The specification is itself an essential part of the hypothesis, and it is a part that is peculiarly likely to be revised and extended as experience accumulates.

In the particular case of falling bodies a more general, though still incomplete, theory is available, largely as a result of attempts to explain the errors of the simple theory, from which the influence of some of the possible disturbing factors can be calculated and of which the simple theory is a special case. However, it does not always pay to use the more general theory because the extra accuracy it yields may not justify the extra cost of using it, so the question under what circumstances the simpler theory works "well enough" remains important. Air pressure is one, but only one, of the variables that define these circumstances; the shape of the body, the velocity attained, and still other variables are relevant as well. One way of interpreting the variables other than air pressure is to regard them as determining whether a particular departure from the "assumption" of a vacuum is or is not significant. For example, the difference in shape of the body can be said to make 15 pounds per square inch significantly different from zero for a feather but not for a compact ball dropped a moderate distance. Such a statement must, however, be sharply distinguished from the very different statement that the theory does not work for a feather because its assumptions are false. The relevant relation runs the other way: the assumptions are false for a feather because the theory does not work. This point needs emphasis, because the entirely valid use of "assumptions" in *specifying* the circumstances for which a theory holds is frequently, and erroneously, interpreted to mean that the assumptions can be used to *determine* the circumstances for which a theory holds, and has, in this way, been an important source of the belief that a theory can be tested by its assumptions.

Let us turn now to another example, this time a constructed one designed to be an analogue of many hypotheses in the social sciences. Consider the density of leaves around a tree. I suggest the hypothesis that the leaves are positioned as if each leaf deliberately sought to maximize the amount of sunlight it receives, given the position of its neighbors, as if it knew the physical laws determining the amount of sunlight that would be received in various positions and could move rapidly or instantaneously from any one position to any other desired and unoccupied position.[14] Now some of the more obvious implications of this hypothesis are clearly consistent with experience: for example, leaves are in general denser on the south than on the north side of trees but, as the hypothesis implies, less so or not at all on the northern

14. This example, and some of the subsequent discussion, though independent in origin, is similar to and in much the same spirit as an example and the approach in an important paper by Armen A. Alchian, "Uncertainty, Evolution, and Economic Theory," *Journal of Political Economy*, LVIII (June, 1950), 211–21.

slope of a hill or when the south side of the trees is shaded in some other way. Is the hypothesis rendered unacceptable or invalid because, so far as we know, leaves do not "deliberate" or consciously "seek," have not been to school and learned the relevant laws of science or the mathematics required to calculate the "optimum" position, and cannot move from position to position? Clearly, none of these contradictions of the hypothesis is vitally relevant; the phenomena involved are not within the "class of phenomena the hypothesis is designed to explain"; the hypothesis does not assert that leaves do these things but only that their density is the same *as if* they did. Despite the apparent falsity of the "assumptions" of the hypothesis, it has great plausibility because of the conformity of its implications with observation. We are inclined to "explain" its validity on the ground that sunlight contributes to the growth of leaves and that hence leaves will grow denser or more putative leaves survive where there is more sun, so the result achieved by purely passive adaptation to external circumstances is the same as the result that would be achieved by deliberate accommodation to them. This alternative hypothesis is more attractive than the constructed hypothesis not because its "assumptions" are more "realistic" but rather because it is part of a more general theory that applies to a wider variety of phenomena, of which the position of leaves around a tree is a special case, has more implications capable of being contradicted, and has failed to be contradicted under a wider variety of circumstances. The direct evidence for the growth of leaves is in this way strengthened by the indirect evidence from the other phenomena to which the more general theory applies.

The constructed hypothesis is presumably valid, that is, yields "sufficiently" accurate predictions about the density of leaves, only for a particular class of circumstances. I do not know what these circumstances are or how to define them. It seems obvious, however, that in this example the "assumptions" of the theory will play no part in specifying them: the kind of tree, the character of the soil, etc., are the types of variables that are likely to define its range of validity, not the ability of the leaves to do complicated mathematics or to move from place to place.

A largely parallel example involving human behavior has been used elsewhere by Savage and me.[15] Consider the problem of predicting the shots made by an expert billiard player. It seems not at all unreasonable that excellent predictions would be yielded by the hypothesis that the billiard player made his shots *as if* he knew the complicated mathematical formulas that would give the optimum directions of travel, could estimate accurately by eye the angles, etc., describing the location of the balls, could make lightning calculations from the formulas, and could then make the balls travel in the direction indicated by the formulas. Our confidence in this hypothesis is not based on the belief that billiard players, even expert ones, can or do go through the process described; it derives rather from the belief that, unless in some way or other they were capable of reaching essentially the same result, they would not in fact be *expert* billiard players.

It is only a short step from these examples to the economic hypothesis that under a wide range of circumstances individual firms behave *as if* they were seeking rationally to maximize their expected returns (generally if misleadingly called "profits")[16] and had full knowledge of the data needed to succeed in this attempt; *as if,* that is, they knew the relevant cost and demand functions,

15. Milton Friedman and L. J. Savage, "The Utility Analysis of Choices Involving Risk," *Journal of Political Economy,* LVI (August, 1948), 298. Reprinted in American Economic Association, *Readings in Price Theory* (Chicago: Richard D. Irwin, Inc., 1952), pp. 57–96.

16. It seems better to use the term "profits" to refer to the difference between actual and "expected" results, between *ex post* and *ex ante* receipts. "Profits" are then a result of uncertainty and, as Alchian (*op. cit.,* p. 212), following Tintner, points out, cannot be deliberately maximized in advance. Given uncertainty, individuals or firms choose among alternative anticipated probability distributions of receipts or incomes. The specific content of a theory of choice among such distributions depends on the criteria by which they are supposed to be ranked. One hypothesis supposes them to be ranked by the mathematical expectation of utility corresponding to them (see Friedman and Savage, "The Expected-Utility Hypothesis and the Measurability of Utility," *op. cit.*). A special case of this hypothesis or an alternative to it ranks probability distributions by the mathematical expectation of the money receipts corresponding to them. The latter is perhaps more applicable, and more frequently applied, to firms than to individuals. The term "expected returns" is intended to be sufficiently broad to apply to any of these alternatives.

The issues alluded to in this note are not basic to the methodological issues being discussed, and so are largely by-passed in the discussion that follows.

calculated marginal cost and marginal revenue from all actions open to them, and pushed each line of action to the point at which the relevant marginal cost and marginal revenue were equal. Now, of course, businessmen do not actually and literally solve the system of simultaneous equations in terms of which the mathematical economist finds it convenient to express this hypothesis, any more than leaves or billiard players explicitly go through complicated mathematical calculations or falling bodies decide to create a vacuum. The billiard player, if asked how he decides where to hit the ball, may say that he "just figures it out" but then also rubs a rabbit's foot just to make sure; and the businessman may well say that he prices at average cost, with of course some minor deviations when the market makes it necessary. The one statement is about as helpful as the other, and neither is a relevant test of the associated hypothesis.

Confidence in the maximization-of-returns hypothesis is justified by evidence of a very different character. This evidence is in part similar to that adduced on behalf of the billiard-player hypothesis—unless the behavior of businessmen in some way or other approximated behavior consistent with the maximization of returns, it seems unlikely that they would remain in business for long. Let the apparent immediate determinant of business behavior be anything at all—habitual reaction, random chance, or whatnot. Whenever this determinant happens to lead to behavior consistent with rational and informed maximization of returns, the business will prosper and acquire resources with which to expand; whenever it does not, the business will tend to lose resources and can be kept in existence only by the addition of resources from outside. The process of "natural selection" thus helps to validate the hypothesis—or, rather, given natural selection, acceptance of the hypothesis can be based largely on the judgment that it summarizes appropriately the conditions for survival.

An even more important body of evidence for the maximization-of-returns hypothesis is experience from countless applications of the hypothesis to specific problems and the repeated failure of its implications to be contradicted. This evidence is extremely hard to document; it is scattered in numerous memorandums, articles, and monographs concerned primarily with specific concrete problems rather than with submitting the hypothesis to test. Yet the continued use and acceptance of the hypothesis over a long period, and the failure of any coherent, self-consistent alternative to be developed and be widely accepted, is strong indirect testimony to its worth. The evidence *for* a hypothesis always consists of its repeated failure to be contradicted, continues to accumulate so long as the hypothesis is used, and by its very nature is difficult to document at all comprehensively. It tends to become part of the tradition and folklore of a science revealed in the tenacity with which hypotheses are held rather than in any textbook list of instances in which the hypothesis has failed to be contradicted.

IV. THE SIGNIFICANCE AND ROLE OF THE "ASSUMPTIONS" OF A THEORY

Up to this point our conclusions about the significance of the "assumptions" of a theory have been almost entirely negative: we have seen that a theory cannot be tested by the "realism" of its "assumptions" and that the very concept of the "assumptions" of a theory is surrounded with ambiguity. But, if this were all there is to it, it would be hard to explain the extensive use of the concept and the strong tendency that we all have to speak of the assumptions of a theory and to compare the assumptions of alternative theories. There is too much smoke for there to be no fire.

In methodology, as in positive science, negative statements can generally be made with greater confidence than positive statements, so I have less confidence in the following remarks on the significance and role of "assumptions" than in the preceding remarks. So far as I can see, the "assumptions of a theory" play three different, though related, positive roles: (*a*) they are often an economical mode of describing or presenting a theory; (*b*) they sometimes facilitate an indirect test of the hypothesis by its implications; and (*c*), as already noted, they are sometimes a convenient means of specifying the conditions under which the theory is expected to be valid. The first two require more extensive discussion.

A. THE USE OF "ASSUMPTIONS" IN STATING A THEORY

The example of the leaves illustrates the first role of assumptions. Instead of saying that leaves seek to maximize the sunlight they receive, we could state the equivalent hypothesis, without any apparent assumptions, in the form of a list of rules for predicting the density of leaves: if a tree stands in a level field with no other trees or other bodies obstructing the rays of the sun, then the density of leaves will tend to be such and such; if a tree is on the northern slope of a hill in the midst of a forest of similar trees, then . . . ; etc. This is clearly a far less economical presentation of the hypothesis than the statement that leaves seek to maximize the sunlight each receives. The latter statement is, in effect, a simple summary of the rules in the above list, even if the list were indefinitely extended, since it indicates both how to determine the features of the environment that are important for the particular problem and how to evaluate their effects. It is more compact and at the same time no less comprehensive.

More generally, a hypothesis or theory consists of an assertion that certain forces are, and by implication others are not, important for a particular class of phenomena and a specification of the manner of action of the forces it asserts to be important. We can regard the hypothesis as consisting of two parts: first, a conceptual world or abstract model simpler than the "real world" and containing only the forces that the hypothesis asserts to be important; second, a set of rules defining the class of phenomena for which the "model" can be taken to be an adequate representation of the "real world" and specifying the correspondence between the variables or entities in the model and observable phenomena.

These two parts are very different in character. The model is abstract and complete; it is an "algebra" or "logic." Mathematics and formal logic come into their own in checking its consistency and completeness and exploring its implications. There is no place in the model for, and no function to be served by, vagueness, maybe's, or approximations. The air pressure is zero, not "small," for a vacuum; the demand curve for the product of a competitive producer is horizontal (has a slope of zero), not "almost horizontal."

The rules for using the model, on the other hand, cannot possibly be abstract and complete. They must be concrete and in consequence incomplete—completeness is possible only in a conceptual world, not in the "real world," however that may be interpreted. The model is the logical embodiment of the half-truth, "There is nothing new under the sun"; the rules for applying it cannot neglect the equally significant half-truth, "History never repeats itself." To a considerable extent the rules can be formulated explicitly—most easily, though even then not completely, when the theory is part of an explicit more general theory as in the example of the vacuum theory for falling bodies. In seeking to make a science as "objective" as possible, our aim should be to formulate the rules explicitly in so far as possible and continually to widen the range of phenomena for which it is possible to do so. But, no matter how successful we may be in this attempt, there inevitably will remain room for judgment in applying the rules. Each occurrence has some features peculiarly its own, not covered by the explicit rules. The capacity to judge that these are or are not to be disregarded, that they should or should not affect what observable phenomena are to be identified with what entities in the model, is something that cannot be taught; it can be learned but only by experience and exposure in the "right" scientific atmosphere, not by rote. It is at this point that the "amateur" is separated from the "professional" in all sciences and that the thin line is drawn which distinguishes the "crackpot" from the scientist.

A simple example may perhaps clarify this point. Euclidean geometry is an abstract model, logically complete and consistent. Its entities are precisely defined—a line is not a geometrical figure "much" longer than it is wide or deep; it is a figure whose width and depth are zero. It is also obviously "unrealistic." There are no such things in "reality" as Euclidean points or lines or surfaces. Let us apply this abstract model to a mark made on a blackboard by a piece of chalk. Is the mark to be identified with a Euclidean line, a Euclidean surface, or a Euclidean solid?

Clearly, it can appropriately be identified with a line if it is being used to represent, say, a demand curve. But it cannot be so identified if it is being used to color, say, countries on a map, for that would imply that the map would never be colored; for this purpose, the same mark must be identified with a surface. But it cannot be so identified by a manufacturer of chalk, for that would imply that no chalk would ever be used up; for his purposes, the same mark must be identified with a volume. In this simple example these judgments will command general agreement. Yet it seems obvious that, while general considerations can be formulated to guide such judgments, they can never be comprehensive and cover every possible instance; they cannot have the self-contained coherent character of Euclidean geometry itself.

In speaking of the "crucial assumptions" of a theory, we are, I believe, trying to state the key elements of the abstract model. There are generally many different ways of describing the model completely—many different sets of "postulates" which both imply and are implied by the model as a whole. These are all logically equivalent: what are regarded as axioms or postulates of a model from one point of view can be regarded as theorems from another, and conversely. The particular "assumptions" termed "crucial" are selected on grounds of their convenience in some such respects as simplicity or economy in describing the model, intuitive plausibility, or capacity to suggest, if only by implication, some of the considerations that are relevant in judging or applying the model.

B. THE USE OF "ASSUMPTIONS" AS AN INDIRECT TEST OF A THEORY

In presenting any hypothesis, it generally seems obvious which of the series of statements used to expound it refer to assumptions and which to implications; yet this distinction is not easy to define rigorously. It is not, I believe, a characteristic of the hypothesis as such but rather of the use to which the hypothesis is to be put. If this is so, the ease of classifying statements must reflect unambiguousness in the purpose the hypothesis is designed to serve. The possibility of interchanging theorems and axioms in an abstract model implies the possibility of interchanging "implications" and "assumptions" in the substantive hypothesis corresponding to the abstract model, which is not to say that any implication can be interchanged with any assumption but only that there may be more than one set of statements that imply the rest.

For example, consider a particular proposition in the theory of oligopolistic behavior. If we assume (*a*) that entrepreneurs seek to maximize their returns by any means including acquiring or extending monopoly power, this will imply (*b*) that, when demand for a "product" is geographically unstable, transportation costs are significant, explicit price agreements illegal, and the number of producers of the product relatively small, they will tend to establish basing-point pricing systems.[17] The assertion (*a*) is regarded as an assumption and (*b*) as an implication because we accept the prediction of market behavior as the purpose of the analysis. We shall regard the assumption as acceptable if we find that the conditions specified in (*b*) are generally associated with basing-point pricing, and conversely. Let us now change our purpose to deciding what cases to prosecute under the Sherman Antitrust Law's prohibition of a "conspiracy in restraint of trade." If we now assume (*c*) that basing-point pricing is a deliberate construction to facilitate collusion under the conditions specified in (*b*), this will imply (*d*) that entrepreneurs who participate in basing-point pricing are engaged in a "conspiracy in restraint of trade." What was formerly an assumption now becomes an implication, and conversely. We shall now regard the assumption (*c*) as valid if we find that, when entrepreneurs participate in basing-point pricing, there generally tends to be other evidence, in the form of letters, memorandums, or the like, of what courts regard as a "conspiracy in restraint of trade."

Suppose the hypothesis works for the first purpose, namely, the prediction of market behavior. It clearly does not follow that it will work for the second purpose, namely, predicting whether there is enough evidence of a "conspiracy in restraint of trade"

17. See George J. Stigler, "A Theory of Delivered Price Systems," *American Economic Review,* XXXIX (December, 1949), 1143–57.

to justify court action. And, conversely, if it works for the second purpose, it does not follow that it will work for the first. Yet, in the absence of other evidence, the success of the hypothesis for one purpose—in explaining one class of phenomena— will give us greater confidence than we would otherwise have that it may succeed for another purpose—in explaining another class of phenomena. It is much harder to say how much greater confidence it justifies. For this depends on how closely related we judge the two classes of phenomena to be, which itself depends in a complex way on similar kinds of indirect evidence, that is, on our experience in other connections in explaining by single theories phenomena that are in some sense similarly diverse.

To state the point more generally, what are called the assumptions of a hypothesis can be used to get some indirect evidence on the acceptability of the hypothesis in so far as the assumptions can themselves be regarded as implications of the hypothesis, and hence their conformity with reality as a failure of some implications to be contradicted, or in so far as the assumptions may call to mind other implications of the hypothesis susceptible to casual empirical observation.[18] The reason this evidence is indirect is that the assumptions or associated implications generally refer to a class of phenomena different from the class which the hypothesis is designed to explain; indeed, as is implied above, this seems to be the chief criterion we use in deciding which statements to term "assumptions" and which to term "implications." The weight attached to this indirect evidence depends on how closely related we judge the two classes of phenomena to be.

Another way in which the "assumptions" of a hypothesis can facilitate its indirect testing is by bringing out its kinship with other hypotheses and thereby making the evidence on their validity relevant to the validity of the hypothesis in question. For example, a hypothesis is formulated for a particular class

18. See Friedman and Savage, "The Expected-Utility Hypothesis and the Measurability of Utility," *op. cit.*, pp. 466–67, for another specific example of this kind of indirect test.

of behavior. This hypothesis can, as usual, be stated without specifying any "assumptions." But suppose it can be shown that it is equivalent to a set of assumptions including the assumption that man seeks his own interest. The hypothesis then gains indirect plausibility from the success for other classes of phenomena of hypotheses that can also be said to make this assumption; at least, what is being done here is not completely unprecedented or unsuccessful in all other uses. In effect, the statement of assumptions so as to bring out a relationship between superficially different hypotheses is a step in the direction of a more general hypothesis.

This kind of indirect evidence from related hypotheses explains in large measure the difference in the confidence attached to a particular hypothesis by people with different backgrounds. Consider, for example, the hypothesis that the extent of racial or religious discrimination in employment in a particular area or industry is closely related to the degree of monopoly in the industry or area in question; that, if the industry is competitive, discrimination will be significant only if the race or religion of employees affects either the willingness of other employees to work with them or the acceptability of the product to customers and will be uncorrelated with the prejudices of employers.[19] This hypothesis is far more likely to appeal to an economist than to a sociologist. It can be said to "assume" single-minded pursuit of pecuniary self-interest by employers in competitive industries; and this "assumption" works well in a wide variety of hypotheses in economics bearing on many of the mass phenomena with which economics deals. It is therefore likely to seem reasonable to the economist that it may work in this case as well. On the other hand, the hypotheses to which the sociologist is accustomed have a very different kind of model or ideal world, in which single-minded pursuit of pecuniary self-interest plays a much less important role. The indirect evidence available to the sociologist on

19. A rigorous statement of this hypothesis would of course have to specify how "extent of racial or religious discrimination" and "degree of monopoly" are to be judged. The loose statement in the text is sufficient, however, for present purposes.

this hypothesis is much less favorable to it than the indirect evidence available to the economist; he is therefore likely to view it with greater suspicion.

Of course, neither the evidence of the economist nor that of the sociologist is conclusive. The decisive test is whether the hypothesis works for the phenomena it purports to explain. But a judgment may be required before any satisfactory test of this kind has been made, and, perhaps, when it cannot be made in the near future, in which case, the judgment will have to be based on the inadequate evidence available. In addition, even when such a test can be made, the background of the scientists is not irrelevant to the judgments they reach. There is never certainty in science, and the weight of evidence for or against a hypothesis can never be assessed completely "objectively." The economist will be more tolerant than the sociologist in judging conformity of the implications of the hypothesis with experience, and he will be persuaded to accept the hypothesis tentatively by fewer instances of "conformity."

V. Some Implications for Economic Issues

The abstract methodological issues we have been discussing have a direct bearing on the perennial criticism of "orthodox" economic theory as "unrealistic" as well as on the attempts that have been made to reformulate theory to meet this charge. Economics is a "dismal" science because it assumes man to be selfish and money-grubbing, "a lightning calculator of pleasures and pains, who oscillates like a homogeneous globule of desire of happiness under the impulse of stimuli that shift him about the area, but leave him intact";[20] it rests on outmoded psychology and must be reconstructed in line with each new development in psychology; it assumes men, or at least businessmen, to be "in a continuous state of 'alert,' ready to change prices and/or pricing rules whenever their sensitive intuitions . . . detect a change in demand and supply conditions";[21] it

20. Thorstein Veblen, "Why Is Economics Not an Evolutionary Science?" (1898), reprinted in *The Place of Science in Modern Civilization* (New York, 1919), p. 73.

21. Oliver, *op. cit.*, p. 381.

assumes markets to be perfect, competition to be pure, and commodities, labor, and capital to be homogeneous.

As we have seen, criticism of this type is largely beside the point unless supplemented by evidence that a hypothesis differing in one or another of these respects from the theory being criticized yields better predictions for as wide a range of phenomena. Yet most such criticism is not so supplemented; it is based almost entirely on supposedly directly perceived discrepancies between the "assumptions" and the "real world." A particularly clear example is furnished by the recent criticisms of the maximization-of-returns hypothesis on the grounds that businessmen do not and indeed cannot behave as the theory "assumes" they do. The evidence cited to support this assertion is generally taken either from the answers given by businessmen to questions about the factors affecting their decisions—a procedure for testing economic theories that is about on a par with testing theories of longevity by asking octogenarians how they account for their long life—or from descriptive studies of the decision-making activities of individual firms.[22] Little if any evidence is ever cited on the conformity of businessmen's actual market behavior—what they do rather than what they say they do—with the implications of the hypothesis being criticized, on the one hand, and of an alternative hypothesis, on the other.

22. See H. D. Henderson, "The Significance of the Rate of Interest," *Oxford Economic Papers,* No. 1 (October, 1938), pp. 1–13; J. E. Meade and P. W. S. Andrews, "Summary of Replies to Questions on Effects of Interest Rates," *Oxford Economic Papers,* No. 1 (October, 1938), pp. 14–31; R. F. Harrod, "Price and Cost in Entrepreneurs' Policy," *Oxford Economic Papers,* No. 2 (May, 1939), pp. 1–11; and R. J. Hall and C. J. Hitch, "Price Theory and Business Behavior," *Oxford Economic Papers,* No. 2 (May, 1939), pp. 12–45; Lester, "Shortcomings of Marginal Analysis for Wage-Employment Problems," *op. cit.*; Gordon, *op. cit.* See Fritz Machlup, "Marginal Analysis and Empirical Research," *op. cit.*, esp. Sec. II, for detailed criticisms of questionnaire methods.

I do not mean to imply that questionnaire studies of businessmen's or others' motives or beliefs about the forces affecting their behavior are useless for all purposes in economics. They may be extremely valuable in suggesting leads to follow in accounting for divergencies between predicted and observed results; that is, in constructing new hypotheses or revising old ones. Whatever their suggestive value in this respect, they seem to me almost entirely useless as a means of *testing* the validity of economic hypotheses. See my comment on Albert G. Hart's paper, "Liquidity and Uncertainty," *American Economic Review,* XXXIX (May, 1949), 198–99.

A theory or its "assumptions" cannot possibly be thoroughly "realistic" in the immediate descriptive sense so often assigned to this term. A completely "realistic" theory of the wheat market would have to include not only the conditions directly underlying the supply and demand for wheat but also the kind of coins or credit instruments used to make exchanges; the personal characteristics of wheat-traders such as the color of each trader's hair and eyes, his antecedents and education, the number of members of his family, their characteristics, antecedents, and education, etc.; the kind of soil on which the wheat was grown, its physical and chemical characteristics, the weather prevailing during the growing season; the personal characteristics of the farmers growing the wheat and of the consumers who will ultimately use it; and so on indefinitely. Any attempt to move very far in achieving this kind of "realism" is certain to render a theory utterly useless.

Of course, the notion of a completely realistic theory is in part a straw man. No critic of a theory would accept this logical extreme as his objective; he would say that the "assumptions" of the theory being criticized were "too" unrealistic and that his objective was a set of assumptions that were "more" realistic though still not completely and slavishly so. But so long as the test of "realism" is the directly perceived descriptive accuracy of the "assumptions"—for example, the observation that "businessmen do not appear to be either as avaricious or as dynamic or as logical as marginal theory portrays them"[23] or that "it would be utterly impractical under present conditions for the manager of a multi-process plant to attempt . . . to work out and equate marginal costs and marginal revenues for each productive factor"[24]—there is no basis for making such a distinction, that is, for stopping short of the straw man depicted in the preceding paragraph. What is the criterion by which to judge whether a particular departure from realism is or is not acceptable? Why is it more "unrealistic" in analyzing business behavior to neglect the magnitude of businessmen's costs than the

23. Oliver, *op. cit.*, p. 382.

24. Lester, "Shortcomings of Marginal Analysis for Wage-Employment Problems," *op. cit.*, p. 75.

color of their eyes? The obvious answer is because the first makes more difference to business behavior than the second; but there is no way of knowing that this is so simply by observing that businessmen do have costs of different magnitudes and eyes of different color. Clearly it can only be known by comparing the effect on the discrepancy between actual and predicted behavior of taking the one factor or the other into account. Even the most extreme proponents of realistic assumptions are thus necessarily driven to reject their own criterion and to accept the test by prediction when they classify alternative assumptions as more or less realistic.[25]

The basic confusion between descriptive accuracy and analytical relevance that underlies most criticisms of economic theory on the grounds that its assumptions are unrealistic as well as the plausibility of the views that lead to this confusion are both strikingly illustrated by a seemingly innocuous remark in an article on business-cycle theory that "economic phenomena are varied and complex, so any comprehensive theory of the business cycle that can apply closely to reality must be very complicated."[26] A fundamental hypothesis of science is that appearances are deceptive and that there is a way of looking at or interpreting or organizing the evidence that will reveal superficially disconnected and diverse phenomena to be manifestations of a more fundamental and relatively simple structure. And the test of this hypothesis, as of any other, is its fruits—a test that science has

25. E.g., Gordon's direct examination of the "assumptions" leads him to formulate the alternative hypothesis generally favored by the critics of the maximization-of-returns hypothesis as follows: "There is an irresistible tendency to price on the basis of average total costs for some 'normal' level of output. This is the yardstick, the short-cut, that businessmen and accountants use, and their aim is more to earn satisfactory profits and play safe than to maximize profits" (*op. cit.*, p. 275). Yet he essentially abandons this hypothesis, or converts it into a tautology, and in the process implicitly accepts the test by prediction when he later remarks: "Full cost and satisfactory profits may continue to be the objectives even when total costs are shaded to meet competition or exceeded to take advantage of a sellers' market" (*ibid.*, p. 284). Where here is the "irresistible tendency"? What kind of evidence could contradict this assertion?

26. Sidney S. Alexander, "Issues of Business Cycle Theory Raised by Mr. Hicks," *American Economic Review*, XLI (December, 1951), 872.

so far met with dramatic success. If a class of "economic phe-nomena" appears varied and complex, it is, we must suppose, be-cause we have no adequate theory to explain them. Known facts cannot be set on one side; a theory to apply "closely to reality," on the other. A theory is the way we perceive "facts," and we cannot perceive "facts" without a theory. Any assertion that economic phenomena *are* varied and complex denies the tentative state of knowledge that alone makes scientific activity meaning-ful; it is in a class with John Stuart Mill's justly ridiculed state-ment that "happily, there is nothing in the laws of value which remains [1848] for the present or any future writer to clear up; the theory of the subject is complete."[27]

The confusion between descriptive accuracy and analytical relevance has led not only to criticisms of economic theory on largely irrelevant grounds but also to misunderstanding of economic theory and misdirection of efforts to repair supposed de-fects. "Ideal types" in the abstract model developed by economic theorists have been regarded as strictly descriptive categories intended to correspond directly and fully to entities in the real world independently of the purpose for which the model is being used. The obvious discrepancies have led to necessarily unsuc-cessful attempts to construct theories on the basis of categories intended to be fully descriptive.

This tendency is perhaps most clearly illustrated by the in-terpretation given to the concepts of "perfect competition" and "monopoly" and the development of the theory of "monopolistic" or "imperfect competition." Marshall, it is said, assumed "per-fect competition"; perhaps there once was such a thing. But clearly there is no longer, and we must therefore discard his theories. The reader will search long and hard—and I predict unsuccessfully—to find in Marshall any explicit assumption about perfect competition or any assertion that in a descriptive sense the world is composed of atomistic firms engaged in perfect competition. Rather, he will find Marshall saying: "At one extreme are world markets in which competition acts directly from all parts of the globe; and at the other those secluded

27. *Principles of Political Economy* (Ashley ed.; Longmans, Green & Co., 1929), p. 436.

markets in which all direct competition from afar is shut out, though indirect and transmitted competition may make itself felt even in these; and about midway between these extremes lie the great majority of the markets which the economist and the business man have to study."[28] Marshall took the world as it is; he sought to construct an "engine" to analyze it, not a photographic reproduction of it.

In analyzing the world as it is, Marshall constructed the hypothesis that, for many problems, firms could be grouped into "industries" such that the similarities among the firms in each group were more important than the differences among them. These are problems in which the important element is that a group of firms is affected alike by some stimulus—a common change in the demand for their products, say, or in the supply of factors. But this will not do for all problems: the important element for these may be the differential effect on particular firms.

The abstract model corresponding to this hypothesis contains two "ideal" types of firms: atomistically competitive firms, grouped into industries, and monopolistic firms. A firm is competitive if the demand curve for its output is infinitely elastic with respect to its own price for some price and all outputs, given the prices charged by all other firms; it belongs to an "industry" defined as a group of firms producing a single "product." A "product" is defined as a collection of units that are perfect substitutes to purchasers so the elasticity of demand for the output of one firm with respect to the price of another firm in the same industry is infinite for some price and some outputs. A firm is monopolistic if the demand curve for its output is not infinitely elastic at some price for all outputs.[29] If it is a monopolist, the firm is the industry.[30]

As always, the hypothesis as a whole consists not only of this abstract model and its ideal types but also of a set of rules, mostly

28. *Principles,* p. 329; see also pp. 35, 100, 341, 347, 375, 546.

29. This ideal type can be divided into two types: the oligopolistic firm, if the demand curve for its output is infinitely elastic at some price for some but not all outputs; the monopolistic firm proper, if the demand curve is nowhere infinitely elastic (except possibly at an output of zero).

30. For the oligopolist of the preceding note an industry can be defined as a group of firms producing the same product.

implicit and suggested by example, for identifying actual firms with one or the other ideal type and for classifying firms into industries. The ideal types are not intended to be descriptive; they are designed to isolate the features that are crucial for a particular problem. Even if we could estimate directly and accurately the demand curve for a firm's product, we could not proceed immediately to classify the firm as perfectly competitive or monopolistic according as the elasticity of the demand curve is or is not infinite. No observed demand curve will ever be precisely horizontal, so the estimated elasticity will always be finite. The relevant question always is whether the elasticity is "sufficiently" large to be regarded as infinite, but this is a question that cannot be answered, once for all, simply in terms of the numerical value of the elasticity itself, any more than we can say, once for all, whether an air pressure of 15 pounds per square inch is "sufficiently" close to zero to use the formula $s = \frac{1}{2}gt.^2$ Similarly, we cannot compute cross-elasticities of demand and then classify firms into industries according as there is a "substantial gap in the cross-elasticities of demand." As Marshall says, "The question where the lines of division between different commodities [i.e., industries] should be drawn must be settled by convenience of the particular discussion."[31] Everything depends on the problem; there is no inconsistency in regarding the same firm as if it were a perfect competitor for one problem, and a monopolist for another, just as there is none in regarding the same chalk mark as a Euclidean line for one problem, a Euclidean surface for a second, and a Euclidean solid for a third. The size of the elasticity and cross-elasticity of demand, the number of firms producing physically similar products, etc., are all relevant because they are or may be among the variables used to define the correspondence between the ideal and real entities in a particular problem and to specify the circumstances under which the theory holds sufficiently well; but they do not provide, once for all, a classification of firms as competitive or monopolistic.

An example may help to clarify this point. Suppose the problem is to determine the effect on retail prices of cigarettes of an

31. *Principles*, p. 100.

increase, expected to be permanent, in the federal cigarette tax. I venture to predict that broadly correct results will be obtained by treating cigarette firms as if they were producing an identical product and were in perfect competition. Of course, in such a case, "some convention must be made as to the" number of Chesterfield cigarettes "which are taken as equivalent" to a Marlborough.[32]

On the other hand, the hypothesis that cigarette firms would behave as if they were perfectly competitive would have been a false guide to their reactions to price control in World War II, and this would doubtless have been recognized before the event. Costs of the cigarette firms must have risen during the war. Under such circumstances perfect competitors would have reduced the quantity offered for sale at the previously existing price. But, at that price, the wartime rise in the income of the public presumably increased the quantity demanded. Under conditions of perfect competition strict adherence to the legal price would therefore imply not only a "shortage" in the sense that quantity demanded exceeded quantity supplied but also an absolute decline in the number of cigarettes produced. The facts contradict this particular implication: there was reasonably good adherence to maximum cigarette prices, yet the quantities produced increased substantially. The common force of increased costs presumably operated less strongly than the disruptive force of the desire by each firm to keep its share of the market, to maintain the value and prestige of its brand name, especially when the excess-profits tax shifted a large share of the costs of this kind of advertising to the government. For this problem the cigarette firms cannot be treated *as if* they were perfect competitors.

Wheat farming is frequently taken to exemplify perfect competition. Yet, while for some problems it is appropriate to treat cigarette producers as if they comprised a perfectly competitive industry, for some it is not appropriate to treat wheat producers as if they did. For example, it may not be if the problem is the differential in prices paid by local elevator operators for wheat.

Marshall's apparatus turned out to be most useful for problems in which a group of firms is affected by common stimuli,

32. Quoted parts from *ibid.*

and in which the firms can be treated *as if* they were perfect competitors. This is the source of the misconception that Marshall "assumed" perfect competition in some descriptive sense. It would be highly desirable to have a more general theory than Marshall's, one that would cover at the same time both those cases in which differentiation of product or fewness of numbers makes an essential difference and those in which it does not. Such a theory would enable us to handle problems we now cannot and, in addition, facilitate determination of the range of circumstances under which the simpler theory can be regarded as a good enough approximation. To perform this function, the more general theory must have content and substance; it must have implications susceptible to empirical contradiction and of substantive interest and importance.

The theory of imperfect or monopolistic competition developed by Chamberlin and Robinson is an attempt to construct such a more general theory.[33] Unfortunately, it possesses none of the attributes that would make it a truly useful general theory. Its contribution has been limited largely to improving the exposition of the economics of the individual firm and thereby the derivation of implications of the Marshallian model, refining Marshall's monopoly analysis, and enriching the vocabulary available for describing industrial experience.

The deficiencies of the theory are revealed most clearly in its treatment of, or inability to treat, problems involving groups of firms—Marshallian "industries." So long as it is insisted that differentiation of product is essential—and it is the distinguishing feature of the theory that it does insist on this point—the definition of an industry in terms of firms producing an identical product cannot be used. By that definition each firm is a separate industry. Definition in terms of "close" substitutes or a "substantial" gap in cross-elasticities evades the issue, introduces fuzziness and undefinable terms into the abstract model where they have no place, and serves only to make the theory analytically meaningless—"close" and "substantial" are in the same category

33. E. H. Chamberlin, *The Theory of Monopolistic Competition* (6th ed.; Cambridge: Harvard University Press, 1950); Joan Robinson, *The Economics of Imperfect Competition* (London: Macmillan & Co., 1933).

as a "small" air pressure.[34] In one connection Chamberlin implicitly defines an industry as a group of firms having identical cost and demand curves.[35] But this, too, is logically meaningless so long as differentiation of product is, as claimed, essential and not to be put aside. What does it mean to say that the cost and demand curves of a firm producing bulldozers are identical with those of a firm producing hairpins?[36] And if it is meaningless for bulldozers and hairpins, it is meaningless also for two brands of toothpaste—so long as it is insisted that the difference between the two brands is fundamentally important.

The theory of monopolistic competition offers no tools for the analysis of an industry and so no stopping place between the firm at one extreme and general equilibrium at the other.[37] It is therefore incompetent to contribute to the analysis of a host of important problems: the one extreme is too narrow to be of great interest; the other, too broad to permit meaningful generalizations.[38]

VI. Conclusion

Economics as a positive science is a body of tentatively accepted generalizations about economic phenomena that can be used to predict the consequences of changes in circumstances.

34. See R. L. Bishop, "Elasticities, Cross-elasticities, and Market Relationships," *American Economic Review,* XLII (December, 1952), 779–803, for a recent attempt to construct a rigorous classification of market relationships along these lines. Despite its ingenuity and sophistication, the result seems to me thoroughly unsatisfactory. It rests basically on certain numbers being classified as "large" or "small," yet there is no discussion at all of how to decide whether a particular number is "large" or "small," as of course there cannot be on a purely abstract level.

35. *Op. cit.,* p. 82.

36. There always exists a transformation of quantities that will make either the cost curves or the demand curves identical; this transformation need not, however, be linear, in which case it will involve different-sized units of one product at different levels of output. There does not necessarily exist a transformation that will make both pairs of curves identical.

37. See Robert Triffin, *Monopolistic Competition and General Equilibrium Theory* (Cambridge: Harvard University Press, 1940), esp. pp. 188–89.

38. For a detailed critique see George J. Stigler, "Monopolistic Competition in Retrospect," in *Five Lectures on Economic Problems* (London: Macmillan & Co., 1949), pp. 12–24.

Progress in expanding this body of generalizations, strengthening our confidence in their validity, and improving the accuracy of the predictions they yield is hindered not only by the limitations of human ability that impede all search for knowledge but also by obstacles that are especially important for the social sciences in general and economics in particular, though by no means peculiar to them. Familiarity with the subject matter of economics breeds contempt for special knowledge about it. The importance of its subject matter to everyday life and to major issues of public policy impedes objectivity and promotes confusion between scientific analysis and normative judgment. The necessity of relying on uncontrolled experience rather than on controlled experiment makes it difficult to produce dramatic and clear-cut evidence to justify the acceptance of tentative hypotheses. Reliance on uncontrolled experience does not affect the fundamental methodological principle that a hypothesis can be tested only by the conformity of its implications or predictions with observable phenomena; but it does render the task of testing hypotheses more difficult and gives greater scope for confusion about the methodological principles involved. More than other scientists, social scientists need to be self-conscious about their methodology.

One confusion that has been particularly rife and has done much damage is confusion about the role of "assumptions" in economic analysis. A meaningful scientific hypothesis or theory typically asserts that certain forces are, and other forces are not, important in understanding a particular class of phenomena. It is frequently convenient to present such a hypothesis by stating that the phenomena it is desired to predict behave in the world of observation *as if* they occurred in a hypothetical and highly simplified world containing only the forces that the hypothesis asserts to be important. In general, there is more than one way to formulate such a description—more than one set of "assumptions" in terms of which the theory can be presented. The choice among such alternative assumptions is made on the grounds of the resulting economy, clarity, and precision in presenting the hypothesis; their capacity to bring indirect evidence to bear on the validity of the hypothesis by suggesting some of its implications that can be readily checked with observation or by bringing out its connection with other hypotheses dealing with related phenomena; and similar considerations.

Such a theory cannot be tested by comparing its "assumptions" directly with "reality." Indeed, there is no meaningful way in which this can be done. Complete "realism" is clearly unattainable, and the question whether a theory is realistic "enough" can be settled only by seeing whether it yields predictions that are good enough for the purpose in hand or that are better than predictions from alternative theories. Yet the belief that a theory can be tested by the realism of its assumptions independently of the accuracy of its predictions is widespread and the source of much of the perennial criticism of economic theory as unrealistic. Such criticism is largely irrelevant, and, in consequence, most attempts to reform economic theory that it has stimulated have been unsuccessful.

The irrelevance of so much criticism of economic theory does not of course imply that existing economic theory deserves any high degree of confidence. These criticisms may miss the target, yet there may be a target for criticism. In a trivial sense, of course, there obviously is. Any theory is necessarily provisional and subject to change with the advance of knowledge. To go beyond this platitude, it is necessary to be more specific about the content of "existing economic theory" and to distinguish among its different branches; some parts of economic theory clearly deserve more confidence than others. A comprehensive evaluation of the present state of positive economics, summary of the evidence bearing on its validity, and assessment of the relative confidence that each part deserves is clearly a task for a treatise or a set of treatises, if it be possible at all, not for a brief paper on methodology.

About all that is possible here is the cursory expression of a personal view. Existing relative price theory, which is designed to explain the allocation of resources among alternative ends and the division of the product among the co-operating resources and which reached almost its present form in Marshall's *Principles of Economics,* seems to me both extremely fruitful and deserving of much confidence for the kind of economic system that characterizes Western nations. Despite the appearance of considerable controversy, this is true equally of existing static monetary theory, which is designed to explain the structural or secular level of absolute prices, aggregate output, and other variables for the economy as a whole and which has had a form of the quantity theory of money as its basic core in all of its major variants from David Hume to the Cambridge School to Irving Fisher to John Maynard Keynes. The weakest and least satisfactory part of current economic theory seems to me to be in the field of monetary dynamics, which is concerned with the process of adaptation of the economy as a whole to changes in conditions and so with short-period fluctuations in aggregate activity. In this field we do not even have a theory that can appropriately be called "the" existing theory of monetary dynamics.

Of course, even in relative price and static monetary theory there is enormous room for extending the scope and improving the accuracy of existing theory. In particular, undue emphasis on the descriptive realism of "assumptions" has contributed to neglect of the critical problem of determining the limits of validity of the various hypotheses that together constitute the existing economic theory in these areas. The abstract models corresponding to these hypotheses have been elaborated in considerable detail and greatly improved in rigor and precision. Descriptive material on the characteristics of our economic system and its operations have been amassed on an unprecedented scale. This is all to the good. But, if we are to use effectively these abstract models and this descriptive material, we must have a comparable exploration of the criteria for determining what abstract model it is best to use for particular kinds of problems, what entities in the abstract model are to be identified with what observable entities, and what features of the problem or of the circumstances have the greatest effect on the accuracy of the predictions yielded by a particular model or theory.

Progress in positive economics will require not only the testing and elaboration of existing hypotheses but also the construction of new hypotheses. On this problem there is little to say on a formal level. The construction of hypotheses is a creative act of inspiration, intuition, invention; its essence is the vision of something new in familiar material. The process must be discussed in psychological, not logical, categories; studied in autobiographies and biographies, not treatises on scientific method; and promoted by maxim and example, not syllogism or theorem.

PART II
Price Theory

The Marshallian Demand Curve[*]

ALFRED MARSHALL's theory of demand strikingly exemplifies his "impatience with rigid definition and an excessive tendency to let the context explain his meaning."[1] The concept of the demand curve as a functional relation between the quantity and the price of a particular commodity is explained repeatedly and explicitly in the *Principles of Economics:* in words in the text, in plane curves in the footnotes, and in symbolic form in the Mathematical Appendix. A complete definition of the demand curve, including, in particular, a statement of the variables that are to be considered the same for all points on the curve and the variables that are to be allowed to vary, is nowhere given explicitly. The reader is left to infer the contents of *ceteris paribus* from general and vague statements, parenthetical remarks, examples that do not purport to be exhaustive, and concise mathematical notes in the Appendix.

In view of the importance of the demand curve in Marshallian analysis, it is natural that other economists should have constructed a rigorous definition to fill the gap that Marshall left. This occurred at an early date, apparently without controversy about the interpretation to be placed on Marshall's comments. The resulting definition of the demand curve is now so much an intrinsic part of current economic theory and is so widely accepted as Marshall's own that the assertion that Marshall himself gave no explicit rigorous definition may shock most readers.

[*] Reprinted from *Journal of Political Economy,* LVII (December, 1949), 463–95.

I am deeply indebted for helpful criticism and suggestions to A. F. Burns, Aaron Director, C. W. Guillebaud, H. Gregg Lewis, A. R. Prest, D. H. Robertson, G. J. Stigler, and, especially, Jacob Viner, to whose penetrating discussion of the demand curve in his course in economic theory I can trace some of the central ideas and even details of this article. The standard comment that none is to be held responsible for the views expressed herein has particular relevance, since most disagreed with my interpretation of Marshall as presented in an earlier and much briefer draft of this article.

1. C. W. Guillebaud, "The Evolution of Marshall's *Principles of Economics,*" *Economic Journal,* LII (December, 1942), 333.

Yet why this particular interpretation evolved and why it gained such unquestioned acceptance are a mystery that requires explanation. The currently accepted interpretation can be read into Marshall only by a liberal—and, I think, strained —reading of his remarks, and its acceptance implicitly convicts him of logical inconsistency and mathematical error at the very foundation of his theory of demand. More important, the alternative interpretation of the demand curve that is yielded by a literal reading of his remarks not only leaves his original work on the theory of demand free from both logical inconsistency and mathematical error but also is more useful for the analysis of most economic problems.

Section I presents the two interpretations of the demand curve and compares them in some detail; Section II argues that a demand curve constructed on my interpretation is the more useful for the analysis of practical problems, whatever may be the verdict about its validity as an interpretation of Marshall; Section III demonstrates that my interpretation is consistent with Marshall's monetary theory and with his work on consumer's surplus; and Section IV presents the textual evidence on the validity of my interpretation. Finally, Section V argues that the change that has occurred in the interpretation of the demand curve reflects a corresponding change in the role assigned to economic theory.

I. Alternative Interpretations of Marshall's Demand Curve

The demand curve of a particular group (which may, as a special case, consist of a single individual) for a particular commodity shows the quantity (strictly speaking, the maximum quantity) of the commodity that will be purchased by the group per unit of time at each price. So far, no question arises; this part of the definition is explicit in Marshall and is common to both alternatives to be discussed. The problem of interpretation relates to the phrase, "other things the same," ordinarily attached to this definition.

In the first place, it should be noted that "same" in this phrase does not mean "same over time." The points on a demand curve are alternative possibilities, not temporally ordered combinations of quantity and price. "Same" means "same for all points on the demand curve"; the different points are to differ in quantity and price and are not to differ with respect to "other things."[2] In the second place, "all" other things cannot be supposed to be the same without completely emasculating the concept. For example, if (a) total money expenditure on all commodities, (b) the price of every commodity other than the one in question, and (c) the quantity purchased of every other commodity were supposed to be the same, the amount of money spent on the commodity in question would necessarily be the same at all prices, simply as a matter of arithmetic, and the demand curve would have unit elasticity everywhere.[3] Different specifications of the "other things" will yield different demand curves. For example, one demand curve will be obtained by excluding b from the list of "other things"; another, quite different one, by excluding c.

A. THE CURRENT INTERPRETATION

The current interpretation of Marshall's demand curve explicitly includes in the list of "other things" (1) tastes and preferences of the group of purchasers considered, (2) their money income, and (3) the price of every other commodity. The quantities of other commodities are explicitly considered as differ-

2. Of course, when correlations among statistical time series are regarded as estimates of demand curves, the hypothesis is that "other things" have been approximately constant over time or that appropriate allowance has been made for changes in them. Similarly, when correlations among cross-section data are regarded as estimates of demand curves, the hypothesis is that "other things" are approximately the same for the units distinguished or that appropriate allowance has been made for differences among them. In both cases the problem of estimation should be clearly distinguished from the theoretical construct to be estimated.

3. Yet Sidney Weintraub not only suggests that Marshall intended to keep a, b, and c simultaneously the same but goes on to say: "Clearly Marshall's assumption means a unit elasticity of demand in the market reviewed and no ramifications elsewhere; that was why he adopted it" ("The Foundations of the Demand Curve," *American Economic Review,* XXXII [September, 1942], 538–52, quotation from n. 12, p. 541). Weintraub even adds the condition of constant tastes and preferences to a, b, and c, speaking of a change in tastes as shifting the demand curve. Obviously, a, b, and c together leave no room for tastes and preferences or, indeed, for anything except simple arithmetic.

ent at different points on the demand curve, and still other variables are ignored.[4]

On this interpretation it is clear that, while money income is the same for different points on the demand curve, real income is not. At the lower of two prices for the commodity in question, more of some commodities can be purchased without reducing the amounts purchased of other commodities. The lower the price, therefore, the higher the real income.

B. AN ALTERNATIVE INTERPRETATION

It seems to me more faithful to both the letter and the spirit of Marshall's writings to include in the list of "other things" (1) tastes and preferences of the group of purchasers considered, (2) their real income, and (3) the price of every closely related commodity.

Two variants of this interpretation can be distinguished, according to the device adopted for keeping real income the same at different points on the demand curve. One variant, which Marshall employed in the text of the *Principles,* is obtained by replacing "(2) their real income" by (2a) their money income and (2b) the "purchasing power of money." Constancy of the "purchasing power of money" for different prices of the commodity in question implies compensating variations in the prices of some or all other commodities. These variations will, indeed, be negligible if the commodity in question accounts for a negligible fraction of total expenditures; but they should not be

---

4. Explicit definition of the demand curve in this way by followers of Marshall dates back at least to 1894 (see F. Y. Edgeworth, "Demand Curves" [art.], *Palgrave's Dictionary of Political Economy,* ed. Henry Higgs [rev. ed.; London: Macmillan & Co., 1926]). Edgeworth's article apparently dates from the first edition, which was published in 1894. While Edgeworth does not explicitly attribute this interpretation to Marshall, it is clear from the context that he is talking about a Marshallian demand curve and that he does not regard his statements as inconsistent in any way with Marshall's *Principles.* Though no explicit listing of "other things" is given by J. R. Hicks, *Value and Capital* (Oxford, 1939), the list given above is implicit throughout chaps. i and ii, which are explicitly devoted to elaborating and extending Marshall's analysis of demand. For statements in modern textbooks on advanced economic theory see G. J. Stigler, *The Theory of Price* (New York: Macmillan Co., 1946), pp. 86–90, and Kenneth E. Boulding, *Economic Analysis* (rev. ed.; New York: Harper & Bros., 1948), pp. 134–35.

disregarded, both because empirical considerations must be sharply separated from logical considerations and because the demand curve need not be limited in applicability to such commodities. On this variant all commodities are, in effect, divided into three groups: (*a*) the commodity in question, (*b*) closely related commodities, and (*c*) all other commodities. The absolute price of each commodity in group *b* is supposed to be the same for different points on the demand curve; only the "average" price, or an index number of prices, is considered for group *c*; and it is to be supposed to rise or fall with a fall or rise in the price of group *a*, so as to keep the "purchasing power of money" the same.

The other variant, which Marshall employed in the Mathematical Appendix of the *Principles,* is obtained by retaining "(2) their real income" and adding (4) the average price of all other commodities. Constancy of real income for different prices of the commodity in question then implies compensating variations in money income. As the price of the commodity in question rises or falls, money income is to be supposed to rise or fall so as to keep real income the same.

These two variants are essentially equivalent mathematically,[5] but the assumption of compensating variations in other prices

5. Let x and y be the quantity and price, respectively, of the commodity in question; x' and y', the quantity and price of a composite commodity representing all other commodities; and m, money income. Let

$$x = g\,(y,\, y',\, m,\, u) \qquad (1)$$

be the demand curve for the commodity in question, given a utility function,

$$U = U\,(x,\, x',\, u)\,, \qquad (2)$$

where u is a parameter to allow for changes in taste, and subject to the condition

$$xy + x'y' = m\,. \qquad (3)$$

From eq. (3) and the usual utility analysis, it follows that eq. (1), like eq. (3), is a homogeneous function of degree zero in y, y', and m; i.e., that

$$g\,(\lambda y,\, \lambda y',\, \lambda m,\, u) = g\,(y,\, y',\, m,\, u)\,. \qquad (4)$$

On the current interpretation, a two-dimensional demand curve is obtained from eq. (1) directly by giving y' (other prices), m (income), and u (tastes) fixed values. A given value of y then implies a given value of x from eq. (1), a given value of x' from eq. (3), and hence a given value of U (i.e., real in-is easier to explain verbally and can be justified as empirically relevant by considerations of monetary theory, which is presumably why Marshall used this variant in his text. On the other hand, the assumption of compensating variations in income is somewhat more convenient mathematically, which is presumably why Marshall used this variant in his Mathematical Appendix.

On my interpretation, Marshall's demand curve is identical with one of the constructions introduced by Slutsky in his famous paper on the theory of choice, namely, the reaction of quantity demanded to a "compensated variation of price," that is, to a variation in price accompanied by a compensating change in money income.[6] Slutsky expressed the compensating change in

---

come) from eq. (2). The value of U will vary with y, being higher, the lower y is.

On my alternative interpretation, u and U are given fixed values and x' is eliminated from eqs. (2) and (3). This gives a pair of equations,

$$x = g\,(y,\, y',\, m,\, u_0)\,, \tag{5}$$

$$U_0 = U_0\left(x,\, \frac{m - xy}{y'},\, u_0\right), \tag{6}$$

where the subscript 0 designates fixed values. The two-dimensional variant involving compensating variations in other prices is obtained by eliminating y' from eqs. (5) and (6) and giving m a fixed value; the variant involving compensating variations in income, by eliminating m from eqs. (5) and (6) and giving y' a fixed value.

The homogeneity of eqs. (5) and (6) in y, y', and m means that x is a function only of ratios among them. Thus eqs. (5) and (6) can be written:

$$x = g\,(y,\, y',\, m,\, u_0) = g\left(\frac{y}{m},\frac{y'}{m},1,\, u_0\right) = g\left(\frac{y}{y'},1,\frac{m}{y'},u_0\right), \tag{5'}$$

$$\left. \begin{aligned} U_0 = U_0\left(x,\, \frac{m - xy}{y'},\, u_0\right) &= U_0\left(x,\, \frac{1 - x\,\dfrac{y}{m}}{\dfrac{y'}{m}},\, u_0\right) \\[2mm] &= U_0\left(x,\, \frac{m}{y'} - x\,\frac{y}{y'},\, u_0\right). \end{aligned}\right\} \tag{6'}$$

The choice of price-compensating variations is equivalent to selecting the forms of these two equations in the next to the last terms of eqs. (5') and (6'); of income-compensating variations, to selecting the forms in the last terms.

6. Eugenio Slutsky, "Sulla teoria del bilancio del consumatore," *Giornale degli economisti*, LI (1915), 1–26, esp. sec. 8. [A translation of this article is now

money income in terms of observable phenomena, taking it as equal to the change in price *times* the quantity demanded at the initial price. Mosak has shown that, in the limit, the change in income so computed is identical with the change required to keep the individual on the same level of utility (on the same indifference curve).[7] It follows that a similar statement is valid for compensating changes in other prices. In the limit the change in other prices required to keep the individual on the same indifference curve when his money income is unchanged but the price of one commodity varies is identical with the change in other prices required to keep unchanged the total cost of the basket of commodities purchased at the initial prices, that is, to keep unchanged the usual type of cost-of-living index number.

C. COMPARISON OF THE INTERPRETATIONS

The relation between demand curves constructed under the two interpretations is depicted in Figure 1. Curve Cc represents a demand curve of an individual consumer for a commodity X drawn on the current interpretation. Money income and the prices of other commodities are supposed the same for all points on it; in consequence, real income is lower at C than at P, since, if the individual sought to buy OM of X at a price of OC, he would be forced to curtail his purchases of something else. As the curve is drawn, of course, he buys none of X at a price of OC, spending the sum of $OHPM$ on other commodities that his action at a price of OH shows him to value less highly than he does OM units of X. The ordinate is described as the ratio of the price of X to the price of other commodities. For the demand curve Cc this is a question only of the unit of measure, since other prices are supposed to be the same for all points on it.

From the definition of the demand curve Cc, OC is obviously the maximum price per unit that an individual would be willing

---

available in American Economic Association, *Readings in Price Theory* (Chicago: Richard D. Irwin, Inc., 1952), pp. 27–56.]

7. Jacob L. Mosak, "On the Interpretation of the Fundamental Equation of Value Theory," in O. Lange, F. McIntyre, and T. O. Yntema (eds.), *Studies in Mathematical Economics and Econometrics* (Chicago: University of Chicago Press, 1942), pp. 69–74, esp. n. 5, pp. 73–74, which contains a rigorous proof of this statement by A. Wald.

to pay for an infinitesimal initial increment of X when his money income and the prices of other commodities have the values assumed in drawing Cc. Let us suppose him to purchase this amount at a price of OC, determine the maximum price per unit he would be willing to pay for an additional increment, and continue in this fashion, exacting the maximum possible amount for each additional increment. Let these successive maximum prices per unit define the curve Cv. The consumer obviously has the same real income at each point on Cv as at C, since the maximum

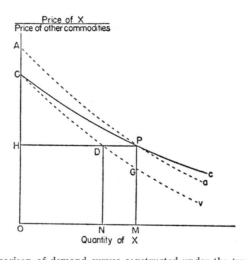

Fig. 1.—Comparison of demand curves constructed under the two interpretations.

price has been extracted from him for each successive unit, so that he has gained no utility in the process.

Cv is now a demand curve constructed according to my interpretation of Marshall. If other prices are supposed to be the same, the necessary compensating variations in money income as the price of X falls are given by triangular areas exemplified by HCD for a price of OH: OH is the maximum price per unit that the individual will give for an additional infinitesimal increment of X when he has spent $OCDN$ for ON of X out of his initial income of, say, m; but his situation is exactly the same if, when the price of X is OH, his income is $(m - HCD)$ and he spends $OHDN$ on X; he has the same amount left to spend on all other commodities, their prices are the same, and he has the same amount of X; accordingly, his demand price will be the same, and he will buy ON of X at a price of OH and an income of $(m - HCD)$.[8]

If compensating variations in other prices rather than in money income are used to keep real income the same, the absolute price of neither X nor other commodities can be read directly from Figure 1. For each ratio of the price of X to the price of other commodities, the quantity of X purchased will be that shown on Cv. But the prices of other goods will vary along Cv, rising as the relative price of X falls, so the absolute price of X can no longer be obtained by multiplying the ordinate by a single scale factor.

Figure 1 is drawn on the assumption that X is a "normal" commodity, that is, a commodity the consumption of which is higher, the higher the income. This is the reason Cv is drawn to the left of Cc—at every point on Cv other than C, real income is

---

8. In the notation of n. 5, except that u is omitted for simplicity, the quantities of X and X' that will be purchased for any given values of y and y' and any given real income, U_0, are obtained by solving simultaneously:

$$\frac{U_x}{U_{x'}} = \frac{y}{y'} , \tag{1}$$

and

$$U(x, x') = U_0 , \tag{2}$$

where U_x and $U_{x'}$ stand for the partial derivatives of U with respect to x and x', respectively, i.e., for the marginal utility of X and X'. The solution of these equations gives the demand curve on my interpretation of Marshall, using compensating variations in money income.

U_0 $(0, m/y')$ is the utility at C in the diagram. For any given amount of X and given value of y', the amount of X' purchased is obtained by solving

$$U(x, x') = U_0 \left(0, \frac{m}{y'}\right), \tag{3}$$

which is identical with eq. (2). The amount paid for X (the area under Cv) is

$$m - x'y' . \tag{4}$$

The maximum price that will be paid per unit of X is the derivative of eq. (4), or

$$y = -\frac{dx'}{dx} y' = \frac{U_x}{U_{x'}} y' , \tag{5}$$

which is identical with eq. (1). It follows that Cv is a demand curve constructed on my interpretation of Marshall.

less than at the corresponding point on Cc; hence less X would be consumed.

Curve Aa represents a demand curve on my interpretation of Marshall for a real income the same as at point P on Cc; it is like Cv but for a higher real income. Real income is higher on Aa than on Cc for prices above OH, lower for prices below OH, which is the reason Aa is to the right of Cc for prices above OH and to the left of Cc for prices below OH.

D. WHY TWO INTERPRETATIONS ARE POSSIBLE

The possibility of interpreting Marshall in these two quite different ways arises in part from the vagueness of Marshall's exposition, from his failure to give precise and rigorous definitions. A more fundamental reason, however, is the existence of inconsistency in the third and later editions of the *Principles*. In that edition Marshall introduced the celebrated passage bearing on the Giffen phenomenon. This passage and a related sentence added at the same time to the Mathematical Appendix fit the current interpretation better than they fit my interpretation. Although these are the only two items that I have been able to find in any edition of the *Principles* of which this is true, they provide some basis for the current interpretation. A hypothesis to explain the introduction of this inconsistency into the *Principles* is offered in Section IV, E, below.

II. THE RELATIVE USEFULNESS OF THE TWO INTERPRETATIONS

The relative usefulness of the two interpretations of the demand curve can be evaluated only in terms of some general conception of the role of economic theory. I shall use the conception that underlies Marshall's work, in which the primary emphasis is on positive economic analysis, on the forging of tools that can be used fairly directly in analyzing practical problems. Economic theory was to him an "engine for the discovery of concrete truth."[9] "Man's powers are limited: almost every one of

9. Alfred Marshall, "The Present Position of Economics" (1885), reprinted in *Memorials of Alfred Marshall*, ed. A. C. Pigou (London: Macmillan & Co., 1925), p. 159.

nature's riddles is complex. He breaks it up, studies one bit at a time, and at last combines his partial solutions with a supreme effort of his whole small strength into some sort of an attempt at a solution of the whole riddle."[10] The underlying justification for the central role of the concepts of demand and supply in Marshall's entire structure of analysis is the empirical generalization that an enumeration of the forces affecting demand in any problem and of the forces affecting supply will yield two lists that contain few items in common. Demand and supply are to him concepts for organizing materials, labels in an "analytical filing box." The "commodity" for which a demand curve is drawn is another label, not a word for a physical or technical entity to be defined once and for all independently of the problem at hand. Marshall writes:

> The question where the lines of division between different commodities should be drawn must be settled by convenience of the particular discussion. For some purposes it may be best to regard Chinese and Indian teas, or even Souchong and Pekoe teas, as different commodities; and to have a separate demand schedule for each of them. While for other purposes it may be best to group together commodities as distinct as beef and mutton, or even as tea and coffee, and to have a single list to represent the demand for the two combined.[11]

A. THE DISTINCTION BETWEEN CLOSELY RELATED
AND ALL OTHER COMMODITIES

A demand function containing as separate variables the prices of a rigidly defined and exhaustive list of commodities, all on the same footing, seems largely foreign to this approach. It may be a useful expository device to bring home the mutual interdependence of economic phenomena; it cannot form part of Marshall's "engine for the discovery of concrete truth." The analyst who attacks a concrete problem can take explicit account of only a limited number of factors; he will inevitably separate commodities that are closely related to the one immediately

10. Alfred Marshall, "Mechanical and Biological Analogies in Economics" (1898), *ibid.,* p. 314.

11. Marshall, *Principles of Economics* (8th ed.; London: Macmillan & Co., 1920), p. 100 n. All subsequent page references to the *Principles,* unless otherwise stated, are to the eighth and final edition.

under study from commodities that are more distantly related. He can pay some attention to each closely related commodity. He cannot handle the more distantly related commodities in this way; he will tend either to ignore them or to consider them as a group. The formally more general demand curve will, in actual use, become the kind of demand curve that is yielded by my interpretation of Marshall.

The part of the Marshallian filing box covered by *ceteris paribus* typically includes three quite different kinds of variables, distinguished by their relation to the variable whose adaptation to some change is directly under investigation (e.g., the price of a commodity): (*a*) variables that are expected both to be materially affected by the variable under study and, in turn, to affect it; (*b*) variables that are expected to be little, if at all, affected by the variable under study but to materially affect it; (*c*) the remaining variables, expected neither to affect significantly the variable under study nor to be significantly affected by it.

In demand analysis the prices of closely related commodities are the variables in group *a*. They are put individually into the pound of *ceteris paribus* to pave the way for further analysis. Holding their prices constant is a provisional step. They must inevitably be affected by anything that affects the commodity in question; and this indirect effect can be analyzed most conveniently by first isolating the direct effect, systematically tracing the repercussions of the direct effect on each closely related commodity, and then tracing the subsequent reflex influences on the commodity in question. Indeed, in many ways, the role of the demand curve itself is as much to provide an orderly means of analyzing these indirect effects as to isolate the direct effect on the commodity in question.

The average price of "all other commodities," income and wealth, and tastes and preferences are the variables in group *b*. These variables are likely to be affected only negligibly by factors affecting primarily the commodity in question. On the other hand, any changes in them would have a significant effect on that commodity. They are put into the pound in order to separate problems, to segregate the particular reactions under study. They are put in individually and explicitly because they are so important that account will have to be taken of them in any application of the analysis.

Price changes within the group of "all other commodities" and an indefinitely long list of other variables are contained in group c. These variables are to be ignored. They are too numerous and each too unimportant to permit separate account to be taken of them.

In keeping with the spirit of Marshallian analysis this classification of variables is to be taken as illustrative, not definitive. What particular variables are appropriate for each group is to be determined by the problem in hand, the amount of information available, the detail required in results, and the patience and resources of the analyst.

B. CONSTANCY OF REAL INCOME

It has just been argued that any actual analysis of a concrete economic problem with the aid of demand curves will inevitably adopt one feature of my interpretation of Marshall—consideration of a residual list of commodities as a single group. For somewhat subtler reasons this is likely to be true also of the second feature of my interpretation of Marshall—holding real income constant along a demand curve. If an analysis, begun with a demand curve constructed on the current interpretation, is carried through and made internally consistent, it will be found that the demand curve has been subjected to shifts that, in effect, result from failure to keep real income constant along the demand curve.

An example will show how this occurs. Let us suppose that the government grants to producers of commodity X a subsidy of a fixed amount per unit of output, financed by a general income tax, so that money income available for expenditure (i.e., net of tax and gross of subsidy) is unchanged. For simplicity, suppose, first, that no commodities are closely related to X either as rivals or as complements, so that interrelations in consumption between X and particular other commodities can be neglected; second, that the tax is paid by individuals in about the same income class and with about the same consumption pattern as those who benefit from the subsidy, so that complications arising from changes in the distribution of income can be neglected; and, third, that there are no idle resources. Let *DD* in Figure 2 be a demand curve for commodity *X*, and *SS* be the initial supply curve for *X*, and let the initial position at their intersection, point *P*, be a position of full equilibrium. The effect of the subsidy is to lower the supply curve to *S'S'*. Since we have ruled out repercussions through consumption relations with other markets and through changes in the level or distribution of money income, it is reason-

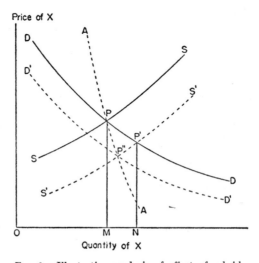

FIG. 2.—Illustrative analysis of effect of subsidy

able to expect that the intersection of this new supply curve and the initial demand curve, point *P'*, will itself be a position of full equilibrium, involving a lower price and larger quantity of *X*. Yet, if the demand curve is constructed on the current interpretation and if the supply curve is not perfectly inelastic,[12] point *P'* is not a position of full equilibrium. This can be seen most easily by supposing *DD* to have unit elasticity, so that the same amount is spent on *X* at *P'* as at *P*. The same amount is then available

12. If it is perfectly inelastic, neither the price nor the quantity of *X* is changed, so the new position of equilibrium coincides with the old; but the demand curve will pass through the initial position of equilibrium whether constructed on the current interpretation or on mine; hence the two coincide at the one point on them that is relevant.

to spend on all other commodities, and, since their prices are supposed to be the same for all points on *DD* under the current interpretation, the same quantity of each of them will be demanded. But then where do the resources come from to produce the extra *MN* units of *X?* Obviously, our assumptions are not internally consistent. The additional units of *X* can be produced only by bidding resources away from the production of other commodities, in the process raising their prices and reducing the amount of them produced. The final equilibrium position will therefore involve higher prices and lower quantities of other commodities. But, on the current interpretation, this means a shift in the demand curve for *X*—say, to *D'D'*—and a final equilibrium position of, say *P.*"[13]

The assumption that the elasticity of *DD* is unity is not, of course, essential for this argument. If the elasticity of *DD* is less than unity, a larger amount than formerly is available to spend on other commodities; at unchanged prices this means a larger quantity demanded. In consequence, while the additional amount of resources required to produce the increased amount of *X* demanded is smaller when *DD* is inelastic than when it has unit elasticity, this is counterbalanced by increased pressure for resources to produce other commodities. Similarly, when *DD* is elastic, the additional amount of resources required to produce the increased quantity of *X* demanded is larger than when *DD* has unit elasticity, but some resources are released in the first instance from the production of other commodities.

No such internal inconsistency as that just outlined arises if the demand curve is constructed by keeping real income the same. Curve *AA* is such a demand curve. At prices of *X* less than *PM*, prices of other commodities are supposed to be sufficiently higher than at *P* to keep real income the same, which involves the release of just enough resources so that the position of final equilib-

---

13. *D'D'* will not necessarily be to the left of *DD* even for a "normal" commodity. The reason is that the ordinate of Fig. 2 measures the absolute price of *X,* so that ordinates of the same height on *DD* and *D'D'* represent different ratios of the price of *X* to the price of other commodities. If the ordinate measured the ratio of the price of *X* to the price of other commodities, *D'D'* would always be to the left of *DD* for "normal" commodities, always to the right for "inferior" commodities.

rium, P'', lies on the demand curve so constructed—at least for small changes in the price of X.[14]

The fundamental principle illustrated by this example can be put more generally. The reason why a demand curve constructed under the current interpretation fails to give the correct solution even when all disturbing influences can be neglected is that each point on it implicitly refers to a different productive capacity of the community. A reduction in the price of the commodity in question is to be regarded as enabling the community, if it so wishes, to consume more of some commodities—this commodity or others—without consuming less of any commodity. But the particular change in supply whose consequences we sought to analyze—that arising from a subsidy—does not make available any additional resources to the community; any increase in the consumption of the commodity in question must be at

14. Let X' be a single composite commodity representing all commodities other than X; x and x', the quantities of X and X'; and y and y', their prices. Let the subscript 1 refer to values at the initial position of equilibrium, P; the subscript 2, to values at the final position, P''. The condition of constant total expenditures means that

$$x_1 y_1 + x'_1 y'_1 = x_2 y_2 + x'_2 y'_2 . \tag{1}$$

As was pointed out above (Sec. I, B), in the limit, holding real income constant is equivalent to holding constant the cost of a fixed basket of commodities. Thus, if P'' is considered close to P,

$$x_1 y_1 + x'_1 y'_1 = x_1 y_2 + x'_1 y'_2. \tag{2}$$

In the neighborhood of P, y_1 can be regarded as the cost per unit of producing X; y'_1, as the cost per unit of producing X'. The condition that sufficient resources be released to permit the production of the requisite additional amount of X is therefore

$$(x_2 - x_1) y_1 = - (x'_2 - x'_1) y'_1 , \tag{3}$$

which is equivalent to

$$x_1 y_1 + x'_1 y'_1 = x_2 y_1 + x'_2 y'_1 . \tag{4}$$

But, in the limit, eqs. (1) and (2) imply eq. (4), as can be seen by subtracting eq. (2) from eq. (1) and replacing y_2 and y'_2 in the result by $(y_2 - y_1 + y_1)$ and $(y'_2 - y'_1 + y'_1)$, respectively.

More generally, constant real income [with constant total expenditures] involves keeping a price index unchanged; constant use of resources involves keeping a quantity index unchanged; and, in the limit, a constant price index and constant total expenditures imply a constant quantity index.

Note that AA need not be steeper than DD in a graph like Fig. 2. The point in question is that commented on in n. 13.

the expense of other commodities. The conditions for which the demand curve is drawn are therefore inconsistent with the conditions postulated on the side of supply. On the other hand, if the demand curve is constructed by keeping "real income" the same, no such inconsistency need arise. True, constant "real income" in the sense of "utility" and constant "real income" in the sense of outputs attainable from a fixed total of resources are different concepts, but they converge and can be treated as the same in the neighborhood of a position of equilibrium.

Of course, not all shifts in supply that it is desired to analyze arise in ways that leave the productive capacity of the community unaltered. Many involve a change in productive capacity —for example, changes in supply arising from improvements in technology or the discovery of previously unknown resources. Even in these cases, however, a demand curve constructed on the current interpretation will not serve. There is no reason to expect the differences in productive capacity implicit in constant money income and constant prices of other goods to bear any consistent relation to the change in productive capacity arising on the side of supply.[15] The better plan, in these cases, is to allow separately and directly for the increase in productive capacity by redrawing the demand curves to correspond to an appropriately higher real income and then to use a demand curve on which all points refer to that higher real income.

The main point under discussion can be put still more generally. The opportunities open to a consumer to satisfy his wants depend principally on two factors—the total resources at his disposal and the terms on which he can exchange one commodity for another, that is, on his real income and on relative prices. The form of analysis that is now fashionable distinguishes three effects of changes in his opportunities—the income effect arising from changes in his money income; the income effect arising from changes in the price of a commodity, with unchanged money

15. Note the difference from the previous case of constant productive capacity. As stated above, there is reason to expect constant real income along a demand curve to bear a consistent relation to constant productive capacity in the neighborhood of equilibrium. The reason, in effect, is provided by one of the conditions of equilibrium: the tangency of consumption and production indifference curves.

income and prices of other commodities; and the substitution effect arising from a change in the relative price of a commodity, with unchanged real income.

The distinction between the so-called "substitution" and "income" effects of a change in price is a direct consequence of defining the demand curve according to the current interpretation of Marshall. Its basis is the arithmetic truism that at given prices for all commodities but one, a given money income corresponds to a higher real income, the lower the price of the remaining commodity—at a lower price for it, more of some commodities can be purchased without purchasing less of others. In consequence, a decline in the price of a commodity, all other prices constant, has, it is argued, two effects: first, with an unchanged real income, it would stimulate the substitution of that commodity for others—this is the substitution effect; second, if the money income of the consumers is supposed to be unchanged, the increase in their real income as a result of the decline in price causes a further change in the consumption of that commodity as well as of others—this is the income effect.[16]

The two different kinds of income effects distinguished in this analysis—one arising from a change in money income, the other from a change in the price of one commodity—are really the same thing, the effect of a change in real income with given relative prices, arising in different ways. It is hard to see any gain from combining the second income effect with the substitution effect; it seems preferable to combine the two income effects and thereby gain a sharp contrast with the substitution effect.

It has often been stated that Marshall "neglected the income effect."[17] On my interpretation of his demand curve, this statement is invalid. One must then say that Marshall recognized the desirability of separating two quite different effects and constructed his demand curve so that it encompassed solely the effect that he wished to isolate for study, namely, the substitution

16. See Slutsky, *op. cit.*; Henry Schultz, *The Theory and Measurement of Demand* (Chicago: University of Chicago Press, 1938), pp. 40–46; J. R. Hicks and R. G. D. Allen, "A Reconsideration of the Theory of Value," *Economica,* XIV (1934), 52–76 and 196–219; Hicks, *op. cit.,* Part I.

17. Hicks, *op. cit.,* p. 32.

effect. Instead of neglecting the income effect, he "eliminated" it.

The conclusion to which the argument of this section leads is identical with that reached by Frank H. Knight in a recent article, in which he says:

> We have to choose in analysis between holding the prices of all other goods constant and maintaining constant the "real income" of the hypothetical consumer. . . . The treatment of the Slutzky school adopts the assumption that . . . the prices of all other goods (and the consumer's money income) are constant. Hence, real income must change. Of the two alternatives, this seems to be definitely the wrong choice. . . . The simple and obvious alternative is to draw the demand curves in terms of a change in *relative* prices, i.e., to assume that the value of money is held constant, through compensating changes in the prices of other goods, and not that these other prices are held constant.[18]

III. The Consistency of the Alternative Interpretation with Other Parts of Marshall's Work

Marshall's demand curve is part of a coherent body of thought; it is designed to fit into the rest of his structure of analysis; and it is used extensively in developing and applying this structure. It would take us too far afield to demonstrate in detail that my interpretation of his demand curve is consistent with the rest of his work. However, two special topics call for some explicit consideration: (1) the relation between the demand curve and Marshall's theory of money, because, in my view, this explains the particular device that he adopted for holding real income constant; and (2) the concept of consumer's surplus, because this is one of the most important applications of the demand curve and certainly the most controversial and because the passages in the later editions of the *Principles* that are inconsistent with my interpretation were introduced into the discussion of consumer's surplus.

A. THE THEORY OF RELATIVE PRICES AND THE THEORY OF MONEY

Granted that real income is to be held constant along the demand curve, why do so by holding money income and the

18. "Realism and Relevance in the Theory of Demand," *Journal of Political Economy,* LII (December, 1944), 289–318, esp. Sec. III, "The Meaning of a Demand Curve," pp. 298–301. Quotation from p. 299.

purchasing power of money constant rather than, for example, by holding prices of other goods constant and permitting compensating variations in money income? What reason is there to treat the prices of all other commodities as moving inversely to the price of the commodity in question?

The answer to these questions is given, I think, by one of Marshall's basic organizing principles, namely, the separation of the theory of relative prices from monetary theory, the theory of the level of prices. The *Principles* is devoted to the theory of relative prices under given monetary conditions; *Money, Credit, and Commerce* to the analysis of monetary conditions and their effect on the "purchasing power of money." With *given monetary conditions,* is it possible for the prices of all commodities other than the one in question to remain the same, on the average, while the price of this one rises or falls? Will not a rise or fall in the price of the commodity in question set in motion *monetary* forces affecting other prices? A complete answer requires explicit specification of the content of "given monetary conditions" and perhaps also of the source of the initial price change.

Marshall's selection of a constant purchasing power of money as a means of impounding monetary forces is presumably the end result of a chain of reasoning about the influence of monetary forces, not the direct content that he gave to "given monetary conditions." The beginning of the chain of reasoning may well be his own version of the quantity theory of money. According to this version, "the value of money is a function of its supply on the one hand, and the demand for it, on the other, as measured by 'the average stock of command over commodities which each person cares to keep in a ready form.' "[19] Given monetary conditions would then imply a given stock of money and a given desired "average stock of command over commodities." A decline in one price alone, all other prices remaining the same, is inconsistent with these "givens." It would increase the real value of a fixed (nominal) stock of money, leave the community with a larger "stock of command over commodities" than previously, and establish an incentive (reflecting "mone-

19. J. M. Keynes, "Alfred Marshall, 1842–1924," *Memorials,* p. 29.

tary" forces) to increase expenditures and thereby raise prices until the fixed stock of money again represented the same "stock of command over commodities," that is, until the "purchasing power of money" reached its former level.[20] This argument suggests that not only was constant purchasing power of money a device for separating the theory of relative prices from monetary theory; it was also a bridge between the two. Marshall separated the two theories in his attempt to reduce problems to manageable proportions, but he constructed them in such a way as to make them mutually consistent and thus facilitate ultimate combination.[21]

Marshall was, of course, very much aware of the interaction between real and monetary factors. The 1879 *Economics of In-*

20. C. W. Guillebaud has pointed out to me that Marshall typically supposed the desired "stock of command over commodities" to be a given fraction of real income (see *ibid.*) and that the argument in the text might not apply if this fraction were taken as the fundamental given. The monetary effects of a change in one price, other prices given, would then depend on the source of the initial price change. If this involved no change in aggregate real income (e.g., arose from a shift in demand), the argument in the text would remain unchanged. If it did involve a change in aggregate real income (e.g., arose from an invention reducing the cost of producing the commodity in question), no inconsistency need arise, since the desired "stock of command over commodities" would change in proportion to the change in real income. These considerations account for the phrase "perhaps also of the source of the initial price change" at the end of the preceding paragraph of the text.

21. This interpretation would, of course, be contradicted if Marshall had devised his theory of money after he had substantially completed his theory of relative prices, as might be inferred from the fact that *Money, Credit, and Commerce* was not published until 1923, thirty-three years after the first edition of the *Principles.* But in Marshall's case, the order of publication is a poor guide to the order of construction. Keynes tells us that the essence of his quantity theory of money is contained in a manuscript "written about 1871"; that "by 1871 his progress along" the lines of the material contained in the *Pure Theory* "was considerably advanced"; that the *Pure Theory* itself was "substantially complete about 1873," though not printed even for private circulation until 1879; that "in 1877 he turned aside to write the *Economics of Industry* with Mrs. Marshall"; and that Mrs. Marshall said "Book III on Demand was largely thought out and written on the roof at Palermo, Nov. 1881—Feb. 1882" (*Memorials*, pp. 28, 21, 23, 39 n.). These dates are extremely suggestive, particularly since the constancy of the purchasing power of money is not explicitly mentioned in the *Pure Theory*, which Marshall was presumably working on at about the same time that he was developing his monetary theory, while it is explicitly mentioned in the 1879 *Economics of Industry*, begun some years later. See also nn. 36 and 37 below.

dustry contains an extremely interesting discussion of the trade cycle, part of which Marshall thought sufficiently important to quote at length in 1886 in answering questions circulated by the celebrated Royal Commission on the Depression of Trade and Industry.[22]

Marshall's decision to keep the purchasing power of money the same for different points on a demand curve may not be the device best suited to abstract from monetary factors. It serves, however, to emphasize the necessity of considering explicitly the monetary arrangements under which the forces affecting relative prices are supposed to operate. The best apparatus for tackling problems of relative prices cannot be determined independently of these arrangements and of their mode of operation. Though price theory and monetary theory can be separated, they are not basically independent. From this point of view it is entirely natural that the recent development of alternative monetary theories should have stimulated re-examination of price theory.

B. CONSUMER'S SURPLUS

Marshall's discussion of consumer's surplus constitutes one of the most extensive applications that he made of his demand curve and has probably given rise to more controversy and discussion than any other part of his theory. Recently, consumer's surplus has come in for renewed attention, primarily as a result of J. R. Hick's attempt to rehabilitate and reinterpret the concept.[23] The

22. See Alfred Marshall and Mary Paley Marshall, *Economics of Industry* (London: Macmillan & Co., 1st ed., 1879; 2d ed., 1881), Book III, chap. i, pp. 150–57. This and all later references are to the first edition. "Answers to Questions on the Subject of Currency and Prices Circulated by the Royal Commission on the Depression of Trade and Industry (1886)," *Official Papers by Alfred Marshall* (London: Macmillan & Co., 1926), pp. 7–9. See also "Remedies for Fluctuations of General Prices" (1887), *Memorials*, pp. 189–92.

23. See Hicks, *op. cit.*, pp. 38–41; "The Rehabilitation of Consumers' Surplus," *Review of Economic Studies*, VIII (February, 1941), 108–16; "Consumers' Surplus and Index Numbers," *ibid.* (summer, 1942), 126–37; "The Four Consumer's Surpluses," *ibid.*, XI (winter, 1943), 31–41. See also A. Henderson, "Consumer's Surplus and the Compensating Variation," *Review of Economic Studies*, VIII (February, 1941), 117–21; Knight, *op. cit.*; Kenneth E. Boulding, "The Concept of Economic Surplus," *American Economic Review*, XXXV (December, 1945), 851–69, reprinted in American Economic Association, *Readings in the Theory of Income Distribution* (Philadelphia: Blakiston Co., 1946), pp. 638–59; E. J. Mishan, "Real-

reason for commenting on it here is not to contribute to the discussion or to evaluate the merits or demerits of the concept but rather to show the relation between Marshall's treatment of consumer's surplus and my interpretation of his demand curve.

Marshall's treatment of consumer's surplus might, offhand, seem inconsistent with my interpretation of his demand curve for either of two different, and almost opposed, reasons. In the first place, consumer's surplus refers to a difference in real income under different situations. But, on my interpretation, all points on the demand curve are to be regarded as corresponding to the same real income. A movement along such a demand curve cannot, therefore, involve a change in consumer's surplus. Does this not eliminate the entire notion of consumer's surplus and make Marshall's entire discussion of it pointless? The answer is clearly "No," the reason being that the two situations compared need not correspond to two points on the *same* demand curve, even though a single demand curve is used to *estimate* the difference in real income between the two situations.

In the second place, Marshall regarded his analysis of consumer's surplus as valid only for commodities that account for a small part of total expenditure. He makes this restriction in order to justify neglecting changes in the marginal utility of money. But, if all points on the demand curve correspond to the same real income, does it not then follow that the marginal utility of money is the same everywhere on the demand curve? And does it not also follow that his estimate of consumer's surplus is exact, so that the assumption that a negligible proportion of expenditures is devoted to the commodity in question becomes unnecessary? Again the answer is "No," and for much the same reason. If the two situations compared differ in real income, the fact that real income is the same along the demand curve becomes something of a vice in using it to measure consumer's surplus. The assumption that a negligible proportion of expenditures is devoted to the commodity in question cannot be dispensed with on my interpretation; indeed, if anything, it is even more necessary than on the current interpretation.

ism and Relevance in Consumer's Surplus," *Review of Economic Studies*, XV (1947–48), 27–33.

To explain and justify these cryptic answers, it will be necessary to examine Marshall's definition of consumer's surplus, his suggested estimate of its magnitude, and the relation of this estimate to the correct value under the two alternative interpretations of the demand curve.

Marshall is more explicit and complete in defining consumer's surplus than was his wont, and his definition admits of little ambiguity: "The excess of the price which he would be willing to pay rather than go without the thing, over that which he actually does pay, is the economic measure of this surplus satisfaction. It may be called *consumer's surplus*."[24]

Marshall then proceeds to argue that consumer's surplus can be *estimated* by the famous triangle under the demand curve. As Hicks remarks, this "association of Consumer's Surplus with the curvilinear triangle under the demand curve . . . is not a definition; it is a theorem, true under certain restrictive assumptions, but only true if these assumptions are granted."[25] The confusion of the suggested estimate with the definition is perhaps the chief source of misunderstanding on this exceedingly complex subject.

Figure 1, introduced in Section I, C, above to illustrate the relation between demand curves drawn on the current and on my interpretation, can also be used to show the relation between consumer's surplus as defined and estimates of it obtained from demand curves constructed according to the two interpretations. Curve *Cc,* it will be recalled, is a demand curve for the commodity *X* constructed according to the current interpretation. Money income and all other prices are the same for all points on it. *Aa* and *Cv* are demand curves constructed according to my interpretation—*Aa* for a real income the same as at *P* on *Cc; Cv* for a real income the same as at *C* on *Cc.* At point *P* on *Aa* and at point *C* on *Cv,* money income and all other prices are the same as on *Cc.* At other points other prices are sufficiently different, or money income is, to compensate for the difference in the price of *X* and thereby keep real income the same.

Now consider the consumer's surplus obtained from this com-

24. *Principles,* p. 124.
25. "The Rehabilitation of Consumers' Surplus," *op. cit.,* p. 109.

modity when the consumer is at P.[26] This is *defined* as "the excess of the price which he would be willing to pay rather than go without the thing, over that which he actually does pay." "Price" is here to be interpreted as "total amount" rather than "price per unit."[27] Further, it is clear that the sum he would pay rather than go without is to be determined for circumstances otherwise the same as at P; in particular, his money income and the other prices are to be the same as at P.[28] Now the amount that he actually does pay for OM of X is given by the rectangle $OHPM$ in the figure. By the argument of Section I, C, the maximum amount that he would be willing to pay for OM of X rather than go without any of it is given by the area under Cv between O and M, or $OCDGM$. The triangular area CDH *minus* the triangular area DPG therefore gives the consumer's surplus. This area is necessarily positive; we know he is willing to pay at least $OHPM$ for OM of X; hence $OCDGM$ must be greater than $OHPM$.

Marshall's *estimate* of the maximum sum is the area under the demand curve: $OCPM$ if we use the current interpretation, $OAPM$ if we use the alternative interpretation. For a "normal" commodity, the case for which the figure is drawn, both are clearly too large. How large the error is depends on the difference between Aa and Cc, on the one hand, and Cv, on the other. Now we have seen (in Sec. I, C) that these differences arise entirely from differences in the real income associated with the different curves; if real incomes differ little, so will the curves. Here is where Marshall's assumption about the fraction of expenditures devoted to the commodity enters the picture. If this fraction is small, the

26. For simplicity, the discussion is restricted to the consumer's surplus obtained from the entire amount of X consumed; and to facilitate this, the demand curves have been drawn to cut the price axis.

27. See Mathematical Note II of the *Principles* (p. 838), in which Marshall defines p as "the price which he is just willing to pay for an amount x of the commodity" and then differentiates p with respect to x to get the price per unit.

28. None of the reasons cited earlier for keeping real income the same along the demand curve applies here. The question being asked is purely hypothetical; no other reactions need be allowed for. Further, to keep his real income the same when he has none of X as when he has OM of X would make the entire discussion of consumer's surplus pointless. The whole point of the discussion is to measure the difference in real income between the two situations.

differences in real income will tend to be small, and both estimates will approach the correct value.[29] Since the error is larger for Aa than for Cc, it is clear that Marshall's assumption is, if anything, even more necessary on my interpretation of the demand curve than on the current one.[30]

29. This statement is not rigorous. As the fraction of expenditures devoted to the commodity diminishes, so will aggregate consumer's surplus. It is not enough that the error become small in absolute terms; its ratio to the correct value must become small. This, in general, will occur, as is well known. The chief qualification has to do with the behavior of a demand curve constructed under the current interpretation (e.g., Cc) for small quantities of X. The crucial question is the difference in real income between P and C. Expenditure on the commodity might be a small fraction of total expenditure at P; yet, if the demand curve constructed under the current interpretation were extremely inelastic, not near C. In this case the difference in real income might be large.

This qualification is emphasized by Marshall. For example: "If however an amount b of the commodity is necessary for existence, $f(z)$ [*sic*] [ordinate of the demand curve] will be infinite, or at least indefinitely great, for values of x less than b. We must therefore take life for granted, and estimate separately the total utility of that part of the supply of the commodity which is in excess of absolute necessaries" (p. 841). See also pp. 133 and 842. $f(z)$ clearly should be $f(x)$, as it is in the first four editions of the *Principles*. See appendix to this paper.

This discussion of the role of the assumption that the commodity absorbs only a small fraction of income throws some light on an issue about which there has been considerable discussion, namely, whether Marshall assumed the marginal utility of money to be roughly constant with respect to a change in price or a change in income. The above analysis suggests that he assumed constancy with respect to a change in income. This is also Hicks's conclusion (*Value and Capital*, p. 40; "The Rehabilitation of Consumers' Surplus," *op. cit.*, p. 109). Samuelson denies this and asserts that he assumed constancy with respect to a change in price (see Paul A. Samuelson, "Constancy of the Marginal Utility of Income," in *Studies in Mathematical Economics and Econometrics*, p. 80).

30. The argument can be easily extended to "inferior" goods. The order of the three curves in Fig. 1 is then reversed; the estimates then become too small, instead of too large; but the error under the alternative interpretation remains larger in absolute value than under the current interpretation.

In the terminology used by Hicks in "The Four Consumer's Surpluses," what I have called the consumer's surplus is what Hicks calls the "quantity-compensating variation." The estimate of consumer's surplus derived from the demand curve constructed under my interpretation (the area APH) Hicks calls the "quantity-equivalent variation." The area CDH in Fig. 1, Hicks calls the "price-compensating variation." Hicks's fourth concept, "price-equivalent variation," is not shown directly in Fig. 1. It is obtained by drawing a horizontal line through C. Designate by E the point at which this line cuts Aa. The "price-equivalent variation" is then equal to the area APH minus AEC. These relations can be checked by noting that curve *mep* in Hicks's Fig. 3 is Aa in our Fig. 1; his curve PCM is Cv in our Fig. 1.

IV. Textual Evidence on What Marshall Really Meant

Marshall's writings on demand bear on three different problems: (1) the definition of the demand curve—the problem of form; (2) the shape of the demand curve—the problem of content; and (3) the use of the demand curve—the problem of application. In his usual manner Marshall gives precedence to the problem of content and does not explicitly separate his discussion of content from his discussion of form. His definitions are characteristically given parenthetically and implicitly. He went to extreme lengths to present his tools in the context of concrete problems, so that definitions grew out of the uses to be made of them.[31] His discussion of utility and diminishing utility in the chapter of the *Principles* which introduces the concept of a demand curve (Book III, chap. iii, "Gradations of Consumers' Demand") is part of the discussion of content, even though it precedes his definition. It is the means whereby he rationalizes his "one general *law of demand:*—The greater the amount to be sold, the smaller must be the price at which it is offered in order that it may find purchasers."[32] It is not part of his definition of the demand curve.

Similarly, one of the major applications that Marshall made of the demand curve was his analysis of consumer's surplus. This analysis, too, must be distinguished from his definition of the demand curve. Assumptions made in his discussion of consumer's

---

Further, in comparing the two figures, the part of Hicks's diagram for quantities less than hN should be neglected. That is, his point P is equivalent to our point C, his p to our P. Our Fig. 1 is also equivalent to Fig. 3B in Boulding, "The Concept of Economic Surplus."

31. Cf. J. M. Keynes, *Memorials,* esp. pp. 33–38; see also Guillebaud, *op. cit.*

32. *Principles,* p. 99. Note that on my interpretation this is truly a *general* law, not subject to the exceptions that have been made in recent literature. It depends for its validity only on (*a*) the postulate that consumers can be treated as if they behaved consistently and attempted to maximize some function of the quantity of commodities consumed; (*b*) the observed fact that consumers choose a higher income in preference to a lower, other things the same; and (*c*) the observed fact that consumers do not spend all their income on one commodity. For proof that a demand curve constructed on my interpretation must slope negatively see Slutsky, *op. cit.,* sec. 8.

surplus cannot, without additional evidence, be supposed to apply equally to other applications of the "demand curve."

A. THE CENTRAL PASSAGES IN THE TEXT
OF THE "PRINCIPLES"

The central passages in the text of the eighth and final edition of the *Principles* bearing on the other things to be kept the same seem to me to be three: one governing the entire volume, and two essentially parenthetical comments in his discussion of the demand curve:

We may throughout this volume neglect possible changes in the general purchasing power of money. Thus the price of anything will be taken as representative of its exchange value relatively to things in general [p. 62].

The larger the amount of a thing that a person has the less, other things being equal (i.e. *the purchasing power of money, and the amount of money at his command being equal*), will be the price which he will pay for a little more of it: or in other words his marginal demand price for it diminishes [p. 95; italics added].

The demand prices in our list are those at which various quantities of a thing can be sold in a market *during a given time and under given conditions.* If the conditions vary in any respect the prices will probably require to be changed; and this has constantly to be done when the desire for anything is materially altered by a *variation of custom, or by a cheapening of the supply of a rival commodity, or by the invention of a new one* [p. 100; second set of italics added].

For our purposes the critical part of the second quotation is the italicized parenthesis and, of the third, the second set of italicized phrases.

Though these quotations are taken from the eighth edition of the *Principles,* their substantive content is contained in Marshall's earliest published work on the theory of demand. All except the constancy of the purchasing power of money is in *The Pure Theory of (Domestic) Values,* printed for private circulation in 1879[33] but, according to Keynes, "substantially complete about 1873"; [34] and the constancy of the purchasing power of money is in his and Mrs. Marshall's *The Economics of Industry,* published

33. Reprinted, together with the companion paper, *The Pure Theory of Foreign Trade,* by the London School of Economics and Political Science (1930).

34. *Memorials,* p. 23.

in 1879.[35] The actual wording of the first and third quotations can be traced back to the first edition of the *Principles* (1890), of the second quotation, to the second edition (1891).[36]

35. This work should not be confused with the condensation of the *Principles,* published, under the same title but with Alfred Marshall as sole author, in 1892.

36. In all editions of the *Principles* the statement corresponding to the first quotation is in a subsection dealing with the meaning of the word "value." In the first (1890), second (1891), and third (1895) editions, the subsection on "value" is at the end of Book I, "Preliminary Survey," chap. i, "Introduction," and contains the statement: "Throughout the earlier stages of our work it will be best to speak of the exchange value of a thing at any place and time as measured by its price, that is, the amount of money for which it will exchange then and there, and to assume that there is no change in the general purchasing power of money" (p. 9, all three editions). In the first edition this assumption is repeated at the beginning of the chapter on "The Law of Demand" (Book III, chap. ii): "The purchasing power of this money may vary from time to time; but in these early stages of our work we assume it to be constant" (1st ed., p. 151). This repetition was eliminated in later editions, apparently in the process of introducing into the second edition the chapter on "Wants in Relation to Activities." In the fourth edition (1898), the subsection on "value" was split, part remaining at the end of Book I, chap. i, the remainder, including the material on the purchasing power of money, being transferred to the end of Book II, "Some Fundamental Notions," chap. ii, "Wealth." The wording was changed to essentially its final form; the only difference is that the first sentence is in the passive voice, reading: "Throughout this volume possible changes in the general purchasing power of money will be neglected" (4th ed., p. 130). In the fifth edition (1907), the rest of the subsection on "value" was transferred to the end of Book II, chap. ii, and the quotation revised to its present form; even the page number is the same in the fifth and eighth editions (p. 62).

In both editions of *The Economics of Industry,* subsection 4 in Book II, "Normal Value," chap. i, "Definitions. Law of Demand," contains essentially the same material as the subsection on "value" in the *Principles* referred to in the preceding paragraph, including the following statement: "But while examining the theory of Normal value we shall, for convenience, assume that the purchasing power of money remains unchanged. So that a rise or fall in the price of a thing will always mean a rise or fall in its general purchasing power or exchange value" (pp. 68–69). No corresponding statement appears in *The Pure Theory.*

The italicized parenthesis in the second quotation is identical in the second and all later editions of the *Principles.* The remainder of the quotation was worded as follows in the second edition: "An increase in the amount of a thing that a person has will, other things being equal . . . diminish his Marginal Demand-price for it" (p. 152). In the third edition, the words "marginal" and "demand" were not capitalized, and the hyphen was eliminated after "Demand" (p. 170). In the fourth edition the end of the statement was expanded to read, "diminish the price which he will pay for a little more of it: or in other words diminishes his marginal demand price for it" (pp. 169–70). In the fifth edition the quotation takes its present form, except for the addition of a comma, even the page number being the same as in the eighth edition (p. 95). In all editions from the second on, the indicated

B. THE BEARING OF THESE PASSAGES ON
THE TWO INTERPRETATIONS

The "other things" listed in the three passages cited above are as follows:

1. "Purchasing power of money"
2. "Amount of money at his command"
3. "Custom"
4. Price of "a rival commodity" (to avoid "cheapening of the supply of a rival commodity")
5. Range of rival commodities available (to avoid "invention of a new one")[37]

---

quotations are in Book III, chap. iii, the chapter first introducing the demand curve. This chapter is entitled "The Law of Demand" in the second and third editions, "Gradations of Demand" in the fourth, and "Gradations of Consumers' Demand" in the fifth and later editions.

The absence of the statement from the first edition reflects a difference in exposition, not in substance. As noted above, an explicit statement that the purchasing power of money is assumed constant appears in the chapter on "The Law of Demand" in the first edition. In all editions this chapter contains a statement covering the second part of the italicized parenthesis, which is worded as follows in the first edition: "Every increase in his resources increases the price which he is willing to pay for any given pleasure. And in the same way every diminution of his resources increases the marginal utility of money to him, and diminishes the price that he is willing to pay for any pleasure" (p. 156). The only change in this statement in later editions was the substitution of "benefit" for "pleasure" (8th ed., p. 96).

The Economics of Industry also contains a statement anticipating the second part of the italicized parenthesis: "The price which he is willing to pay for a thing depends not only on its utility to him but also on *his means;* that is, the amount of money or general purchasing power at his disposal" (p. 70).

In all editions of the *Principles* the statement corresponding to the third quotation is in the final subsection of the chapter first introducing the demand curve (1st ed., Book III, chap. ii; in later editions, Book III, chap. iii). In the first edition it reads: "It must be remembered that the demand schedule gives the prices at which various quantities of a thing can be sold in a market during a given time and under given conditions. If the conditions vary in any respect the figures of the schedule will probably require to be changed. One condition which it is especially important to watch is the price of rival commodities, that is, of commodities which can be used as substitutes for it" (p. 160). A footnote is attached to the word "rival," the first sentence of which

[Footnote 36 concluded on p. 77]

---

37. The adequacy of this list as a summary of Marshall's views may be checked by comparing it with two others in Marshall's writings. In *The Pure*

[Footnote 37 continued on pp. 77 and 78]

1. *The current interpretation.*—The current interpretation of Marshall's demand curve treats item 2 as referring to the money

[Footnote 36 concluded]

reads: "Or to use Jevons' phrase (*Theory of Political Economy,* Ch. IV), commodities that are nearly 'equivalent'" (1st ed., p. 160, n. 2).

The part of the second sentence of the third quotation following the semicolon assumed its final form in the second edition (p. 157), the footnote reference to Jevons being dropped. The rest of the quotation is the same in the second and third editions as in the first and assumes its final form in the fourth (p. 174). The change made in the second sentence from the first to the second edition argues that the list was not intended to be exhaustive, but illustrative. No change in substance is involved (see 1st ed., p. 155). In all editions the quoted statement is followed by the example of tea and coffee to illustrate the necessity of assuming the prices of rival commodities to be known; in the second edition the example of gas and electricity was added, and in the third edition the example of different varieties of tea. The passage itself, the changes in it, and the examples all indicate that Marshall considered the price of "rival" commodities particularly important. The examples, together with the footnote in the first edition, make it clear that he meant "close" rivals.

For a statement in the *Pure Theory* covering the substance of these quotations, except the constancy of the purchasing power of money, see n. 37 below.

[Footnote 37 continued from p. 76]

Theory of (Domestic) Values, he writes: "The periods with which we are concerned . . . are sufficiently long to eliminate . . . casual disturbances. . . . But they are sufficiently short to exclude fundamental changes in the circumstances of demand and in those of supply. On the side of demand for the ware in question it is requisite that the periods should not include (i) any very great change in the prosperity and purchasing power of the community; (ii) any important changes in the fashions which affect the use of the ware; (iii) the invention or the great cheapening of any other ware which comes to be used largely as a substitute for it; (iv) the deficiency of the supply of any ware for which the ware in question may be used as a substitute, whether this deficiency be occasioned by bad harvests, by war, or by the imposition of customs or excise taxes; (v) a sudden large requirement for the commodity, as e.g. for ropes in the breaking out of a maritime war; (vi) the discovery of new means of utilizing the ware, or the opening up of important markets in which it can be sold" (p. 15).

Item i in this list presumably corresponds with 2 in my list; ii corresponds with 3, and iii and iv with 4 and 5, iii excluding a fall in the price of a rival commodity and iv a rise. Items v and the first part of vi would seem to be contained in 3 and largely redundant with ii. The rest of vi is presumably covered by the restriction of the discussion to a demand curve for a particular market.

The other list is in Marshall's discussion in the *Principles* of the difficulties of the statistical study of demand (Book III, chap. iv), where he writes: "Other

[Footnote 37 concluded on p. 78]

income of the group of purchasers to whom the demand curve relates, item 3 to their tastes and preferences, and item 4 to the price of every other commodity rather than of *rival* commodities alone. It ignores entirely items 1 and 5.

Item 2 is not entirely unambiguous. It might be interpreted as referring to the cash balances of the purchasers or to their wealth instead of, or in addition to, their income. On the whole, the most reasonable course seems to be to interpret it as referring to both income and wealth,[38] particularly since wealth qualifies for the list of "other things" by virtue of its possible importance as a factor affecting consumption. This expansion of the current interpretation does not alter it materially; it merely transfers "wealth"

[Footnote 37 concluded]

things seldom are equal in fact over periods of time sufficiently long for the collection of full and trustworthy statistics. . . . To begin with, [a] the purchasing power of money is continually changing. . . . Next come the changes in [b] the general prosperity and in the total purchasing power at the disposal of the community at large. . . . Next come the changes due to [c] the gradual growth of population and wealth. . . . Next, allowance must be made for changes in [d] fashion, and taste and habit, for [e] the opening out of new uses of a commodity, for [f] the discovery or improvement or cheapening of other things that can be applied to the same uses with it" (*Principles*, pp. 109–10; letters in brackets added). This statement dates from the first edition (pp. 170–71); only trivial editorial changes were made in later editions.

Item *a* in this list corresponds with 1 in my list; *b* with 2; *d* and presumably *e* with 3; and *f* with 4 and 5. Item *c* is presumably in part covered by restriction of the discussion to a demand curve for a particular market; in part it contains an item that may deserve to be added to the list, namely, "wealth." The wording of *f* is ambiguous, since it could refer to substitutes for the good in question, to complements, or to both. The subsequent text and the examples cited make it clear that it refers to substitutes; one example, of petroleum and petroleum lamps, itself ambiguously worded, suggests that it may refer to complements as well.

38. In the quotations from Book III, chap. iv, in the preceding footnote, "wealth" is mentioned explicitly, though separately from "general prosperity" and "total purchasing power." See also the quotations in the fourth and fifth paragraphs of n. 36. Marshall repeatedly refers to "rich" and "poor" rather than to high- and low-income people (e.g., pp. 19, 95, 98). However, in an illustrative case, a rich man and a poor man are identified by their annual incomes (p. 19). And in Book III, chap. vi, he remarks: "We have throughout this and preceding chapters spoken of the rich, the middle classes and the poor as having respectively large, medium and small incomes—not possessions" (p. 134).

from the category of "other things" implicitly supposed to be the same to the list of things mentioned explicitly.

Item 3 requires no discussion, since the only reasonable interpretation of it is that it refers to tastes and preferences.[39]

The important defect of the current interpretation is its treatment of item 4, which is, in turn, responsible for the neglect of items 1 and 5. "Rival commodity" is replaced by, or read to mean, "any other commodity," and hence item 4 is taken to mean that the price of every other commodity is to be supposed the same. For example, Henry Schultz says, as if it were obvious and without citing any statements of Marshall: "Marshall also assumes, in giving definite form to the law of demand for any one commodity, that the prices of all other commodities remain constant."[40] Numerous other statements to the same effect could be cited. It is an amusing commentary on our capacity for self-delusion that the only reference to Marshall for support that I have seen are to the page containing the third quotation in Section IV, A, above—the source of the words quoted in item 4.[41] The first set of italicized words in that quotation are the only words on the page even remotely supporting the substitution of

39. See n. 37 above. In discussing the law of diminishing marginal utility, Marshall says: "We do not suppose time to be allowed for any alteration in the character or tastes of the man himself" (p. 94).

40. *Op. cit.*, p. 53. Immediately after making this statement he quotes from Edgeworth's article on "Demand Curves" cited in n. 4 above, not as evidence for the validity of his interpretation of Marshall but rather as an indication of the difficulties that it raises.

41. Joan Robinson states without citation: "Marshall instructs us to draw up a demand schedule on the assumption that the prices of all other things are fixed" (*The Economics of Imperfect Competition* [London: Macmillan & Co., 1934], p. 20). Paul Samuelson says, also without citation: "All other prices and income are held constant by *ceteris paribus* assumptions" in the "Marshallian partial equilibrium demand functions" (*Foundations of Economic Analysis* [Cambridge: Harvard University Press, 1947], p. 97). In an unpublished exposition of income and substitution effects prepared for class use about 1939, I stated, also without citation: "There is no question but that it [the Marshallian demand curve] was not intended to be . . . interpreted" as "showing the effect of *compensated* variations in price." Similar statements, all citing p. 100 of the *Principles* as authority, are made by Robert Triffin, *Monopolistic Competition and General Equilibrium Theory* (Cambridge: Harvard University Press, 1940), p. 44; Ruby Turner Norris, *The Theory of Consumer's Demand* (New Haven: Yale University Press, 1941), p. 82; and Weintraub, *op. cit.*, p. 539.

"any other" for rival. The specific examples that follow the quotation—tea and coffee, gas and electric lighting, different varieties of tea, beef and mutton—make it clear that Marshall was using the word "rival" in a narrow sense and not in that broad sense in which it may be said that all commodities are "rivals" for the consumer's income.[42] Whatever the merits of the current interpretation, it cannot be found explicitly in Marshall.

The interpretation of item 4 as referring to all other commodities makes item 5 unnecessary and contradicts item 1. Item 5 is unnecessary because the introduction of a new commodity is equivalent to a decline in its price from infinity to a finite amount; hence is ruled out if the price of every other commodity is to be unchanged. Item 1 is contradicted because, if all other prices are unchanged, the purchasing power of money will be lower, the higher the price of the commodity in question. The purchasing power of money cannot, therefore, be the same for all points on the demand curve.

The redundancy of item 5 on this interpretation of item 4 is unimportant; this item is in a list that is illustrative rather than exhaustive, and there is no reason why Marshall should have scrupulously avoided overlapping. The logical inconsistency between items 1 and 4 cannot, however, be dismissed so lightly. Retention of the current interpretation requires either that item 1 be eliminated, on the grounds that the quotations on which it is based are exceptional and peripheral, or that Marshall be convicted of logical inconsistency on a fundamental point in his theory of demand.[43] Item 1 cannot, I think, be eliminated. The constancy of the purchasing power of money is clearly fundamental in Mar-

42. If any doubt remains, it is removed by the footnote in the first edition attached to the word "rival" referring to Jevons' phrase "commodities that are nearly 'equivalent'" (see n. 36 above).

43. The extent to which the current interpretation dominates economic thought could not be more strikingly illustrated than by the fact that so acute an economic theorist as J. R. Hicks can write: "No doubt it [the constancy of the marginal utility of money] was . . . associated in his [Marshall's] mind with the assumption of a constant value of money (constant prices of other consumers' goods than the one, or sometimes ones, in question)" ("The Rehabilitation of Consumers' Surplus," *op. cit.*, p. 109). Hicks here treats constancy of all other prices as an alternative statement of item 1, when, in fact, it is logically inconsistent with item 1.

shall's thought, probably more fundamental than any other item on our list.[44]

One excuse for retaining the current interpretation of Marshall, despite the logical inconsistency that it introduces, is to suppose that Marshall intended to restrict the use of his demand curve to commodities that account for only a small fraction of total expenditures. A change in the price of such a commodity would have only a small effect on the purchasing power of money, and it could be argued that Marshall neglected it as a "second-order effect." On this rationalization, item 1 becomes redundant, but, in the limit, not logically inconsistent with an item 4 taken to refer to all other commodities.

I do not believe that Marshall intended to restrict the use of the demand curve to commodities accounting for only a small fraction of total expenditure. He speaks of a demand curve for wheat (p. 106), for houseroom (p. 107), and for other commodities that he cannot have regarded as unimportant. He first explicitly introduces the restriction to unimportant commodities in connection with his discussion of consumer's surplus, which comes well after the initial discussion of the demand curve—in the eighth edition, three chapters later; and the restriction is repeated at most points at which the argument depends on it. At one point the restriction is said to be "generally," not universally, justifiable. This evidence may not be conclusive, but it certainly establishes a strong presumption that Marshall did not intend the restriction to carry over to all uses of the demand curve.[45]

44. See nn. 36 and 37 above. Note also that constancy of the purchasing power of money was a standard assumption of economic theory long before Marshall's day. It was made by Ricardo in his price theory, and Marshall refers to Cournot's discussion of the reasons for making this assumption (see Marshall, *Principles,* pp. ix, 62; Augustin Cournot, *Researches into the Mathematical Principles of the Theory of Wealth* [1838], trans. Nathaniel Bacon [New York: Macmillan Co., 1897], p. 26).

45. In connection with the discussion of consumer's surplus and the assumption of a constant marginal utility of money implicit in that discussion, Marshall says: "The assumption . . . underlies our whole reasoning, that the expenditure on any one thing . . . is only a small part of his whole expenditure" (p. 842). The first sentence of the paragraph from which this quotation is taken explicitly limits it to "the discussion of consumers' surplus" (p. 842). The quotation is followed by a cross-reference to the part of Marshall's famous analysis of the process by which

It should be noted that Marshall's explicit introduction of the restriction to unimportant commodities has no bearing on the relative validity of the two interpretations of his demand curve. The restriction is necessary on either of the two interpretations at each point at which Marshall explicitly makes it. So the restriction cannot be regarded as called for by the inconsistency of items 1 and 4 on the current interpretation of 4.

2. *The alternative interpretation.*—My interpretation of the Marshallian demand curve resolves almost all the difficulties that plague the current interpretation, since it accepts at face value the five "other things" listed at the beginning of Section IV, B. Marshall's words can be taken to mean what they say without uncomfortable stretching, and there is no logical inconsistency in the constancy of both item 1, the purchasing power of money, and item 4, the prices of rival commodities. Item 5, the range of rival commodities available, is still redundant, since, if "rival" has the same meaning in 4 and 5, the invention of a new rival commodity means a change in its price from infinity to a finite value.

My interpretation explains also the precise wording of the second quotation in Section IV, A, which reads, in part: "The larger the amount of a thing that a person has the less . . . will

---

equilibrium is reached in a corn market in which he discusses "the latent assumption, that the dealers' willingness to spend money is nearly constant throughout" (p. 334). "This assumption," he says, "is justifiable with regard to most of the market dealings with which we are practically concerned. When a person buys anything for his own consumption, he generally spends on it a small part of his total resources" (p. 335).

Nowhere in Book III, chap. iii, does Marshall explicitly restrict his discussion to unimportant commodities. The one statement in that chapter that might be regarded as so restricting the discussion is the statement on p. 95 that "the marginal utility of money to him is a fixed quantity." But the context argues and Note II in the Mathematical Appendix demonstrates that this is merely a verbal statement of an identity (if income is unchanged, so is marginal utility of money), and thus is not really relevant to the issue. In the eighth edition, Note II is referred to only at the end of the subsection following the paragraph containing the passage quoted. However, in the first edition, the corresponding note (Note III) is referred to at the end of the paragraph containing the passage quoted, and hence clearly covers it (pp. 155–56, 737–38).

The above quotations are essentially unchanged from the first edition on. The restriction to unimportant commodities is, however, mentioned neither in Marshall and Marshall, *Economics of Industry,* nor in the *Pure Theory.*

be the price which he will pay for a little more of it." This is a curious form of phrasing on the current interpretation. Why emphasize the amount of a thing that a person has and the marginal expenditure that he can be induced to make rather than the amount he purchases and the average price he pays? On my interpretation, this phrasing follows directly from the argument of Section I, C, above (and Note II of Marshall's Mathematical Appendix), according to which a demand curve constructed on my interpretation can be viewed as showing the maximum price per unit that a person can be induced to pay for successive increments of the commodity.

One minor puzzle remains on my interpretation. Why does Marshall restrict his attention to "rival" commodities? Why not to "closely related" commodities, whether rivals or complements? His use of the word "rivals" in discussing the demand curve is apparently not a mere verbal accident. He uses the word repeatedly; almost all his examples deal with the effect of, or through, substitutes. I have no very good answer to this puzzle; the only one that seems at all persuasive is that he thought the concept of "joint demand" and the associated analytical apparatus better suited to problems involving complementary goods.[46]

My interpretation follows so directly from Marshall's words that further defense of it would be unnecessary were it not for the unquestioned dominance of the current interpretation in the economic thinking and writing of the past half-century. This circumstance explains the presentation of additional textual evidence bearing on the validity of the alternative interpretation.

C. COUNTEREVIDENCE FROM THE TEXT OF THE "PRINCIPLES"

I have been able to find only one passage in the text of the eighth edition of the *Principles* that is in any way inconsistent with my interpretation of Marshall. This is the celebrated pas-

46. In Note VII of the Mathematical Appendix, Marshall qualifies a suggested formula for combining consumer's surplus from different commodities by saying: "if we could find a plan for grouping together in one common demand curve all those things which satisfy the same wants, and are rivals; and also for every group of things of which the services are complementary (see Book V, chap. vi) . . ." (p. 842). Book V, chap. vi, contains the discussion of joint demand. The qualification quoted appears first in the third edition.

sage, adverted to above, which deals with the so-called "Giffen phenomenon" and which was first introduced in the third edition:

> For instance, as Sir R. Giffen has pointed out, a rise in the price of bread makes so large a drain on the resources of the *poorer labouring families* and raises so much the marginal utility of money to them, that they are forced to curtail their consumption of meat and the more expensive farinaceous foods: and bread being still the cheapest food which they can get and will take, they consume more, and not less of it [p. 132; italics added].

This passage clearly offsets an income effect against a substitution effect, whereas, on my interpretation of Marshall, real income is the same at all points on the demand curve, so there is no "income effect" (see Sec. II, B, above). The passage is thus in the spirit of the current interpretation. Yet the words I have italicized indicate that it does not necessarily contradict my interpretation of Marshall. The purchasing power of money and the real income of the community at large may remain constant; yet the real income of a particular group in the community that has a special consumption pattern may be adversely affected by the rise in the price of a particular commodity.[47]

D. THE EVIDENCE OF THE MATHEMATICAL APPENDIX

The Mathematical Appendix to the *Principles* confirms and extends the evidence already presented from the text of the *Principles* and from Marshall's other writings. Note II (III in the first edition) explicitly derives a relation between price and quantity demanded that is identical with a demand curve on my interpretation, in which real income is kept constant by compensating variations in money income. Indeed, my derivation of such a demand curve in Section I, C, above is a verbal paraphrase of Marshall's mathematics. Marshall does not explicitly say that the relation he derives is a demand curve, but Note II is attached to his intitial discussion of the demand curve (Book III, chap. iii, in the eighth edition) and is given as the authority for statements made about the demand curve; hence there can be no doubt that it presents the pure theory of his demand curve.

47. See Marshall's explicit discussion of, and emphasis on, this possibility in "Remedies for Fluctuations of General Prices" (1887), *Memorials,* p. 207.

In all editions of the *Principles* Note VI, attached to Marshall's discussion of consumer's surplus, contains a sentence that is definitely wrong on the current interpretation of his demand curve but correct on my interpretation.

Finally, a sentence added to Note VI in the third edition, referred to in the text of the *Principles* in connection with the material added on the Giffen phenomenon, contains an implicit mathematical proposition that is correct on the current interpretation but incorrect on my interpretation. The mathematical point in question is considerably more subtle than those referred to in the two preceding paragraphs, so it cannot be given the same weight.

These two notes are examined in some detail in the appendix to this paper, to which the reader is referred for proof of the above statements.

E. A SYNTHESIS OF THE EVIDENCE

There are two differences between the current interpretation of Marshall's demand curve and my interpretation: (1) On the current interpretation, account is taken of the price of each other commodity individually; on my interpretation, only of the average price of all commodities other than the one in question and its close rivals. (2) On the current interpretation, real income varies along the demand curve with the price of the good in question; on my interpretation, real income is constant along the demand curve.

On the first, and less important, point, it is mathematically convenient to consider each other price separately, and this procedure might well have recommended itself to the writer of mathematical Notes XIV and XXI. On the other hand, it is impossible to consider each price separately in a practical analysis; so the use of an average price would clearly have recommended itself to the writer of the text of the *Principles* and is entirely in the spirit of Marshall's explicit methodological statements (see Sec. II, A, above). Marshall does not discuss this point explicitly; hence the textual evidence is all indirect.

On the second and basic point of difference the evidence leaves little room for doubt: Marshall's theory of demand, in the form in which it is presented in the first edition of the *Principles,* is explicitly based on constancy of real income along the demand curve. This interpretation not only is consistent with both the letter and the spirit of the entire text of the first edition of the *Principles* but is almost conclusively established by the evidence cited above from two notes in the Mathematical Appendix of the first edition. In his determined effort to be persuasive and to make his work accessible to educated laymen, Marshall might well have been vague in his verbal presentation, though even there it seems unlikely that he would have been logically incon-sistent. It is hardly credible that he would have been not merely vague but downright wrong on simple mathematical points stated in mathematical language, especially since the mathematical points in question could hardly even have arisen if he had been explicitly using the current interpretation of the demand curve.

I am inclined to believe, however, that by the time Marshall made the revisions incorporated in the third edition of the *Prin-ciples*—presumably between 1891, when the second edition ap-peared, and 1895, when the third edition appeared—he had him-self been influenced by the current interpretation, probably with-out realizing that it was different from his own. This conjecture is based primarily on the two passages cited above as incon-sistent with my interpretation: the passage dealing with the Giffen phenomenon and the last sentence of Note VI of the Mathematical Appendix. Both were added in the third edition— and these are the only passages I have been able to find in any edition of the *Principles* that fit the current interpretation better than they fit my interpretation. Further, both show some evi-dence of confusion about the fine points of his theory of de-mand (see last paragraph of appendix to this paper).

The hypothesis that Marshall did not recognize the contra-diction between the current interpretation and his earlier work would hardly be tenable if the lapse of time between the work incorporated in the first and the third editions of the *Principles* were as short as between their publication. But, as already noted, this is not the case. The essence of both his theory of demand and his analysis of consumer's surplus is contained in the *Pure Theory of (Domestic) Values,* which, though not printed until

1879, "must have been substantially complete about 1873."[48] The one important point in the theory of demand that is not in the *Pure Theory*—explicit mention of constancy of the purchasing power of money—is in the 1879 *Economics of Industry*. The only important addition in the *Principles* is the concept of "elasticity of demand"; and even this concept, which is not relevant to the present problem, was worked out in 1881–82.[49] No important substantive changes were made in the theory of demand in successive editions of the *Principles,* though the exposition was amplified and rearranged, the wording changed in detail, and some examples modified. The only important change of substance introduced into the discussion of consumer's surplus (in the third edition) was in connection with a point that has no bearing on the present issue.[50]

48. Keynes, *Memorials,* p. 23.

49. *Ibid.,* p. 39, n. 3.

50. This change does not reflect favorably on Marshall's willingness to admit error. The first edition states: "Subject to these corrections then we may regard the aggregate of the money measures of the total utility of weath as a fair measure of that part of the happiness which is dependent on wealth" (pp. 179–80), the corrections referred to being for "differences in the wealth of different purchasers" (p. 178) and "elements of collective wealth which are apt to be overlooked" (p. 179). A footnote to the first quotation refers to mathematical Note VII, in which he says, subject to the same two qualifications: "if a_1, a_2, a_3 . . . be the amounts consumed of the several commodities of which b_1, b_2, b_3 . . . are necessary for existence, if $y = f_1(x)$, $y = f_2(x)$, $y = f_3(x)$ . . . be the equations to their demand curves . . . , then the total utility of his wealth, subsistence being taken for granted, is represented by

$$\sum \int_b^a f(x)\,dx"$$

(1st ed.; p. 741)

The eighth edition does not contain the first statement. Instead, the text contains an explicit warning against adding consumer's surpluses for different commodities, and a footnote says: "Some ambiguous phrases in earlier editions appear to have suggested to some readers the opposite opinion" (p. 131). Note VII in the Mathematical Appendix was modified by replacing "his wealth" by "income" and, of more importance, "is represented" by "might be represented" and by adding after the formula the significant qualification, "if we could find a plan for grouping together in one common demand curve all those things which satisfy the same wants, and are rivals; and also for every group of things of which the services are complementary. . . . But we cannot do this; and therefore the formula remains a mere general expression, having no practical application" (p. 842). As noted, these changes date from the third edition.

Marshall himself writes: "My main position as to the theory
of value and distribution was practically completed in the years
1867 to 1870. . . . By this time [from the context, 1874] I had
practically completed the whole of the substance of my Mathematical Appendix."[51] Thus Marshall appears to have completed
his fundamental work on the theory of demand in the early
1870's and to have made no important substantive changes
thereafter. The third edition appeared some twenty or more years
later—an ample lapse of time for the precise details of an essentially mathematical analysis to have become vague and their
difference from a superficially similar set of details to pass unnoticed. This seems especially plausible in view of the acceptance of the current interpretation by others and the absence
of controversy about it.

Further circumstantial evidence that Marshall did not recognize the contradiction between the current interpretation and
his earlier work is provided by the apparent absence of any explicit discussion of the question in the writings of either Marshall
or the more prominent of his students or even of any comments
that could reasonably be interpreted as implying recognition of
the existence of alternative interpretations of the demand curve.
Yet, as noted earlier (n. 4), the current interpretation is explicitly given by Edgeworth as early as 1894 in an article on
"Demand Curves" in *Palgrave's Dictionary of Political Economy*
that Marshall must be presumed to have read. Though the assumption of constant prices of commodities other than the one
in question is not explicitly attributed to Marshall, most of the
article is based on Marshall; and there is no suggestion that
this assumption does not apply to Marshall's demand curve.
Further, Walras' definition of the demand curve, which presumably influenced Edgeworth, is identical with the current interpretation of Marshall's demand curve, and Marshall refers to
Walras several times in the first edition of the *Principles,* though
it seems clear that Marshall developed his theory of demand
independently of Walras.[52] So Marshall must have been exposed

51. Letter to J. B. Clark, *Memorials,* p. 416.

52. *Principles* (1st ed.), pp. xi, xii, 425; Keynes, *Memorials,* pp. 19–24; Marshall's
letter to J. B. Clark, *ibid.,* pp. 416–18.

to a definition of the demand curve corresponding to the current interpretation at a time when he was still making substantial revisions in the *Principles*. If he had recognized that this interpretation was incorrect, would he not have taken the opportunity to clarify his statements in later editions?

V. ALTERNATIVE CONCEPTIONS OF ECONOMIC THEORY

There remains the mystery how the current interpretation of Marshall's demand curve gained such unquestioned dominance at so early a date and retained it so long, not only as an interpretation of Marshall, but also as "the" definition of "the" demand curve.

One obvious explanation is that mathematical economists were more likely than others to state explicitly and precisely their assumptions about the behavior of other prices; that mathematical economists were likely to be familiar with Walras' independent definition and to take it as a point of departure; and that, in any event, the current interpretation is mathematically more convenient. Other economists, it could be argued, followed the lead of the mathematical economists, and thus the current interpretation was taken for granted and accepted without question.

This explanation seems to me a significant part of the answer; however, I do not believe that it is the entire answer. If, as I have argued above, my interpretation of Marshall is more useful for most practical problems, why has its use been so rarely proposed; why has there been no general feeling of dissatisfaction with the current interpretation? There must, it would seem, be something about the role that has been assigned to economic theory that has made the current interpretation acceptable.

I am inclined to believe that this is, in fact, the case; that, by slow and gradual steps, the role assigned to economic theory has altered in the course of time until today we assign a substantially different role to theory than Marshall did. We curtsy to Marshall, but we walk with Walras.

The distinction commonly drawn between Marshall and Walras is that Marshall dealt with "partial equilibrium," Walras with "general equilibrium." This distinction is, I believe, false and unimportant. Marshall and Walras alike dealt with general equilibrium; partial equilibrium analysis as usually conceived is but a special kind of general equilibrium analysis—unless, indeed, partial equilibrium analysis is taken to mean erroneous general equilibrium analysis. Marshall wrote to J. B. Clark in 1908: "My whole life has been and will be given to presenting in realistic form as much as I can of my Note XXI."[53] Note XXI, essentially unchanged from the first edition of the *Principles* to the last, presents a system of equations of general equilibrium. It ends with the sentence: "Thus, however complex the problem may become, we can see that it is theoretically determinate, because the number of unknowns is always exactly equal to the number of equations which we obtain."[54] The explanation given above why Marshall might have decided to hold the purchasing power of money constant was entirely in terms of constructing the demand curve so that it would be consistent with general equilibrium in those parts of the system not under direct study.

The important distinction between the conceptions of economic theory implicit in Marshall and Walras lies in the purpose for which the theory is constructed and used. To Marshall—to repeat an expression quoted earlier—economic theory is "an engine for the discovery of concrete truth." The "economic organon" introduces "systematic and organized methods of reasoning." Marshall wrote:

> Facts by themselves are silent. . . . The most reckless and treacherous of all theorists is he who professes to let facts and figures speak for themselves, who keeps in the background the part he has played, perhaps unconsciously, in selecting and grouping them, and in suggesting the argument *post hoc ergo propter hoc.* . . . The economist . . . must be suspicious of any direct light that the past is said to throw on problems of the present. He must stand fast by the more laborious plan of interrogating facts in order to learn the manner of action of causes singly and in combination, applying this knowledge to build up the organon of economic theory, and then making use of the aid of the organon in dealing with the economic side of social problems.[55]

53. *Memorials,* p. 417.

54. *Principles,* p. 856. This note was numbered XX in the first edition.

55. The quotations are all taken from Marshall, "The Present Position of Economics" (1885), *Memorials,* pp. 159, 161, 164, 166, 168, 171.

Economic theory, in this view, has two intermingled roles: to provide "systematic and organized methods of reasoning" about economic problems; to provide a body of substantive hypotheses, based on factual evidence, about the "manner of action of causes." In both roles the test of the theory is its value in explaining facts, in predicting the consequences of changes in the economic environment. Abstractness, generality, mathematical elegance—these are all secondary, themselves to be judged by the test of application. The counting of equations and unknowns is a check on the completeness of reasoning, the beginning of analysis, not an end in itself.

Doubtless, most modern economic theorists would accept these general statements of the objectives of economic theory. But our work belies our professions. Abstractness, generality, and mathematical elegance have in some measure become ends in themselves, criteria by which to judge economic theory. Facts are to be described, not explained. Theory is to be tested by the accuracy of its "assumptions" as photographic descriptions of reality, not by the correctness of the predictions that can be derived from it. From this viewpoint the current interpretation of the demand curve is clearly the better. It is more general and elegant to include the price of every commodity in the universe in the demand function rather than the average price of a residual group. Any price may affect any other, so a demand equation including every price is a more accurate photographic description. Of course, it cannot be used in discovering "concrete truth"; it contains no empirical generalization that is capable of being contradicted—but these are Marshallian objections. From the "Walrasian" viewpoint, to take one other example from recent developments in economic theory, it is a gain to eliminate the concept of an "industry," to take the individual firm as the unit of analysis, to treat each firm as a monopoly, to confine all analysis to either the economics of the individual firm or to a general equilibrium analysis of the economy as a whole.[56] From the Marshallian viewpoint this logical terminus of monopolistic competition analysis is a blind alley. Its categories are rigid, determined not by the problem at hand but by mathematical

56. See Triffin, *op. cit.*, pp. 188–89.

considerations. It yields no predictions, summarizes no empirical generalizations, provides no useful framework of analysis.

Of course, it would be an overstatement to characterize all modern economic theory as "Walrasian" in this sense. For example, Keynes's theory of employment, whatever its merits or demerits on other grounds, is Marshallian in method. It is a general equilibrium theory containing important empirical content and constructed to facilitate meaningful prediction. On the other hand, much recent work based on Keynes's theory of employment is Walrasian.[57]

VI. Conclusion

Modern economic theory typically defines the demand curve as showing the relation between the quantity of a commodity demanded and its price for given tastes, money income, and prices of other commodities. This definition has also been uniformly accepted as a correct interpretation of the demand curve defined and used by Alfred Marshall in his *Principles of Economics*. Rarely has the view been expressed that a different definition would be preferable.

Despite its unquestioned acceptance for over half a century, this interpretation of Marshall is, in my view, wrong. Marshall's early writings, the text of the *Principles*, and, even more definitely, the Mathematical Appendix provide almost conclusive proof that Marshall's demand curve differs in two respects from the one commonly used and attributed to him: first, commodities other than the one in question and its close rivals are treated as a group rather than individually, and only their average price is explicitly taken into account; second, and far more important, real income is considered the same at all points on the demand curve, whereas constant money income and other prices imply a higher real income, the lower the price of the commodity in question. Two variants of Marshall's demand curve can be distinguished: one, employed in the text of the *Principles*, uses variations in the prices of other commodities to compensate for variations in the price of the commodity in question and thereby

57. O. Lange, *Price Flexibility and Employment* (Bloomington, Ind.: Principia Press, 1944), is perhaps as good an example as any.

keeps the purchasing power of money constant; the other, employed in the Mathematical Appendix, uses variations in money income to compensate for variations in the price of the commodity in question.

The only textual evidence that conflicts with this interpretation is a passage in the text and a related sentence in the Mathematical Appendix that were added to the third edition of the *Principles*. The inconsistency of these with the rest of the *Principles* can be explained by the hypothesis that Marshall himself was after a point influenced by the current interpretation of the demand curve without recognizing its inconsistency with his earlier work. Some circumstantial evidence also supports this hypothesis.

The alternative interpretation of the demand curve not only is faithful to both the letter and the spirit of Marshall's work but also is more useful for the analysis of concrete problems than is the demand curve commonly employed. The acceptance of a less useful definition seems to me to be a consequence of a changed conception of the role of theory in economic analysis. The current interpretation of the demand curve is Walrasian; and so is current economic theory in general.

APPENDIX ON TWO NOTES IN THE MATHEMATICAL APPENDIX TO THE *PRINCIPLES*

I. Note II of the Eighth Edition

This note is numbered III in the first edition of the *Principles,* II in the rest. In the first edition the relevant parts are worded as follows (pp. 737–38):

"If m is the amount of money or general purchasing power at a person's disposal at any time, and μ represents its total utility to him, then $d\mu/dm$ represents the marginal utility of money to him.

"If p is the price which he is just willing to pay for an amount x of the commodity which gives him a total pleasure u, then

$$\frac{d\mu}{dm} \Delta p = \Delta u \; ; \text{and} \qquad \frac{d\mu}{dm} \frac{dp}{dx} = \frac{du}{dx} \cdots$$

"Every increase in his means diminishes the marginal utility of money to him; . . .

"Therefore, du/dx, the marginal utility to him of an amount x of a commodity remaining unchanged, an increase in his means . . . increases dp/dx, that is, the rate at which he is willing to pay for further supplies of it. Treating u as a variable, that is to say, allowing for possible variations in the person's liking for the commodity in question, we may regard dp/dx as a function of m, u, and x. . . ."

The wording in the eighth edition is identical except that "marginal utility of money" is replaced by "marginal degree of utility of money" and that "du/dx" and the words "Treating u . . . in question" are omitted from the last paragraph quoted (pp. 838–39). The changes were first made in the third edition.

In the second sentence of this note the word "price" is to be interpreted as "total amount," not as "price per unit." This is clear from the context and is demonstrated by the equation that follows and the designation of dp/dx as "the rate at which he is willing to pay for further supplies of it." The words "just willing" in the second sentence and the equations that follow demonstrate that p is the maximum amount he can pay for an amount x and have the same utility as if he had none of the commodity. Thus Marshall is describing a process like that outlined in Section I, C, of this paper, whereby the maximum possible amount is extracted from the individual for each successive increment of the commodity, the individual retaining the same "real income," that is, remaining on the same indifference curve, throughout the process.

The last sentence quoted shows that u is to be regarded as a parameter to allow for changes in tastes. The rest of that sentence simply describes a function like that obtained by eliminating y' from equations (5) and (6) of note 5 of this paper. The parameter m in Marshall's function takes the place of U_o in our footnote, since dp/dx is still to be regarded as the price per unit paid for an additional increment of the commodity rather than as the price per unit at which any amount can be purchased. In consequence, no explicit statement is needed as yet about the compensating variations in income that are implicit in Marshall's analysis.

The word "demand" does not appear in this note. But the note is attached to the chapter in the *Principles* in which Marshall first introduces the demand curve (Book III, chap. ii, in the first edition; Book III, chap. iii, in later editions) and is cited as proof of statements about the demand curve; hence there can be no doubt that the "function" mentioned in the last sentence quoted is the counterpart of Marshall's demand curve.

I have been able to construct no interpretation of this note that would render it consistent with the current interpretation of Marshall's demand curve.

II. Note VI

This note has the same number in all editions. In the first edition the relevant parts are worded as follows (p. 740):

"If y be the price at which an amount x of a commodity can find purchasers in a given market, and $y = f(x)$ be the equation to the demand-curve, then the total utility of the commodity is measured by

$$\int_o^a f(x)\,dx\,,$$

where a is the amount consumed.

"If however an amount b of the commodity is necessary for existence, $f(x)$ will be infinite, or at least indefinitely great, for values of x less than b. We must therefore take life for granted, and estimate separately the total utility of that part of the supply of the commodity which is in excess of absolute necessaries: it is of course

$$\int_b^a f(x)\,dx\ldots.$$

"It should be noted that, in the discussion of Consumers' Rent, we assume that the marginal utility of money to the individual purchaser is the same throughout. . . ."

Only trivial changes were made in these sentences in subsequent editions: a typographical error in the fifth edition, which remained uncorrected thereafter, substituted $f(z)$ for $f(x)$ in the second sentence; and "consumers' surplus" replaced "Consumers' Rent." In the third edition the following sentence was added at the end of the note:

"If, for any reason it be desirable to take acount of the influence which his expenditure on tea exerts on the value of money to him, it is only necessary to multiply $f(x)$, within the integral given above by that function of $xf(x)$ (i.e. of the amount which he has already spent on tea) which represents the marginal utility to him of money when his stock of it has been diminished by that amount" (3d ed., p. 795). The only subsequent changes were the addition of a comma after "reason" and the deletion of the comma before "within" (8th ed., p. 842).

In its final form Note VI seems internally inconsistent: the second sentence is wrong on the current interpretation of Marshall's demand curve, correct on my interpretation; the final sentence, added in the third edition, seems correct on the current interpretation, wrong on my interpretation.

A. THE SECOND SENTENCE

The second sentence is wrong on the current interpretation, which holds money income and other prices constant along the demand curve, since the ordinate of the demand curve for any quantity x cannot then exceed money income divided by x, and this is not "indefinitely great" for a fixed value of x—say, x_o—*whether* x_o is greater or less than b. True, $f(x)$ might approach infinity as x approaches zero, but this is not what Marshall says; he says it is "indefinitely great, for values of x less than b," i.e., for any particular value of x less than b—say, $x_o = 0.99b$.

On the variant of my interpretation involving compensating variations in money income—the variant that the note numbered II in the eighth edition leads me to believe Marshall used in the Mathematical Appendix—this sentence is entirely valid. As x declines from a value larger than b, the compensating variation in money income required to keep the individual's real income the same becomes larger and larger, approaching infinity as x approaches b, the minimum amount necessary for existence. This permits the ordinate of the demand curve likewise to approach infinity as x approaches b. On the variant involving compensating variations in other prices—the one Marshall used in the text—the definition of the demand curve breaks down for values of x less than b: for a finite price of the commodity in question, sufficiently high so that the given money income could purchase only a quantity x less than b, there will exist no set of nonnegative prices for the remaining commodities that will keep the purchasing power of money constant in the sense of enabling the same money income to provide the same level of utility; money income and real income cannot both be held constant and at the same time all prices be kept nonnegative. This sentence can therefore be defended as valid on either variant of my interpretation.

One possible ground for dismissing this sentence as evidence against the current interpretation is that the so-called "error" on that interpretation is of my own making, arising from a too subtle and too literal reading of the note. Marshall, it could be argued, was using "demand curve" to mean "utility curve" and $f(x)$ to mean "marginal utility," and therefore he did not consider whether the sentence would be valid if $f(x)$ were to be interpreted literally as the ordinate of the demand curve. A note that Marshall published in 1893 on "Consumer's Surplus" could be cited as evidence for this contention. In this note he quotes part of Note VI as follows: " 'If, however, an amount b of the commodity is necessary for existence, [the utility of the first element] a will be infinite.' "[58] The bracketed expression that Marshall substituted for $f(x)$ would support the notion that he was using "demand curve" and "utility curve" interchangeably.

I do not myself accept this argument; it seems to me to do much less than justice to Marshall. In the first place, I am inclined to give little weight to an incidental, explanatory, phrase inserted by Marshall as late as 1892 or 1893, some twenty years after the fundamental analysis incorporated in Note VI had been completed. I have noted above and shall presently cite evidence that Marshall may have been somewhat confused about the fine points of his own theory of demand by the early 1890's. In the second place, and more important, Marshall clearly distinguishes in the earlier notes in the Mathe-

---

58. "Consumer's Surplus," *Annals of the American Academy of Political and Social Science,* III (March, 1893), 618–21 (brackets in original). This note is a reply to some comments by Simon Patten. The letter a after the brackets which appears in the *Annals* note does not appear in the *Principles,* and I can explain it only as a typographical error.

matical Appendix between a utility curve and a demand curve, repeatedly using the word "utility," and in the first sentence of Note VI says that "the total utility of the commodity is *measured by*

$$\int_0^a f(x)\, dx'$$

(1st ed., p. 740; italics added). If he had been using $f(x)$ to stand for marginal utility, the words I have italicized could have been omitted. Finally, Note VI, like most of the rest of the Mathematical Appendix, summarizes a subtle, closely reasoned, and by no means obvious, mathematical argument, in which, so far as I know, few errors have ever been found. Is it credible that it would have been worded as loosely and carelessly as the argument being criticized requires; or that, if at one stage it had been, Marshall would have failed to see the simple mathematical error implicit in a literal reading of his words on the current interpretation of the demand curve? It seems to me far more credible that he meant what he said and that the correctness of what he said on my interpretation of his demand curve is strong evidence for that interpretation.

B. THE FINAL SENTENCE

The explanation that follows of the final sentence added to Note VI in the third edition, though not completely satisfactory, is reasonably so, and I have been able to construct no other even remotely satisfactory explanation.

Let U be the utility function of the "individual purchaser" and U_x the marginal utility of x units of tea to him, i.e., the partial derivative of U with respect to x. Now the increase in utility attributable to having a rather than b units of tea—consumer's surplus in utility units—is given by

$$\int_b^a U_x dx\ ,\qquad\qquad (1)$$

where the integral is computed for constant quantities of other commodities equal to the amounts consumed when a units of tea are consumed and other conditions are those corresponding to the demand curve $y = f(x)$.

At every point along the demand curve,

$$U_x = ny = n(x) f(x)\ ,\qquad\qquad (2)$$

where n is the marginal utility of money—itself, of course, a function of x along the demand curve. Integrating both sides of equation (2) gives

$$\int_b^a U_x dx = \int_b^a n(x) f(x)\, dx\ .\qquad\qquad (3)$$

The left-hand side of equation (3) is symbolically identical with equation (1); yet there is an important difference between them. In equation (1), U_x is computed, holding the quantities of other commodities constant as x varies; in equation (3), U_x is computed, holding constant whatever is held constant along the demand curve (money income and other prices on the current interpretation; real income on my interpretation). In general, quantities of other commodities vary along the demand curve (on either interpretation), and U_x may depend on the quantities of other commodities, so the U_x in equation (3) may be numerically different from the U_x in equation (1) for a value of x other than a. This difficulty disappears if U_x is supposed to be independent of the quantities of other commodities—an assumption that Marshall pretty clearly makes as a general rule (e.g., see Notes I and II of the Mathematical Appendix). On this assumption, then, the right-hand side of equation (3) measures consumer's surplus in utility units.

It is at this point that difficulties of interpretation arise; for the right-hand side of equation (3) is obtained by multiplying "$f(x)$ within the integral given above by that function of" x "which represents the marginal utility . . . of money." Why does Marshall say "that function of $xf(x)$" rather than of x alone? And is it valid to make this substitution? One can argue that to each value of x there corresponds a value of $f(x)$ and hence of $xf(x)$, so that the two forms of statement are equivalent: Marshall has simply made the transformation $z = xf(x)$ and converted $n(x)$ into $n(z)$. This argument is not, however, rigorous. In general, x will not be a single-valued function of z; hence to any given value of z there may correspond more than one value of x and hence more than one value of n. The two forms of statement are equivalent if and only if n is a single-valued function of z, i.e., if $n(x)$ is the same for all values of x for which $xf(x)$ is the same.

Given independence between the marginal utility of tea and the quantity of other commodities, this condition is always satisfied on the current interpretation of the demand curve but not on the alternative interpretation. Let x' stand for the quantity of a composite commodity representing all commodities other than tea, y' for its price, and $U_{x'}$, for its marginal utility. At each point on the demand curve,

$$\frac{U_x}{y} = \frac{U_{x'}}{y'} = n .$$

On the current interpretation of the demand curve, money income and the prices of other commodities are the same for all points on the demand curve. It follows that, for all values of x that yield the same value of $xf(x)$, the same amount will be spent on other commodities; so x' is the same (since y' is by definition); so $U_{x'}$ is (since, on the assumption of independence, $U_{x'}$ depends only on x'); and so n is. Marshall's use of $xf(x)$ instead of x is thus valid on the current interpretation of the demand curve.

On my interpretation, either money income varies along the demand curve, so as to keep real income constant, or other prices do; hence the preceding argument is no longer valid. That the two forms of statement are no longer always equivalent can be shown by a counterexample. If other prices are held constant and compensating variations of income are used to keep real income constant,

$$U = \sqrt{x} + \sqrt{x'}$$

is a utility function that gives different values of n for different values of x yielding the same value of $xf(x)$. If money income is held constant and compensating variations of other prices are used to keep real income constant,

$$U = 3 + x - \tfrac{1}{10} x^2 + \sqrt{x'}$$

is such a utility function. Hence Marshall's use of $xf(x)$ instead of x is invalid on either variant of the alternative interpretation.

This explanation leaves a number of Marshall's verbal statements wrong or ambiguous, whichever interpretation of the demand curve is accepted. (1) The parenthetical explanation of the meaning of $xf(x)$ seems wrong—why the word "already"? If one is thinking of going through the process of extracting as much as possible from the consumer for each successive unit of tea and is supposing the maximum price that he will pay for successive units to be given by the demand curve, then

$$\int_b^x f(x)\,dx$$

and not $xf(x)$ is the amount he has "already spent on tea." If one is thinking of the amount spent on tea at a given price for tea, then $xf(x)$ is the amount spent when the price is $f(x)$, not the amount "already spent." The explanation offered above accepts the latter rendering of the parenthesis, i.e., supposes the word "already" omitted. (2) The last clause—"when his stock of money has been diminished by that amount"—is ambiguous. To make it consistent with the explanation offered above, one must add "and tea is unavailable, so that the balance is spent solely on other commodities at the prices assumed in drawing the demand curve for tea." The reference to "stock of money" suggests that Marshall was supposing money income constant and so, independently of the rest of the quotation, would tend to rule out compensating variations in money income. It should be noted that there are no such ambiguities in the original version of Note VI, either in the parts quoted above or in the parts not quoted.

The "Welfare" Effects of an Income Tax and an Excise Tax[*]

THIS paper discusses the relative effects on welfare of an excise tax and an income tax. It demonstrates that an alleged "proof" of the superiority of the income tax is no proof at all, though it has repeatedly been cited as one. It then outlines a "correct" analysis of the problem.[1]

The explicit content of the paper is, however, only indirectly related to its major aim, which is to show by example the difference between two approaches to economic analysis. From this point of view, the present paper is an extended footnote to a recent article in the *Journal of Political Economy* in which I contrasted two definitions of the demand curve—the usual one, which supposes *money* income and money prices of other commodities the same for different points on a single demand curve, and an alternative definition, which I attributed to Alfred Marshall and which supposes *real* income to be the same.[2] I argued that the usual definition has arisen out of, and reflects, an essentially arithmetical and descriptive approach to economic analysis; the alternative definition, an analytical and problem-solving approach; and that the usual definition is in consequence less useful for most purposes. The quantitative difference between the two demand curves is small if the percentage of income spent on the commodity in question is small, as it generally is in actual applications, and approaches zero as that percentage approaches zero. Nonetheless, the difference in concept is highly important

* Reprinted from *Journal of Political Economy*, LX (February, 1952), 25–33, with revisions to eliminate error in original version pointed out by Cecil G. Phipps in *Journal of Political Economy*, LX (August, 1952), 332–36.

1. This paper is written in the spirit of the "new" welfare economics, because the technical problem it deals with has been considered primarily in those terms and despite serious doubts about the acceptability and validity of this approach to normative economics. The value of the general approach is a separate and broader issue, not considered here, except for the parenthetical comment in n. 5.

2. "The Marshallian Demand Curve," *supra*, pp. 47–99.

precisely because it does reflect a fundamental difference in approach.

The following discussion makes no explicit use of a demand curve. Yet it will be seen that the widely used analysis of the welfare effects of income and excise taxes, which it shows to be erroneous, is cut from the same cloth as the usual definition of the demand curve—both reflect the arithmetical approach to economic analysis. Of course, no approach makes error inevitable. An analyst may win through to correct results despite deficiencies in his approach and tools. Yet the fact that able and sophisticated analysts have been misled affords ample evidence that the defect is not unimportant.

I. The Alleged "Proof" of the Superiority of an Income Tax

Figure 1 summarizes an analysis that has frequently been offered as a "proof" that an income tax is superior to an excise tax yielding the same revenue.[3]

3. Most presentations of the "proof" derive from M. F. W. Joseph, "The Excess Burden of Indirect Taxation," *Review of Economic Studies,* VI (June, 1939), 226–31; or J. R. Hicks, *Value and Capital* (Oxford, 1939), p. 41. T. Peacock and D. Berry, in "A Note on the Theory of Income Distribution," *Economica,* XVIII (new ser.; February, 1951), 83–90, which applies Joseph's analysis to a slightly different problem and hence is equally invalid, point out that Joseph was anticipated by Gino Borgatta in an article in the 1921 volume of the *Giornale degli economisti.* The "proof" is also repeated in George J. Stigler, *Theory of Price* (New York: Macmillan Co., 1946), pp. 81–82; Edward D. Allen and O. H. Brownlee, *Economics of Public Finance* (New York: Prentice-Hall, Inc., 1947), pp. 343–45; M. W. Reder, "Welfare Economics and Rationing," *Quarterly Journal of Economics,* LVII (November, 1942), 153–55 (the rest of Reder's article is characterized by the same fallacy as the "proof" he reproduces, attributing it to Hicks); Haskell Wald, "The Classical Indictment of Indirect Taxation," *Quarterly Journal of Economics,* LIX (August, 1945), 577–96, esp. pp. 579–82; and A. Henderson, "The Case for Indirect Taxation," *Economic Journal,* LVIII (December, 1948), 538–53, esp. pp. 538–40. A logically equivalent argument is used to discuss the welfare effects of alternative forms of direct taxation by Kenneth E. Boulding, *Economic Analysis* (rev. ed.; New York: Harper & Bros., 1948), pp. 773–75, and is repeated by Eli Schwartz and Donald A. Moore, who dispute Boulding's specific conclusions but do not question the validity of his argument, in "The Distorting Effects of Direct Taxation: A Re-evaluation," *American Economic Review,* XLI (March, 1951), 139–48.

The analysis of this problem by Joseph and Hicks is often considered identical with the earlier analysis of the same problem by Harold Hotelling in "The General

Consider a world of two goods, X and Y. Let the quantity of X be measured along the horizontal axis and that of Y along the vertical and draw the indifference curves of a consumer (a "representative" consumer [?]). Let AB represent the initial budget line, so P_1 is the initial equilibrium position. Let an excise tax of, say, 50 per cent of the price inclusive of tax be placed on X (call this "Excise Tax A"), and let it be entirely shifted to the consumer, so that the price of X to the consumer doubles. On the assumption (underlying the usual demand curve) that money income and other prices are to be held fixed in analyzing the effect of a change in one price, the budget line shifts to AC and the equilibrium position to P_2. Suppose, now, that instead of the excise tax an income tax had been imposed to yield the same revenue ("Income Tax A"). The budget line corresponding to this income tax is parallel to AB, since prices are assumed to be unaffected. Moreover, it must go through P_2 if the revenue from the income tax is to be equal to the revenue from the

---

Welfare in Relation to Problems of Taxation and of Railway and Utility Rates," *Econometrica,* VI (July, 1938), 242–69, esp. pp. 249–51. But this is a serious error, since Hotelling avoids the fallacy that mars the analyses listed in the preceding paragraph. An interchange between Hotelling and Ragnar Frisch on Hotelling's article, *Econometrica,* VII (April, 1939), 45–60, deals rather obliquely with the point with which the present note is concerned. At bottom, the major difference between Frisch and Hotelling is that Frisch interprets Hotelling's proof as identical with that given by Joseph, although, of course, Joseph's proof is not referred to and had not appeared in print when Frisch wrote. Frisch fails to see the force of Hotelling's emphasis on the essential point of difference, namely, that Hotelling takes account of conditions of cost of production.

The "proof" is critically examined and correctly criticized by Earl R. Rolph and George F. Break, in "The Welfare Aspects of Excise Taxes," *Journal of Political Economy,* LVII (February, 1949), 46–54. Their analysis has much in common with that of the present paper; they point out essentially the same defects in the "proof" and give an essentially correct analysis of the problem. A correct analysis of the problem is also given by I. M. D. Little, *A Critique of Welfare Economics* (Oxford, 1950), pp. 157–79. In a recent article, "Direct versus Indirect Taxes," *Economic Journal,* LXI (September, 1951), 577–84, which came to my attention only after the present paper was in the hands of the printer, Little also points out the defects in the usual analysis. The chief difference between the present paper and the relevant parts of the papers by Rolph and Break and by Little is that the present paper is primarily concerned with the methodological issue involved in the analysis; the others, with the substantive issue.

excise tax: under the excise tax the individual spends his whole money income, which is taken to be the same whichever tax is imposed, on the bundle of goods indicated by P_2; this expenditure equals the tax payment plus the cost of P_2 at pretax prices. In consequence, if he pays the same amount in taxes under an income tax, he will be able to buy the bundle indicated by P_2 at the pretax prices with the rest of his income. The budget line

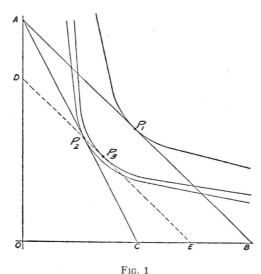

Fig. 1

under the income tax is therefore DE. But, with this budget line, the individual will not in fact buy the bundle indicated by P_2; he will instead buy the bundle indicated by P_3, which is on a higher indifference curve. It is therefore concluded that an income tax permits a consumer to attain a higher indifference curve than an excise tax yielding the same revenue;[4] that is, that

4. Total revenue from all taxes will necessarily be the same at P_2 and P_3 only if there are no differential excise taxes or subsidies in force at the initial position. If, for example, there is an excise tax on Y at the initial position, its yield will be less at P_3 than at P_2, and the preferability of the former may be interpreted as reflecting this smaller tax payment rather than the different form of the tax. The existence of a tax on Y at P_1 does not alter the argument in the text; it does change the meaning or interpretation of the conclusion.

(1) *Income Tax A is preferable to Excise Tax A.*[5]

So far we have dealt with only a single individual. The *analysis* generally ends at this point, but the *conclusion* is immediately generalized to the community as a whole to yield the proposition that all members of the community would be better off (on higher indifference curves) if an excise tax were replaced by an income tax so levied that each member pays the same amount as an income tax that he formerly paid as an excise tax.

II. The Fallacy in the Alleged "Proof"

This "proof" contains two essential steps: first, the derivation of proposition (1) for an isolated individual; second, the generalization of this proposition to the community at large.

The analysis for an isolated individual is entirely valid. If Excise Tax A or Income Tax A were imposed solely on one individual among many, they would have negligible indirect effects beyond those summarized in Figure 1, and that figure could serve as an adequate representation of the final position attained by the individual in question. Its arithmetic is impeccable, and arithmetic alone is relevant in this case.

The immediate generalization of the analysis to the community at large, on the other hand, is invalid. While Figure 1 is an adequate representation of the final position when taxes are imposed on one person alone, it is not adequate when taxes are imposed on all members of a community alike—as would indeed be painfully obvious except for the habitual patterns of thought engendered by the usual approach to demand curves. Consider, for example, the budget lines *AB* and *AC* in Figure 1. It is obvious directly, and without the use of indifference curves,

5. The reader should perhaps be warned that the identification of "being on a higher indifference curve" with "is preferable to" is a far less innocent step than may appear on the surface. Indeed, the view expressed in n. 1 about the validity of the "new" welfare economics in general rests in considerable measure on the belief that this step cannot be justified within the utilitarian framework of that approach, though it can be within a different, and in my judgment preferable, philosophical framework. For a criticism of this step on somewhat different grounds see Little, *A Critique of Welfare Economics,* pp. 38–50. These considerations are not, however, relevant to the particular technical point made in this paper.

that the alternatives available to the consumer when the budget line is AC are clearly inferior to those available when the budget line is AB. When it is AB, he can, if he wishes, have any of the alternatives available when it is AC *plus* all the bundles in the triangle ACB. Generalization of the analysis for an isolated individual to the community as a whole therefore supposes that the mere imposition of the excise tax reduces the range of alternatives open to every consumer in a way that is calculable by simple arithmetic. How can this be? The imposition of the excise tax per se does not change any of the technical production possibilities; it does not by itself lessen the physical resources available to the community. It may reduce the quantity of resources available to produce X and Y if the proceeds are used to produce goods under state direction which formerly were not produced (say, goods Z). But, in that case, Figure 1 is not at all adequate, since an additional axis would be needed to represent goods Z. More important, the reduction in the alternatives open to the consumer would then depend on physical and technical possibilities, the kinds of resources needed for the goods produced by the state, and similar factors; the reduction cannot be computed by simple arithmetic from the knowledge summarized in Figure 1.

The above analysis says nothing about the destination of the proceeds of the excise tax; it would not be changed if the proceeds were impounded or used to give a per-unit subsidy on Y or an income subsidy to consumers. But in any of these cases the tax would not have reduced the range of alternatives technically available. If prices were temporarily rigid, the supply of money fixed except for the changes brought about by the tax, and the proceeds of the tax impounded, unemployment might of course occur in the short run (though there is then considerable ambiguity in the assumption that X and Y are the only goods in the world). This would not, however, be a stable position; prices would tend to fall relative to money income, which would shift the line AC to the right. More important, if prices did not fall relative to money income, the most significant implication of either the excise tax or the income tax would be the same, namely, that either tended to produce unemployment and a reduction

in the alternatives available to consumers. The difference between P_3 and a point at the original prices equivalent in utility
to P_2 (the point of tangency between a budget line parallel to
AB and the indifference curve through P_2) is small compared to
the difference between either and P_1; indeed, the ratio of the
former difference to the latter difference approaches zero as the
excise tax (or equivalent income tax) approaches zero.[6] It follows that, if rigidity of prices and creation of unemployment are
considered the major consequences, the conclusion would have
to be that the income tax and excise tax have essentially identical
effects on "welfare" and that any difference between their effects
is of the "second order of smalls."

The analysis cannot be saved by this route. It is clearly intended to be a "long-run" analysis—comparative "statics," not
dynamics—as is amply demonstrated by both the considerations
just cited and the assumed complete shifting of the excise tax.
We can therefore abstract from any short-run price rigidities and
suppose complete adaptation to the the new circumstances. But
then it is clear that Figure 1 alone tells nothing about the final
effects of either the income tax or the excise tax. For example,
suppose the excise tax is used to give a per-unit subsidy on Y.
The slope of the new budget line would then be known (and
might be that shown by AC if the excise tax and subsidy were
adjusted appropriately), but its position would not be; for its
position would be determined not alone by the tastes of consumers and by arithmetic calculation but also by the technical
possibilities open to the community.

III. A "CORRECT" ANALYSIS

In order to bring the technical possibilities into the picture,
let us suppose that we are dealing with a community of many

6. The difference between P_1 and P_3 corresponds to the "income effect" as defined by Slutsky; between P_1 and the point at the original prices on the same
indifference curve as P_2, to the "income effect" as defined by Hicks. As Mosak has
shown, the difference between the two income effects approaches zero relative to
the income effect itself as the price change approaches zero. See Jacob T. Mosak,
"On the Interpretation of the Fundamental Equation of Value Theory," in Oscar
Lange, Francis McIntyre, and Theodore S. Yntema (eds.), *Studies in Mathematical
Economics and Econometrics* (Chicago: University of Chicago Press, 1942), pp.
69–74.

identical individuals—identical in tastes and preferences and also in kind and quantity of resources owned by each individual. In this community every individual will have the same income and consume the same bundle of goods, so we can represent the position of the community by the position of any one individual, as in Figure 2. Given the resources available to the community, there will be some set of combinations of X and Y that it is technically possible to produce. These can be represented by a production indifference curve. Since in our hypothetical community

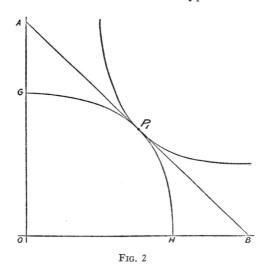

Fig. 2

every individual will consume an aliquot share of each commodity, we can divide the coordinates of this production curve by the number of individuals and plot the result on any one individual's indifference map. GH on Figure 2 is such a production possibility curve. It shows the alternative combinations of X and Y that are technically available to each individual, given that every individual ends up with the same combination. It should be emphasized that Figure 2 is for an individual and therefore does not involve interpersonal comparisons; we are interested here in an "allocative," not a "distributive," problem and can abstract from the distributive problem by dealing with a society composed of identical individuals.

If the society were initially at a position of full competitive equilibrium, each individual would be at P_1. At this point the rate of substitution in consumption (the slope of the consumption indifference curve) is equal to the rate of substitution in purchase on the market (the price ratio shown by the slope of the budget line), which, in turn, is equal to the rate of substitution in production (the slope of the production indifference curve). Technical possibilities are being fully exploited, as shown by the fact that P_1 is on the frontier of the alternatives technically capable of being produced (these obviously include not only those on GP_1H but also those between the production indifference curve and the origin).

How can we represent a proportional income tax on this diagram? If the proceeds are impounded or returned to individuals in the form of a per-capita subsidy, the diagram obviously remains completely unchanged. For such an income tax and subsidy do not alter the relative prices of X and Y, the consumption indifference curves, or the production possibilities. They are a purely nominal matter on the present level of analysis. If the proceeds of the income tax are spent by the state to produce, say, Z, with resources formerly used to produce X or Y, the production possibilities are clearly changed. There will now be a new production indifference curve, showing the alternative combinations of X and Y capable of being produced, given the production of a specified amount of Z. But the change in the production indifference curve depends only on the amount of Z produced, not on how the funds are raised. If we suppose this amount of Z to be given and fixed, the new production indifference curve will be the same whether an income tax or an excise tax is imposed; hence, in investigating any difference between an income tax and an excise tax, we can, without loss of generality, suppose GP_1H to be the production indifference curve after the subtraction of resources to produce Z. Figure 2 can therefore represent the situation both before and after a proportional income tax for purposes of comparing such a tax with an excise tax.

What now of an excise tax? One condition is obvious. The position of equilibrium must be on the production indifference

curve *GH*. Any position above the production indifference curve
is technically impossible with the available resources; any position below it does not involve full use of available resources
and is therefore unstable. Beyond this, the essential feature of
an excise tax for our purposes is that it leads to a divergence between two prices—the price paid by the consumer and the price
received by the producer—and, hence, between two price ratios
that were formerly the same—the price ratio relevant to the consumer and the price ratio relevant to the producer. The terms
on which the consumer can substitute one commodity for the
other in purchase on the market, while keeping total expenditures
the same, must be calculated from prices inclusive of tax; the
terms on which the producer can substitute one commodity for
the other in sale on the market, while keeping total receipts the
same, must be calculated from the prices exclusive of tax. Equilibrium for consumers requires that the rate at which consumers
can substitute in purchase be equal to the rate at which they
are willing to substitute in consumption; that is, that the consumer budget line be tangent to a consumption indifference
curve. Equilibrium for producers requires that the rate at which
producers can substitute in sale be equal to the rate at which they
can substitute in production; that is, that a constant-receipts
line be tangent to the production indifference curve. A position
of equilibrium satisfying these conditions is given by P_6 in Figure 3. The line *IJ* is the budget line as it appears to the consumer; the line *KL,* the constant-receipts line as it appears to
producers. The two diverge because of Excise Tax A on *X*,
which may be regarded as determining the angle between the
two lines and which means that the extra amount of *X* consumers
can purchase by giving up one unit of *Y* is less than the extra
amount of *X* producers need to sell to recoup the loss from selling one fewer units of *Y*. At P_6, *KL* is tangent to the production
indifference curve and *IJ* to a consumption indifference curve.

The ratio of the price of *Y* to the price of *X* when the excise
tax is in effect (at P_6) cannot, as is assumed in drawing Figure
1, be calculated simply from the initial price ratio at P_1 and the
rate of the tax. It depends also on production considerations.
The less concave the production possibility curve, the larger

the fraction of the tax that will be shifted to the consumer and the smaller the fraction that will be shifted to the producer, and conversely. The whole of the tax will be shifted to the consumer, in the sense that the relative price of the two commodities exclusive of tax will be the same at P_6 as at P_1, only if the production possibility curve is identical with AB.

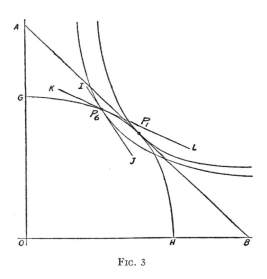

Fig. 3

Given the shapes of the curves as in Figure 3, P_6 is necessarily inferior to P_1, in the sense that the individual is on a lower indifference curve. Given that the initial position is one of full competitive equilibrium with no taxes or subsidies, that is, that it is P_1, Excise Tax A is inferior to Income Tax A.

Suppose, however, that the initial position had been P_6 instead of P_1, not because of governmental taxes or subsidies but because of some other deviation from fully competitive conditions, say, because of monopolistic conditions in the production of X which produce the same position of equilibrium as Excise Tax A imposed under fully competitive conditions. Let an excise tax now be imposed on commodity Y of the same percentage as Excise Tax A, say 50 per cent (call this Excise Tax B), and let us compare this with an income tax (Income Tax B) yielding the same revenue to the government.

The analysis summarized in Section I could be repeated for this excise tax and income tax, and it would yield the same conclusion—that the income tax is preferable to the excise tax, since nothing is said in that analysis about the nature of the initial position, except possibly that it be a position in which there are no differential excise taxes or subsidies.[7]

Yet Figure 3 shows that this conclusion is wrong. Excise Tax B precisely offsets the effect of the assumed monopoly in the production of X; it eliminates the divergence produced by that monopoly between the price ratio relevant to consumers (the ratio of market prices inclusive of taxes) and that relevant to producers (the ratio of marginal revenues exclusive of taxes). The two ratios coincide, and, in consequence, P_1 is the equilibrium position with Excise Tax B imposed on an initial position P_6. On the other hand, the imposition of Income Tax B leaves the divergence between the two ratios unchanged and leaves P_6 the equilibrium position. Hence Excise Tax B is preferable to Income Tax B, given that both are imposed when the initial position is P_6.

IV. Conclusion

At this point the reader may well be tempted to regard the alleged proof of Section I as rehabilitated, to say that "of course" its validity depends on the assumption that the initial position is one of full competitive equilibrium and that, while the users of the "proof" have been careless in not stating this assumption explicitly, they have doubtless recognized its necessity. A reexamination of the "proof" will, however, show that no "assumption" about the nature of the initial position will render it a valid proof of the relevant economic proposition. The conclusion to which it is said to lead may be correct when the initial position is a position of full competitive equilibrium; but the argument does not demonstrate that it is correct or why it is correct. The alleged syllogism, "Socrates is a man; Socrates is X; therefore, all men are X," happens to lead to a correct "conclu-

7. This qualification is necessary if the two taxes compared are to have not only the same direct tax yield but also to *add* the same amount to the total tax yield (see n. 4).

sion" when X stands for "mortal," though not when X stands for "Greek." Nonetheless, the assumption that X stands for "mortal" will not render it a valid syllogism. The parallel is exact: the alleged proof that an income tax is superior to an excise tax is not a proof at all; no *step* in the alleged proof depends for its validity on the character of the initial position; hence, no "assumption" about the initial position can convert it into a valid proof, though the final statement in the "proof" may be correct for some conditions and not for others.[8]

The analysis in Section III shows that no general statement can be made about the relative effects on "welfare" of what we have been calling "income taxes" and "excise taxes." Everything depends on the initial conditions under which the taxes are imposed. But even this statement does not sufficiently indicate the limitations on the direct applicability of the results. What I, in common with the other writers on this problem, have called an "income tax" has little or no kinship with the taxes actually levied under that name. The latter are fundamentally excise taxes more or less broad in scope. Even a straight proportional income tax on a broadly defined tax base does not fall equally on all goods and services produced with available resources; inevitably it leaves untouched goods and services not produced through the market—leisure, household activities, etc. It therefore makes the rate at which the consumer can substitute them for marketable goods and services different from the rate at which it is technically possible to substitute them. This effect is clearly greater if the income-tax base is more narrowly defined, an exemption is allowed, or the rates are progressive. The most that one can infer from the analysis is perhaps a presumption that, the broader the scope of the tax and the more equal its incidence, the less likely it is to falsify rates of substitution. But even this is at best a presumption to be tested in each case. Unfortunately, formal analysis can seldom if ever give easy answers to hard

8. Note the difference between this case for the community and the case for an isolated individual when the initial position already involves a special excise tax. In that case, though the analysis is no different, the meaning and interpretation of the conclusion is, as noted in nn. 4 and 7 above. But, even for the individual, other deviations from competitive conditions at the initial position do not affect the validity or meaning of any step in the proof.

problems. Its role is quite different: to suggest the considerations relevant to an answer and to provide a useful means of organizing the analysis.

The analysis in Section III is clearly applicable to many problems other than the particular one to which it is there applied. Forces other than taxes may produce divergences between the rates of substitution whose equality is the essential condition of an "optimum" in the sense implicit in the above discussion. For example, as already noted, monopoly produces such a divergence, and it is this divergence that constitutes the fundamental argument, on strictly allocative grounds, against monopoly. Similarly, Marshall's argument for taxes on decreasing-return industries and subsidies to increasing-return industries, to the extent that it is valid, involves a divergence between the production indifference curve relevant to the producer and the production indifference curve relevant to society and hence a divergence between the rate at which a producer judges that he can substitute commodities in production and the rate at which producers as a whole can actually do so. In fact, our simple Figure 3 contains the essence of much of modern welfare economics.

To return to the initial theme, the approach to economics underlying the usual demand curve is the approach underlying the superficial analysis embodied in Figure 1; the approach underlying the alternative demand curve along which "real income" is held constant is the approach embodied in Figures 2 and 3; one who started with this approach would be heavily insulated against analyses such as that embodied in Figure 1. The great defect of the approach underlying the usual demand curve is that it emphasizes arithmetic considerations; the great virtue of the approach underlying the alternative demand curve is that it emphasizes economic considerations.

PART III
Monetary Theory and Policy

The Effects of a Full-Employment Policy on Economic Stability: A Formal Analysis*

A FULL-EMPLOYMENT policy has come in recent years to mean both the adoption by government of a "high" and "stable" level of employment as a leading policy objective and the promotion of this objective by deliberate actions taken from time to time to add to or subtract from aggregate money demand for goods and services. It is by no means clear that this objective is capable of attainment by these means. Government actions undertaken to eliminate or offset economic instability may instead increase instability. They obviously will do so if they tend for some reason to be persistently perverse, so that government generally takes expansionary action when, at least from hindsight, contraction is called for, and conversely. But government countercyclical actions may also be destabilizing—and this is both less obvious and more important—even though they are more often in the right than in the wrong direction and even though they are smaller in magnitude than the fluctuations they are designed to offset.

Under what conditions will countercyclical action succeed in its objective of reducing instability? Under what conditions will it actually increase instability? How does its effectiveness depend on the magnitude of action? What is the optimum magnitude of countercyclical action? The present note considers these questions on a highly formal level. Its purpose is primarily to make it clear that they are important and relevant questions; secondarily, to indicate in general terms the considerations on which an answer in any particular case depends. It does not attempt to answer them for any particular case.

* A slightly revised version of a manuscript translated into French by Jacques Mayer and published as "Les effets d'une politique de plein emploi sur la stabilité économique: Analyse formelle," *Économie appliquée,* IV (July–December, 1951), 441–56.

I

Despite the enormous literature on full-employment policy, these questions have been almost completely neglected. The many proponents of full-employment policies seem to take it for granted that a full-employment policy will not be destabilizing, that this will be true regardless of the precise character of the policy, and that there is no serious problem about the magnitude of government measures to promote stability except to make them large enough. On the other hand, opponents have seldom attacked full-employment policies on the grounds that they may increase instability but rather on the grounds that such policies would strengthen the role of the government and threaten political freedom, or would reduce the rate of progress, or would strengthen pressure groups and promote inflation, etc.

The failure to recognize that there is a basic problem about the effectiveness of countercyclical action, that it is possible to do too much as well as too little, is paralleled by a frequent failure on the part of proponents of full-employment policies to specify precisely the policies they favor. And both, it seems to me, largely reflect the naïve theoretical model in terms of which full-employment policies have been defended and alternative policies judged, either implicitly or explicitly, even by economists who are fully aware, in other contexts, of the deficiencies of the model. This model, in its simplest form, takes investment as given by external circumstances and unaffected by government action, consumption as determined by current income, and current income as the sum of investment, consumption, and government expenditure. It largely neglects price movements, generally by regarding prices as essentially rigid when money income is below the minimum level consistent with "full employment" and as changing in proportion with money income when money income exceeds the minimum level consistent with "full employment."[1]

1. In symbols, if Y stands for income; C, for consumption; I, for investment; and G, for government expenditure on goods and services, all in "real" terms:

$$Y = C + I + G ,\qquad (1)$$

from which
$$C = f(Y),\qquad (2)$$
$$Y = f(Y) + I + G .\qquad (3)$$

If I is fixed, Y clearly becomes a function of G.

This model neglects such complications as the difference between gross national

According to this model, increased government expenditure adds to income directly and thereby stimulates consumption, which leads to further additions to income through the consumption "multiplier." More important for our purposes, the system has no lags. In consequence, it implies for each time unit a particular value of real government expenditure, and a minimum value of money government expenditure, that would produce full employment, and these values do not depend on what has occurred in preceding time units.[2] If actual government expenditure were below this level, income would be below the full-employment level; if money government expenditure were above the minimum level consistent with full employment, prices would be unnecessarily high to produce full employment. Fluctuations in investment are the only important factor regarded as making for fluctuations in income, and these can always be offset by appropriate fluctuations in government expenditure. Finally, it is generally assumed—though this assumption is not strictly implicit in the model—that government expenditure (or the government contribution to the

---

product and national income and between national income and personal income; it takes national income as the determinant of consumption expenditures, thereby supposing direct taxes to be either zero or a function of national income. The model could readily be extended to allow for these various complications as well as for others and in this way to make explicit the possibility of using changes in taxes as well as in expenditures to promote full employment. But such extensions would only complicate the exposition without changing the fundamental character of the model for our purpose.

For recent examples of the explicit use of such a model see E. Cary Brown, "Analysis of Consumption Taxes in Terms of the Theory of Income Determination," *American Economic Review,* XL (March, 1950), 74–89; Ta-Chung Liu and Ching-Gwan Chang, "Consumption and Investment Propensities Pre-war and Post-war," *American Economic Review,* XL (September, 1950), 565–82.

The model is nearly as explicit in John M. Clark, Arthur Smithies, Nicholas Kaldor, Pierre Urie, and E. Ronald Walker, *National and International Measures for Full Employment: A Report by a Group of Experts Appointed by the Secretary General* (Lake Success, N.Y.: United Nations, December, 1949), pp. 20–23, particularly pars. 37, 38, 45. This report is hereafter referred to as *"UN Report."*

2. If Y_0 is the "full-employment" income, then

$$G_0 = Y_0 - f(Y_0) - I_0$$

is the level of government expenditure that on this model will produce full employment. It should be noted that this can all be expressed in terms of the "government contribution" and so take account of tax changes as well. If the model is taken literally, real government expenditure cannot exceed this level. Any attempt to have it do so will simply mean higher prices.

income stream) can be altered at will and without significant lag, so that the "appropriate" fluctuations in government expenditure can be produced by deliberate action.[3]

With this model it is easy to see that there is no great problem, at least so far as maintaining a desired level of aggregate income is concerned. In any period in which income would otherwise be below the full-employment level, it is only necessary for government to spend more (or tax less) in order to raise income, and to spend more in any way whatsoever; so long as government does not spend more than the amount, in principle calculable, required to produce full employment, it can do no harm. Mistakes may lead to temporarily overshooting or undershooting the mark, but this is of no great moment, since errors do not affect the future and so can readily be corrected. The real danger is that government will not do enough; there is little reason to suppose it will do too much.[4] The techniques used to spend more or less (or tax less or more) may matter for other reasons—equity, economic efficiency, etc.—but are irrelevant to the technical effectiveness of countercyclical policy. Similarly, grasping trade-unions or producer pressure groups may by their actions steadily raise the minimum money value of the full-employment income and so make stable prices and full-employment incompatible, but again this is a "political" problem and is irrelevant to the technical effectiveness of countercyclical policy.

Few would explicitly accept this simple model as an adequate representation of the forces determining the level of economic activity. For example, it clearly provides no "theory" of cyclical fluctuations worthy of the name; it interprets cyclical fluctuations as simply a reflection of fluctuations in investment, which are themselves taken as given. Lagged reactions are the essence of cyclical fluctuations regarded as self-generating. In consequence, when those who follow this general approach seek to "explain"

3. The *UN Report* exemplifies almost ideally the position I am describing. See especially pars. 45, 67, 68, and 76.

4. Compare the following quotation from the *UN Report:* "Some decline in demand is therefore bound to occur before effective measures can be taken to check and reverse the movement. In present circumstances, this may be inevitable; what is essential is to ensure that such counter-measures are not taken too late, and that when they are taken they should be adequate for dealing with the situation" (p. 39).

cyclical fluctuations, they complicate their models by introducing lagged reactions of one kind or another and in this way have developed an embarrassingly wide variety of different cycle-generating models. Yet I think it is correct to say that these complications are neglected in discussions of the feasibility of full-employment policy and of the merits of alternative policies. For this purpose the analysis generally proceeds as if the simple model I have sketched were completely adequate.[5]

II

This model cannot, of course, be used to investigate the questions considered in this note—which is, indeed, a major reason why these questions have been so generally neglected. It answers them in a way that is almost equivalent to denying their significance. According to this model, countercyclical action by government can be destabilizing only if it goes so far as to convert what would otherwise be conditions of depression into conditions of boom, and conversely; the optimum magnitude of government action is that which produces complete stability of income, and there is nothing in the model to indicate that this result is incapable of attainment or that it requires knowledge not now available or what factors will interfere with its attainment. We shall, instead, investigate these questions by an altogether different route, one suggested by the theory of statistics rather than economic theory.[6]

Our problem is to compare the results of two alternative structures of economic policy: one including and the other excluding a specified "full-employment policy." Of course, the absence of the specified "full-employment policy" does not mean that government actions do not impinge on economic activity or that they may not in some sense be responsible for fluctuations in economic activity. It merely means that we take this latter set of actions

5. A striking example is the *UN Report*, which cites, as the reason why the above model is "a drastic simplification of reality," its neglect of the behavior of prices and does not even mention the problem of lags in reaction.

6. The formal analysis that follows is an expansion of footnotes in two earlier articles. See "Lerner on the Economics of Control," *infra*, p. 316, n. 12; "Rejoinder" to comment by Philip Neff, *American Economic Review*, XXXIX (September, 1949), 951, n. 2.

for granted and inquire about the effects of the additional actions grouped under the title "full-employment policy." We shall judge the effects of the two alternative policies by the behavior of national income, without specifying whether "real" or "money" income. The formal analysis that follows will apply equally well to either as well as to any other criterion of performance.

Let $X(t)$ represent income at time t in the absence of the specified full-employment policy. The full-employment policy may be regarded as having effects that add to or subtract from income. Let $Y(t)$ represent the amount so added to or subtracted from $X(t)$, so that

$$Z(t) = X(t) + Y(t) \tag{1}$$

represents income at time t in the presence of the specified full-employment policy.

Note that $Y(t)$ does *not* measure the effect of the countercyclical actions *taken* at time t. It measures instead the combined effect at time t of countercyclical action whenever taken. Thus it may reflect action taken very much earlier; it may even reflect action to be taken in the future in so far as anticipation that such action will be taken affects current income. Note also that nothing special is involved in writing $Y(t)$ as a magnitude to be *added* to $X(t)$. This is a matter of definition: we could have defined $X(t)$ and $Z(t)$ as income in the absence and presence, respectively, of a specified full-employment policy and then have defined $Y(t)$ as the difference between Z and X.

Income may, and generally will, display a trend as well as fluctuations about the trend. Similarly, the introduction of the policies whose effect is measured by $Y(t)$ may alter the average level of income or may introduce a trend into income. Since our interest is primarily in fluctuations, rather than in level or trend, we shall assume in the discussion that follows that all our variables have horizontal trends, that is, that the expected value of each variable is the same for all values of t.[7] This involves no loss of generality for our purpose, since we could equally well have defined Z, X, and Y as deviations from trends.

7. In other words, we shall regard $Z(t)$, $X(t)$, and $Y(t)$ as stationary stochastic series. The expected value of $Y(t)$ will be positive, zero, or negative according as the existence of countercyclical policy tends to raise the average level of income, leave it unchanged, or lower it.

We can measure the magnitude of fluctuations in many different ways, and it is somewhat arbitrary to select any one. At the same time I do not see that the results we reach will be critically affected by the particular measure we use, and it is mathematically most convenient to use the variance (or square of the standard deviation), that is, the mean square deviation of the series from its mean. Accordingly, we shall use the variance, which we shall designate σ^2 with a subscript to indicate the series considered.[8] For X or Z the variance measures the fluctuations in income in the absence or presence of a countercyclical policy. For Y the variance may be regarded as measuring the magnitude of the countercyclical action taken: if no action were taken, the variance of Y would be zero; the greater the magnitude of action, for a given kind and time pattern of action, the greater the variance of Y.

We can now rephrase our initial questions in terms of these concepts and symbols. Under what conditions will the variance of $Z(\sigma_Z^2)$ be less than the variance of $X(\sigma_X^2)$, so that the countercyclical policy succeeds in its objective of reducing instability? Under what conditions will σ_Z^2 exceed σ_X^2? How does the difference between σ_Z^2 and σ_X^2 depend on the magnitude of countercyclical action, that is, on σ_Y^2? What is the optimum size of σ_Y^2?

By a well-known statistical theorem

$$\sigma_Z^2 = \sigma_X^2 + \sigma_Y^2 + 2r_{XY}\sigma_X\sigma_Y \qquad (2)$$

where r_{XY} is the correlation coefficient between X and Y.[9] Just as σ_Y measures one dimension of countercyclical policy—its magnitude—so r_{XY} measures another dimension—roughly speaking, its timing or "fit." If countercyclical policy were always timed and proportioned correctly, its *effects* would uniformly be in the opposite direction to the deviation of X from its mean and a fixed proportion of this deviation. In this case, Y would be perfectly negatively correlated with X, and r_{XY} would equal -1. On the other hand, if countercyclical policy were thoroughly random in its impact, its effects would be as likely to be in the same direction

8. Let X be the expected value of X. Then

$$\sigma_X^2 = E(X - \bar{X})^2,$$

where E stands for expected value.

9. $r_{XY}\sigma_X\sigma_Y = E(X - \bar{X})(Y - \bar{Y})$.

as the deviation of X from its mean as in the opposite direction, and r_{XY} would equal zero. A perfectly perverse cyclical policy would be described by an r_{XY} equal to $+1$. Thus σ_Y and r_{XY} provide a two-dimensional classification of all countercyclical policies by the only characteristics that are relevant for our present purposes.

It is clear from (2) that a countercyclical policy for which $r_{XY} = 0$, that is, which is about as likely to have effects in the wrong as in the right direction, is not "neutral" in its impact but rather destabilizing. For if $r_{XY} = 0$, the variance of Z exceeds the variance of X by the variance of Y; that is, by the magnitude of the countercyclical action. In order, therefore, for countercyclical action to succeed in its objective, its effects must be in the right direction more often than in the wrong.

For a more precise statement divide both sides of (2) by σ_X^2. This gives

$$\frac{\sigma_Z^2}{\sigma_X^2} = 1 + \frac{\sigma_Y^2}{\sigma_X^2} + 2 r_{XY} \frac{\sigma_Y}{\sigma_X}. \tag{3}$$

The left-hand side of (3) is the ratio of the variance of income when the countercyclical policy is present to its variance when the countercyclical policy is absent. If this ratio is unity, the countercyclical policy may be regarded as having had no effect on stability; if the ratio is less than unity, the countercyclical policy has succeeded in its objective of promoting stability; if the ratio is greater than unity, the countercyclical policy has failed in its objective and has been destabilizing rather than stabilizing.

Clearly,

$$\frac{\sigma_Z^2}{\sigma_X^2} \underset{>}{\overset{<}{}} 1$$

according as

$$\frac{\sigma_Y^2}{\sigma_X^2} + 2 r_{XY} \frac{\sigma_Y}{\sigma_X} \underset{>}{\overset{<}{}} 0$$

or

$$r_{XY} \underset{>}{\overset{<}{}} -\frac{1}{2} \frac{\sigma_Y}{\sigma_X}. \tag{4}$$

This equation indicates the conditions under which countercyclical policy will succeed in its objectives: if r_{XY} is between -1 and $-\frac{1}{2}\,\sigma_Y/\sigma_X$, the countercyclical policy will be stabilizing in its effects; if it is between $-\frac{1}{2}\,\sigma_Y/\sigma_X$ and $+1$, the countercyclical policy will be destabilizing. For example, suppose that, in line with the simple model described earlier, an attempt were made to produce complete stability. This would require making $\sigma_Y = \sigma_X$. Assume that this magnitude of countercyclical action were attained. In that case the actions taken would be destabilizing unless r_{XY} were between $-.5$ and -1. We shall have something to say later about the factors determining the magnitude of r_{XY}; but it is clear that the requirement that it exceed .5 in absolute value is a rather stringent one; yet, unless it does, the indicated countercyclical policy will do more harm than good.

For a given magnitude of countercyclical effects (i.e., a given σ_Y), it is obvious that, the closer the correlation coefficient between X and Y is to -1, the better, since this means that the countercyclical effects will be better adapted to needs. If r_{XY} were -1, and $\sigma_Y = \sigma_X$, the countercyclical policy would be ideal in the sense that the variance of Z would be zero. It is less obvious what the consequence is of varying the magnitude of countercyclical effects for a given correlation; though perhaps it is reasonably obvious that, for each value of the correlation, there is some optimum value of σ_Y and that this optimum value is zero if r_{XY} is zero or positive (i.e., countercyclical policy is perverse in its timing) and equal to σ_Y if r_{XY} is -1.[10] For a more precise statement differentiate the right-hand side of (3) with respect to σ_Y, set the result equal to zero, and solve for σ_Y. This gives

$$\hat{\sigma}_Y = -r_{XY}\sigma_X \qquad (5)$$

where $\hat{\sigma}_Y$ stands for the optimum value of σ_Y. Equation (5) gives the general rule and checks the above statements for $r_{XY} = 0$ and -1. For r_{XY} positive, equation (5) gives a negative value for $\hat{\sigma}_Y$,

10. If σ_Y is zero, r_{XY} as given by the formula in n. 9 will, of course, be the indeterminate form 0/0. We can, nevertheless, speak of this correlation as being zero or positive by evaluating the indeterminate form through a limiting process. The appropriate process is to let σ_Y approach zero by multiplying each deviation of Y from its mean by a common multiple that itself approaches zero. This change of scale of Y does not affect the correlation coefficient, which has the same value throughout the limiting process.

which is, of course, impossible. The best attainable value is then zero.

It is clear from these results that countercyclical policy can be "too" strong as well as "too" weak and that this can be true even though its effects are smaller in magnitude than the cyclical fluctuations that the policy is designed to offset. For example, suppose $r_{XY} = -\frac{1}{2}$. The optimum value of σ_Y would then be $\frac{1}{2}$ of σ_X. If this value were achieved, σ_Z^2/σ_X^2 would be equal to $\frac{3}{4}$; that is, this policy would reduce the variance of fluctuations in income by 25 per cent. Suppose, however, σ_Y were increased by engaging in larger countercyclical operations of the same time pattern. The result would be not so good as before: if σ_Y were made equal to $\frac{3}{4}\sigma_X$, the final variance would be reduced by only $18\frac{3}{4}$ per cent instead of 25 per cent; if σ_Y were made equal to σ_X, the improvement would be completely canceled.

Suppose that the countercyclical policy were of the optimum magnitude, so that σ_Y satisfied equation (5). If we substitute this value in (3), we can determine the maximum reduction in instability capable of being achieved as a function of r_{XY}. The result is:

$$\left(\frac{\sigma_Z^2}{\sigma_X^2}\right)_{\sigma_Y=-r_{XY}\sigma_X} = 1 - r_{XY}^2. \tag{6}$$

This equation strikingly shows the crucial importance of the size of r_{XY} for the effectiveness of countercyclical policy. In order to be able to cut the variance of income fluctuations in half (which would cut the standard deviation by less than a third), r_{XY} must exceed .7, and σ_Y must be optimally related to σ_X.

III

We have so far described alternative countercyclical policies exclusively in terms of their statistical characteristics—σ_Y and r_{XY}. The relation of these characteristics to substantive countercyclical policy is clearly of crucial importance in applying the above results. From this point of view, the two characteristics are clearly very different. The average magnitude of effect, σ_Y, can be more readily increased or decreased—though it may be no easier to measure—than the timing of the effect, r_{XY}, can be improved. The former may well be a parameter of action capable of being readily controlled for each type of countercyclical policy separately. The latter is, I conjecture, a relatively fixed (albeit unknown) characteristic of each type of policy that can be changed only by changing to a qualitatively different kind of policy or by an increase in knowledge about the sources of fluctuations.

The magnitude of effect can in general be expected to vary directly with the magnitude of the initial stimulus. For example, suppose the countercyclical policy takes the form of deliberately produced changes in the government budget, a deficit being produced (or increased or surplus decreased) when it is desired to expand income, a surplus being produced when it is desired to contract income. So far as the mechanical linkages are concerned between the government budget and aggregate income, twice as large a deficit or surplus would have approximately twice as large an effect on aggregate income. Similarly, a decrease or increase in the quantity of money may be expected to have a larger contractionary or expansionary effect the greater the decrease or increase. Of course, these relations may be altered by other effects of the actions, such as their effects on "confidence" and the like, and these may not be strictly proportionate to the stimulus or even in the same direction, so that there may be some magnitude of stimulus beyond which the magnitude of effect is reduced rather than increased. But we may neglect these complications for our present purpose.

It follows that a larger magnitude of effect can be produced by taking more vigorous action when it is decided to take action, and conversely. While it is therefore relatively easy to change the magnitude of effect, it is much more difficult to measure what magnitude of effect is being produced. An example may illustrate some of the difficulties. A proposal for stabilization policy that I have elsewhere made avoids discretionary monetary or fiscal policy and relies exclusively on reactions automatically produced by the impact of changes in aggregate income on a stable monetary and fiscal framework.[11] Given a progressive tax and transfer structure, and a stable expenditure program, any increase in aggregate income would tend to increase government receipts in greater pro-

11. "A Monetary and Fiscal Framework for Economic Stability," *infra,* pp. 133–56.

portion than government expenditures and so tend to halt the increase in income, and conversely. What magnitude of effect might be expected from this policy?

It has been estimated that, given the current fiscal system of the United States, this policy would mean a change in the government's budget of approximately one-quarter to one-third of any change in income; that is, that an increase in national income of $10 billion would tend to involve changes in government income and expenditures that would have the effect of reducing a deficit or increasing a surplus by something between $2.5 and $3.3 billion.[12]

If this change in the government's budget had no other effects and if it bore a constant temporal relation to the changes in income producing it (e.g., lagged a fixed number of time units), it would follow that σ_Y was between $\frac{1}{4}$ and $\frac{1}{3}$ of σ_X. But clearly neither of these assumptions can be accepted. The change in the government's budget will have indirect as well as direct effects on income: through the multiplier process, through effects on the stock of money, and perhaps in other ways as well. And these effects will be spread over time with lags that will vary from time to time. In our previous notation the value of Y in any time unit will itself be a sum of components produced by budget changes in each of a series of preceding time units, and the number of such components is likely itself to change over time. The size of σ_Y will depend on the size and character of the indirect effects, on the variability in the time pattern of effects, and on the correlation among the components of Y in any time unit. This last will, in turn, depend on the correlation among successive stimuli and so, ultimately, on the correlation among successive values of X—on the serial correlation of the time series involved.

It seems reasonable that these complications would not reduce σ_Y below the value of $\frac{1}{4}$ to $\frac{1}{3}$ of σ_X that would be assigned to it

12. This estimate is based primarily on R. A. Musgrave and M. H. Miller, "Built-in Flexibility," *American Economic Review*, XXXVIII (March, 1948), 122–28. Subsequent changes in tax legislation have doubtless affected the exact figure but have probably not significantly changed its order of magnitude.

if they were absent, but even this is not certain.[13] They could easily multiply this figure several fold, so that about all that can be said about the magnitude of effect under this proposal is that it cannot plausibly be put lower than $\frac{1}{4}$ of σ_X and may be very much greater.

The timing of effect, r_{XY}, is even more difficult either to control or to measure. As was suggested by our earlier discussion of the simple model implicitly accepted by most proponents of full-employment policy, r_{XY} is likely to be larger (in absolute value) the smaller the lags in the economic system relative to the movements it is desired to offset. If the need for action could be recognized immediately, the recognition translated immediately into action, and the action immediately effective, it is clear that r_{XY} could be extremely close to -1; and, indeed, this is the implicit assumption to which the simple model leads those who use it. In the absence of such instantaneous reactions, a high (absolute) value of r_{XY} requires a high ability to predict both the behavior of the system in the absence of action and the effect of action; for this would permit action to be taken in advance that would turn out to be correct when its effects occurred. I need hardly belabor the point that to date there is no reason for confidence in our ability to make such predictions.

If forecasting is ruled out, the value of r_{XY} can be controlled only by affecting the lags involved: the shorter and less variable the lags can be made, the higher is likely to be the absolute value of r_{XY}. These lags can, for this purpose, be thought of as composed of three parts: (1) the lag between the need for action and the recognition of this need; (2) the lag between recognition of the need for action and the taking of action; and (3) the lag between the action and its effects. The third component clearly depends on the fundamental characteristics of the economic system but may be different for different types of action—for example, it may be shorter for fiscal than for monetary action. The first two, on the other hand, may be capable of

---

13. σ_Y could be reduced below $\frac{1}{4}$ to $\frac{1}{3}$ of σ_X if there were a sufficiently high negative serial correlation in X and if the effects of the budget change in any time unit were spread over several successive time units.

deliberate control (successful forecasting may be viewed as making the first component negative). Even here, however, there are drastic limits on what can be done. I have elsewhere argued that there is a strong presumption that the automatic policy alluded to above would have a shorter total lag, and so a higher r_{XY}, than discretionary actions of the kind proposed but that even for such a policy the lags are likely to be substantial relative to the length of the movement it is desired to offset, so that r_{XY} may be very far from — 1 in value.[14] In the present state of knowledge we cannot, of course, know what the potential magnitude of r_{XY} is, but it would certainly be wishful thinking to suppose that it is very large for any currently proposed policy.

In the present state of knowledge we cannot even be sure whether the completely automatic policy alluded to above would be "too strong" or "too weak." I have argued that, for the United States, it is reasonable to suppose that σ_Y is larger than $\frac{1}{4}$ of σ_X and perhaps much larger. Suppose the value of σ_Y for this policy is $\frac{1}{2}$ of σ_X. This will be "too strong" a policy if r_{XY} is less than $\frac{1}{2}$ in absolute value; "too weak," if r_{XY} is larger than $\frac{1}{2}$.

These conclusions suggested by our analysis are strikingly at variance with views commonly held. The proposal for relying exclusively on automatic reactions is generally criticized as not doing enough; it is seldom explicitly recognized that it may do too much. For example, in their report to the United Nations on full-employment measures the group of experts write:

> Such "built-in" . . . stabilizers, by the nature of the case, can only have the effect of dampening the range of economic fluctuations. They can mitigate the fall in consumers' demand that occurs in response to a fall in investment demand; they cannot conjure up an actual *rise* in consumers' demand that would be needed to offset the fall in investment demand. . . . A rise in consumers' demand could, however, be secured through budgetary measures if governments did not content themselves with the "built-in" stabilizers . . . , but undertook positive counter-measures through counter-cyclical variations in the rates of taxation in force. If the rates of taxation were lowered in times of declining demand, and raised in times of rising demand, the purchasing power in the hands of consumers could be altered sufficiently to maintain total demand at a stable level.[15]

14. See "A Monetary and Fiscal Framework for Economic Stability," *infra*, pp. 144–48.

15. *UN Report*, pp. 37–38.

In the light of our analysis this statement is, at best, misleading; at worst, downright wrong.

Whereas one method of controlling r_{XY} is to change the kind of action taken, another method is to limit the objective. The effect of action is clearly likely to be in the right direction much more frequently if action is taken to counteract only substantial movements in income than if it is taken to counteract mild movements as well. In the case of substantial movements the lag between action and its effects is likely to be much shorter relative to the movement itself—even if not in absolute terms—than for mild movements, and so r_{XY} is likely to be greater. This is the fundamental idea behind such proposals as the "two-part policy" suggested by Bach, who proposes to rely on automatic reactions so long as a price index stays within a fairly broad band and to supplement these reactions by discretionary action if the index moves outside the specified band.[16]

According to our analysis, in any such multipart approach, a larger magnitude of effect is called for, the larger the movement to be countered, for two reasons: first, σ_Y should be larger, the larger σ_X; second, σ_Y should be larger, the larger (in absolute value) r_{XY}, and it is assumed that r_{XY} is larger in absolute value for those movements giving a large σ_X.

The preceding discussion is by no means exhaustive. Indeed, it raises many more questions, and more difficult questions, than it answers. Its purpose is much more modest, namely, to suggest the relation between the substantive content of policies designed to promote stability and the two statistical parameters describing their operations that we found to play so fundamental a role in determining their effectiveness.

IV

In writing this note, I feel at one and the same time as if I were preaching in the wilderness and belaboring the obvious. For the major conclusions of this paper are important and widely neglected, yet they seem distressingly obvious.

There is some limit to the possibilities of stabilizing the level

16. G. L. Bach, "Monetary-Fiscal Policy Reconsidered," *Journal of Political Economy*, LVII (October, 1949), 383–94.

of economic activity by policy measures intended to do so. This limit depends on two major characteristics of the action taken: the extent to which the effects of the action are proportioned to the effects needed—to put it loosely, the frequency with which the effects are in the "right" direction—and the magnitude of the action taken. For any given magnitude of action the total effects of the policy may be destabilizing even if effects of the actions taken are more frequently in the "right" than in the "wrong" direction; there is some minimum frequency of "right" to "wrong" action required in order that the actions on balance be stabilizing. Similarly, for any given frequency of "right" to "wrong" actions, there is an optimum magnitude of action. More vigorous action than this, however well intended, will do more harm than good. A relatively high frequency of right to wrong actions is required if fluctuations are to be substantially reduced; and this frequency is not readily subject to control except as the advance of economic science may enable us to predict more accurately than we now can the consequences of action. In short, good intentions, however admirable, are not enough. They will be abortive unless matched by the capacity to put them into effect.

Obvious though these conclusions are, I believe them to be of the greatest importance for discussions of full-employment policy. Much of this discussion is vitiated by a failure to distinguish between objectives and means and simply consists of exhortation to do the right thing with no advice how to know what is the right thing to do. There has been little realistic examination of the inevitable limitations to the effectiveness of countercyclical action. There has been almost no recognition that vigorous countercyclical action may result in more instability than milder action. In this field, as in all others, the "will" is too often mistaken for the "deed."

A Monetary and Fiscal Framework for Economic Stability[*]

DURING the late nineteenth and early twentieth centuries the problems of the day were of a kind that led economists to concentrate on the allocation of resources, and, to a lesser extent, economic growth, and to pay little attention to short-run fluctuations of a cyclical character. Since the Great Depression of the 1930's, this emphasis has been reversed. Economists now tend to concentrate on cyclical movements, to act and talk as if any improvement, however slight, in control of the cycle justified any sacrifice, however large, in the long-run efficiency, or prospects for growth, of the economic system. Proposals for the control of the cycle thus tend to be developed almost as if there were no other objectives and as if it made no difference within what general framework cyclical fluctuations take place. A consequence of this attitude is that inadequate attention is given to the possibility of satisfying both sets of objectives simultaneously.

In constructing the monetary and fiscal framework proposed in this paper, I deliberately gave primary consideration to long-run objectives. That is, I tried to design a framework that would be appropriate for a world in which cyclical movements, other than those introduced by "bad" monetary and fiscal arrangements, were of no consequence. I then examined the resulting proposal to see how it would behave in respect of cyclical fluctuations. It behaves surprisingly well; not only might it be expected not to contribute to cyclical fluctuations but it tends to offset them and therefore seems to offer considerable promise of providing a tolerable degree of short-run economic stability.

* Reprinted from *American Economic Review*, XXXVIII (June, 1948), 245–64.

An earlier version of this paper was presented before the Econometric Society on September 17, 1947, at a meeting held in conjunction with the International Statistical Conferences in Washington, D.C. I am deeply indebted for helpful criticisms and constructive suggestions to Arthur F. Burns, Aaron Director, Albert G. Hart, H. Gregg Lewis, Lloyd W. Mints, Don Patinkin, and George J. Stigler.

This paper is devoted to presenting the part of the analysis dealing with the implications of the proposal for cyclical stability. Nonetheless, in view of the motivation of the proposal, it seems well to begin by indicating the long-run objectives adopted as a guide, even though a reasonably full discussion of these long-run objectives would not be appropriate here.

The basic long-run objectives, shared, I am sure, by most economists, are political freedom, economic efficiency, and substantial equality of economic power. These objectives are not, of course, entirely consistent, and some compromise among them may be required. Moreover, objectives stated on this level of generality can hardly guide proximate policy choices. We must take the next step and specify the general institutional arrangements we regard best suited for the attainment of these objectives. I believe—and at this stage agreement will be far less widespread—that all three objectives can best be realized by relying, as far as possible, on a market mechanism within a "competitive order" to organize the utilization of economic resources. Among the specific propositions that follow from this general position, three are particularly relevant: (1) government must provide a monetary framework for a competitive order, since the competitive order cannot provide one for itself; (2) this monetary framework should operate under the "rule of law" rather than the discretionary authority of administrators; and, (3) while a truly free market in a "competitive order" would yield far less inequality than currently exists, I should hope that the community would desire to reduce inequality even further. Moreover, measures to supplement the market would need to be taken in the interim. For both purposes general fiscal measures (as contrasted with specific intervention) are the most desirable non-free-market means of decreasing inequality.

The extremely simple proposal which these long-run objectives lead me to advance contains no new elements. Indeed, in view of the number of proposals that have been made for altering one or another part of the present monetary or fiscal framework, it is hard to believe that anything completely new remains to be added. The combination of elements that emerges is somewhat less hackneyed; yet no claim of originality can be made even for this. As is perhaps not surprising from what has already been said, the proposal is something like the greatest common denominator of many different proposals. This is perhaps the chief justification for presenting it and urging that it receive full professional discussion. Perhaps it, or some variant, can approach a minimum program for which economists of the less extreme shades of opinion can make common cause.

This paper deals only with the broad outlines of the monetary and fiscal framework and neglects, or deals superficially with, many difficult, important, and closely related problems. In particular, it neglects almost entirely the transition from the present framework to that outlined here, the implications of the adoption of the recommended framework for international monetary arrangements, and the special requirements of war finance. These associated problems are numerous and serious and are likely to justify compromise at some points. It seems well, however, to set forth the ultimate ideal as clearly as possible before beginning to compromise.

I. THE PROPOSAL

The particular proposal outlined below involves four main elements: the first relates to the monetary system; the second, to government expenditures on goods and services; the third, to government transfer payments; and the fourth, to the tax structure. Throughout, it pertains entirely to the federal government, and all references to "government" should be so interpreted.[1]

1. *A reform of the monetary and banking system to eliminate both the private creation or destruction of money and discretionary control of the quantity of money by central-bank authority.—* The private creation of money can perhaps best be eliminated by adopting the 100 per cent reserve proposal, thereby separating the depositary from the lending function of the banking system.[2]

1. The reason for restricting the discussion to the federal government is simply that it alone has ultimate monetary powers, not any desire to minimize the role of smaller governmental units. Indeed, for the achievement of the long-run objectives stated above it is highly desirable that the maximum amount of government activity be in the hands of the smaller governmental units to achieve as much decentralization of political power as possible.

2. This proposal was advanced by Henry C. Simons. See his *A Positive Program for Laissez Faire: Some Proposals for a Liberal Economic Policy* ("Public Policy Pamphlets," No. 15 [Chicago: University of Chicago Press, 1934]) ; "Rules versus

The adoption of 100 per cent reserves would also reduce the discretionary powers of the reserve system by eliminating rediscounting and existing powers over reserve requirements. To complete the elimination of the major weapons of discretionary authority, the existing powers to engage in open-market operations and the existing direct controls over stock market and consumer credit should be abolished.

These modifications would leave as the chief monetary functions of the banking system the provision of depositary facilities, the facilitation of check clearance, and the like, and as the chief function of the monetary authorities the creation of money to meet government deficits or the retirement of money when the government has a surplus.[3]

2. *A policy of determining the volume of government expenditures on goods and services—defined to exclude transfer expenditures of all kinds—entirely on the basis of the community's desire, need, and willingness to pay for public services.*—Changes in the level of expenditure should be made solely in response to alterations in the relative value attached by the community to public services and private consumption. No attempt should be made to vary expenditures, either directly or inversely, in response to cyclical fluctuations in business activity. Since the community's basic objectives would presumably change only slowly—except in time of war or immediate threat of war—this policy would, with the same exception, lead to a relatively stable volume of expenditures on goods and services.[4]

Authorities in Monetary Policy," *Journal of Political Economy*, XLIV (February, 1936), 1–30. Both of these are reprinted in Henry C. Simons, *Economic Policy for a Free Society* (Chicago: University of Chicago Press, 1948).

3. The adoption of 100 per cent reserves is essential if the proposed framework is to be entirely automatic. It should be noted, however, that the same results could, in principle, be achieved in a fractional reserve system through discretionary authority. In order to accomplish this, the monetary authorities would have to adopt the rule that the quantity of money should be increased only when the government has a deficit, and then by the amount of the deficit, and should be decreased only when the government has a surplus, and then by the amount of the surplus.

4. The volume of expenditures might remain stable either in money or in real terms. The principle of determining the volume of expenditures by the community's objectives would lead to a stable real volume of expenditures on current goods and

3. *A predetermined program of transfer expenditures, consisting of a statement of the conditions and terms under which relief and assistance and other transfer payments will be granted.*[5] —Such a program is exemplified by the present system of social security under which rules exist for the payment of old age and unemployment insurance. The program should be changed only in response to alterations in the kind and level of transfer payments the community feels it should and can afford to make. The program should not be changed in response to cyclical fluctuations in business activity. Absolute outlays, however, will vary automatically over the cycle. They will tend to be high when unemployment is high and low when unemployment is low.[6]

4. *A progressive tax system which places primary reliance on the personal income tax.*—Every effort should be made to collect as much of the tax bill as possible at source and to minimize the delay between the accrual of the tax liability and the actual collection of the tax. Rates, exemptions, etc., should be set in light of the expected yield at a level of income corresponding to reasonably full employment at a predetermined price level. The budget principle might be either that the hypothetical yield should balance government expenditure, including transfer payments (at the same hypothetical level of income), or that it should lead to a deficit sufficient to provide some specified secular increase in the quantity of money.[7] The tax structure should not

---

services. On the other hand, the usual legislative procedure in budget-making is to grant fixed sums of money, which would lead to stability of money expenditures and provide a slight automatic contracyclical flexibility. If the volume of real expenditures were stabilized, money expenditures would vary directly with prices.

5. These transfer payments might perhaps more appropriately be regarded as negative revenue.

6. It may be hoped that the present complex structure of transfer payments will be integrated into a single scheme co-ordinated with the income tax and designed to provide a universal floor to personal incomes. But this is a separate issue.

7. These specifications about the hypothetical level of income to be used and the budget principle to be followed are more definite and dogmatic than is justified. In principle, the economic system could ultimately adjust to any tax structure and expenditure policy, no matter what level of income or what budget principle they were initially based on, provided that the tax structure and expenditure policy remained stable. That is, there corresponds some secular position appropriate to each possible tax structure and expenditure policy. The best level of income and the best

be varied in response to cyclical fluctuations in business activity, though actual receipts will, of course, vary automatically.[8] Changes in the tax structure should reflect changes in the level of public services or transfer payments the community chooses to have. A decision to undertake additional public expenditures should be accompanied by a revenue measure increasing taxes. Calculations of both the cost of additional public services or transfer payments and the yield of additional taxes should be made at the hypothetical level of income suggested above rather than at the actual level of income. The government would thus keep two budgets: the stable budget, in which all figures refer to the hypothetical income, and the actual budget. The principle of balancing outlays and receipts at a hypothetical income level would be substituted for the principle of balancing actual outlays and receipts.

---

budget principle to choose depend therefore on short-run adjustment considerations: what choice would require the least difficult adjustment? Moreover, the level of income and budget principle must be chosen jointly; the same final result can obviously be obtained by combining a high hypothetical income with a surplus budget principle or a low hypothetical income with a deficit budget principle or by any number of intermediate combinations. My own conjecture is that the particular level of income and budget principles suggested above are unlikely to lead to results that would require radical short-run adjustments to attain the corresponding secular position. Unfortunately, our knowledge about the relevant economic interrelationships is too meager to permit more than reasonably informed conjecture (see Sec. IV below, esp. n. 22).

8. The principle of setting taxes so as to balance the budget at a high level of employment was suggested by Beardsley Ruml and H. Chr. Sonne, *Fiscal and Monetary Policy* ("National Planning Pamphlets," No. 35 [Washington, D.C., July, 1944]).

Since the present paper was written, the Committee for Economic Development has issued a policy statement in which it makes essentially the same tax and expenditure recommendations—that is, it calls for adoption of a stable tax structure capable of balancing the budget at a high level of employment, a stable expenditure policy, and primary reliance on automatic adjustments of absolute revenue and expenditures to provide cyclical stability. They call this policy the "stabilizing budget policy." The chief difference between the present proposal and the CED proposal is that the CED is silent on the monetary framework and almost silent on public debt policy, whereas the present proposal covers both. Presumably the CED plans to cover monetary and debt policy in separate statements still to be issued (see *Taxes and the Budget: A Program for Prosperity in a Free Economy,* a statement on national policy by the Research and Policy Committee of the Committee for Economic Development [November, 1947]).

II. Operation of the Proposal

The essence of this fourfold proposal is that it uses automatic adaptations in the government contribution to the current income stream to offset, at least in part, changes in other segments of aggregate demand and to change appropriately the supply of money. It eliminates discretionary action in response to cyclical movements as well as some extraneous or perverse reactions of our present monetary and fiscal structure.[9] Discretionary action is limited to the determination of the hypothetical level of income underlying the stable budget; that is, essentially to the determination of a reasonably attainable objective. Some decision of this kind is unavoidable in drawing up the government's budget; the proposal involves a particular decision and makes it explicit. The determination of the income goal admittedly cannot be made entirely objective or mechanical. At the same time, this determination would need to be made only at rather long intervals—perhaps every five or ten years—and involves a minimum of forecasting. Further, as will be indicated later, errors in the income goal tend to be automatically neutralized and do not require a redetermination of the goal.

Under the proposal, government expenditures would be financed entirely by either tax revenues or the creation of money, that is, the issue of noninterest-bearing securities. Government would not issue interest-bearing securities to the public; the Federal Reserve System would not operate in the open market. This restriction of the sources of government funds seems reasonable for peacetime. The chief valid ground for paying interest to the public on government debt is to offset the inflationary pressure of abnormally high government expenditures when, for one reason or another, it is not feasible or desirable to levy sufficient taxes to do so. This was the justification for wartime issuance

9. E.g., the tendency under the existing system of fractional reserve banking for the total volume of money to change when there is a change in the proportion of its total stock of money the community wishes to hold in the form of deposits; the tendency to reduce tax rates and increase government expenditures in booms and to do the reverse in depressions; and the tendency for the government to borrow from individuals at the same time as the Federal Reserve System is buying government bonds on the open market.

of interest-bearing securities, though, perversely, the rate of interest on these securities was pegged at a low level. It seems inapplicable in peacetime, especially if, as suggested, the volume of government expenditures on goods and services is kept relatively stable. Another reason sometimes given for issuing interest-bearing securities is that in a period of unemployment it is less deflationary to issue securities than to levy taxes. This is true. But it is still less deflationary to issue money.[10]

Deficits or surpluses in the government budget would be reflected dollar for dollar in changes in the quantity of money; and, conversely, the quantity of money would change only as a consequence of deficits or surpluses. A deficit means an increase in the quantity of money; a surplus, a decrease.[11]

Deficits or surpluses themselves become automatic consequences of changes in the level of business activity. When national money income is high, tax receipts will be large and transfer payments small; so a surplus will tend to be created, and, the higher the level of income, the larger the surplus. This ex-

10. See Henry C. Simons, "On Debt Policy," *Journal of Political Economy,* LII (December, 1944), 356–61.

This paragraph deliberately avoids the question of the payment of interest to banks on special issues of government bonds, as has been proposed in some versions of the 100 per cent reserve proposal. The fundamental issue involved in judging such proposals is whether government should subsidize the use of deposit money and a system of check clearance and, if so, what form the subsidy should take.

The large volume of government bonds now outstanding raises one of the most serious problems in accomplishing the transition from the present framework. This problem would be eased somewhat by the monetization of bonds that would occur in the process of going over to 100 per cent reserves. But there would still remain a substantial volume. Two alternatives suggest themselves: (1) freeze the volume of debt at some figure, preferably by converting it into perpetuities ("consols"), or (2) use the monetization of the debt as a means of providing a secular increase in the quantity of money. Under the second plan, which, on a first view, seems more attractive, the principle of balancing the stable budget would be adopted, and the government would commit itself to retiring, through the issuance of new money, a predetermined amount of the public debt annually. The amount to be retired would be determined so as to achieve whatever secular increase in the quantity of money seemed desirable. This problem, however, requires much additional study.

11. These statements refer, of course, to the ultimate operation of the proposal. Under the second of the alternatives suggested in the preceding footnote, the change in the quantity of money during the transitional period would equal the excess of government expenditures over receipts plus the predetermined amount of money issued to retire debt.

traction of funds from the current income stream makes aggregate demand lower than it otherwise would be and reduces the volume of money, thereby tending to offset the factors making for a further increase in income. When national money income is low, tax receipts will be small and transfer payments large, so a deficit will tend to be created, and, the lower the level of income, the larger the deficit. This addition of funds to the current income stream makes aggregate demand higher than it otherwise would be and increases the quantity of money, thereby tending to offset the factors making for a further decline in income.

The size of the effects automatically produced by changes in national income obviously depends on the range of activities government undertakes, since this will in turn determine the general order of magnitude of the government budget. Nonetheless, an essential element of the proposal is that the activities to be undertaken by government be determined entirely on other grounds. In part, this element is an immediate consequence of the motivation of the proposal. The motivation aside, however, it seems a desirable element of any proposal to promote stability. First, there is and can be no simple, reasonably objective, rule to determine the optimum share of activity that should be assigned to government—short of complete socialization—even if stability were the only objective. Changes in circumstances are likely to produce rapid and erratic variations in the share that seems desirable. But changes in the share assigned government are themselves likely to be destabilizing, both directly and through their adverse effects on anticipations. The attempt to adapt the magnitude of government operations to the requirements of stability may therefore easily introduce more instability than it corrects. Second, the share of activity assigned government is likely to have far more important consequences for other objectives—particularly political freedom and economic efficiency—than for stability.[12] Third, means other than changes in the

12. An example of the relevance of these two points is provided by the tendency during the thirties to recommend an increase in the progressiveness of the tax structure as a means of increasing the propensity to consume and hence, it was argued, employment. Applied to the postwar period, the same argument would call for a shift to regressive taxes, yet I wonder if many economists would wish to recommend regressive taxes on these grounds.

share of activity assigned government are readily available for changing the size of the reaction to changes in income, if experience under the proposal should prove this desirable. And some of these means need not have anything like the same consequences for other objectives.

Under the proposal the aggregate quantity of money is automatically determined by the requirements of domestic stability. It follows that changes in the quantity of money cannot also be used—as they are in a fully operative gold standard—to achieve equilibrium in international trade. The two criteria will by no means always require the same changes in the quantity of money; when they conflict, one or the other must dominate. The decision, implicit in the framework recommended, to select domestic stability means that some other technique must be used to bring about adjustments to changes in the conditions of international trade. The international arrangement that seems the logical counterpart of the proposed framework is flexible exchange rates, freely determined in foreign exchange markets, preferably entirely by private dealings.[13]

III. Effect of Proposal under Present Institutional Conditions

The fluctuations in the government contribution to the income stream under the proposed monetary and fiscal framework are clearly in the "right" direction. Nonetheless, it is not at all clear that they would, without additional institutional modifications, necessarily lead either to reasonably full employment or to a reasonable degree of stability. Rigidities in prices are likely to make this proposal, and indeed most if not all other proposals for attaining cyclical stability, inconsistent with reasonably full employment and, when combined with lags in other types of response, to render extremely uncertain their effectiveness in stabilizing economic activity.

13. Though here presented as a byproduct of the proposed domestic framework, flexible exchange rates can be defended directly. Indeed, it would be equally appropriate to present the proposed domestic framework as a means of implementing flexible exchange rates. The heart of the matter is that domestic and international monetary and trade arrangements are part of one whole. [See "The Case for Flexible Exchange Rates," *infra*, pp. 157–203.]

A. PRICE RIGIDITIES

Under existing circumstances, when many prices are moderately rigid, at least against declines, the monetary and fiscal framework described above cannot be expected to lead to reasonably full employment of resources, even though lags in other kinds of response are minor. The most that can be expected under such circumstances is a reasonably stable or moderately rising level of money income. As an extreme example, suppose that the economy is in a relatively stable position at reasonably full employment and with a roughly balanced actual government budget and that the great bulk of wage rates are rigid against downward pressure. Now, let there be a substantial rise in the wage rates of a particular group of workers as a consequence either of trade-union action or of a sharp but temporary increase in the demand for that type of labor or decrease in its supply, and let this higher wage rate be rigid against downward pressure. Employment of resources as full as previously would imply a higher aggregate money income, since, under the assumed conditions of rigidity, other resources would receive the same amount as previously, whereas the workers whose wage rates rose would receive a larger aggregate amount if fully employed. But if this higher money income, which also of course would imply a higher price structure, were attained, the government would tend to have a surplus, since receipts would rise by more than expenditures. There is nothing that has occurred that would, in the absence of other independent changes, offset the deflationary effect of the surplus. The assumed full-employment position would not therefore be an equilibrium position. If attained by accident, the resultant budgetary surplus would reduce effective demand, and, since prices are assumed rigid, the outcome could only be unemployment. The equilibrium level of income will be somewhat higher than before, primarily because transfer payments to the unemployed will be larger, so that some of the unemployment will be offset. But there is no mechanism for offsetting the rest. The only escape from this situation is to permit inflation.

As is widely recognized, the difficulty just described is present also in most other monetary and fiscal proposals; they, too, can produce full employment under such circumstances only by inflation. This dilemma often tends, however, to be concealed in their formulation, and, in practice, it seems fairly likely that inflation would result. The brute fact is that a rational economic program for a free-enterprise system (and perhaps even for a collectivist system) must have flexibility of prices (including wages) as one of its cornerstones. This need is made clear by a proposal like the present. Moreover, the adoption of such a proposal would provide some assurance against cumulative deflation and thereby tend to make flexibility of prices a good deal easier to achieve, since government support for monopolistic practices of special occupational and industrial groups derives in large measure from the obvious waste of general deflation and the need for protection against it.

B. LAGS IN RESPONSE

Our economy is characterized not only by price rigidities but also by significant lags in other types of response. These lags make impossible any definitive statement about the actual degree of stability likely to result from the operation of the monetary and fiscal framework described above. One could reasonably expect smaller fluctuations than currently exist, though our ignorance about lags and about the fundamental causes of business fluctuations prevents complete confidence even in this outcome. The lag between the creation of a government deficit and its effects on the behavior of consumers and producers could conceivably be so long and variable that the stimulating effects of the deficit were often operative only after other factors had already brought about a recovery rather than when the initial decline was in progress. Despite intuitive feelings to the contrary, I do not believe we know enough to rule out completely this possibility. If it were realized, the proposed framework could intensify rather than mitigate cyclical fluctuations; that is, long and variable lags could convert the fluctuations in the government contribution to the income stream into the equivalent of an additional random disturbance.[14]

14. See "Lerner on the Economics of Control," *infra*, p. 316, n. 12. [See also "The Effects of a Full-Employment Policy on Economic Stability: A Formal Analysis," *supra*, pp. 117–32.]

About all one can say about this possibility is that the completely automatic proposal outlined above seems likely to do less harm under the circumstances envisaged than alternative proposals which provide for discretionary action in addition to automatic reactions. There is a strong presumption that these discretionary actions will in general be subject to longer lags than the automatic reactions and hence will be destabilizing even more frequently.

The basis for this presumption can best be seen by subdividing into three parts the total lag involved in any action to offset a disturbance: (1) the lag between the need for action and the recognition of this need; (2) the lag between recognition of the need for action and the taking of action; and (3) the lag between the action and its effects.

The first lag, which is nonexistent for automatic reactions of the kind here proposed, could be negative for discretionary proposals if it were possible to forecast accurately the economic changes that would occur in the absence of government action. In view of the record of forecasters, it hardly needs to be argued that it would be better to shun forecasting and rely instead on as prompt an evaluation of the current situation as possible. The lag between the need for action and the recognition of that need then becomes positive. Its exact magnitude depends on the particular discretionary proposal, though the past record of contemporary interpreters of business conditions indicates that it is not likely to be negligible.[15]

The second lag is present even for automatic reactions because all taxes will not or cannot be collected at source simultaneously with the associated payments, and transfer payments will not or cannot be made immediately without some kind of a waiting period or processing period. It is clear, however, that this lag can be reduced to a negligible time by appropriate construction and administration of the system of taxes and transfer payments. For discretionary action the length of the lag between the recognition of the need for action and the taking of action depends very much on the kind of action taken. Action can be taken very promptly to change the form or amount of the community's

15. *Ibid.*, pp. 314–15, esp. n. 11.

holdings of assets by open-market purchases or sales of securities or by changes in rediscount rates or reserve requirements. A considerably longer time is required to change the net contribution of the government to the income stream by changing the tax structure. Even though advance prescription for alternative possibilities eliminates any delay in deciding what changes to make in tax rates, exemptions, kinds of taxes levied, or the like, administrative considerations will enforce a substantial delay before the change becomes effective. Taxpayers, businesses or individuals acting as intermediaries in collecting the taxes, and tax administrators must all be informed of the change and be given an opportunity to make the appropriate adjustments in their procedures; new forms must be printed or at least circulated; and so on.

The longest delay of all is likely to be involved in changing the net contribution of government to the income stream by changing government expenditure policy, particularly for goods and services. No matter how much advance planning may have been done, the rate of expenditure cannot be stepped up or curtailed overnight unless the number of names on the payroll is to be the only basis in terms of which the expenditure is to be controlled or judged. Time is involved in getting projects under way with any degree of efficiency; and considerable waste in ceasing work on projects abruptly.

The third lag, that between the action and its effects, is present and significant both for automatic reactions and for discretionary actions, and little if anything can be done about it by either legal or administrative reform of the fiscal and monetary structure.[16] We have no trustworthy empirical evidence on the length of this lag for various kinds of action, and much further study of this problem is clearly called for. Some clues about the direction such study should take are furnished by a priori considerations which suggest, as a first approximation, that the order of the various policies with respect to the length of this lag is the reverse of their order with respect to the length of the lag between the recognition of the need for action and the taking of action. Changes

16. Reforms of other types (e.g., reforms increasing the flexibility of prices) might affect this lag.

in government expenditures on goods and services lead to almost immediate changes in the employment of the resources used to produce those goods and services. They have secondary effects through the changes thereby induced in the expenditures of the individuals owning the resources so employed.

The lag in these induced changes might be expected to be less than the lag in the adjustment of expenditures to changed taxes or to a changed amount or form of asset holdings. Changes in taxes make the disposable incomes of individuals larger or smaller than they would otherwise be. Individuals might be expected to react to a change in disposable income as a result of a tax change only slightly less rapidly than to a change in disposable income as a result of a change in aggregate income.

These indications are, however, none too trustworthy. There are likely to be important indirect effects that depend on such things as the kinds of goods and services directly affected by changed government expenditures, the incidence of the changes in disposable income that result from changed expenditures or taxes, and the means employed to finance government deficits. For example, if deficits are financed through increases in the quantity of money and surpluses are used to reduce the quantity of money, part of the effect of changes in government expenditures or taxes will be produced by changes in interest rates and the kind and volume of assets held by the community. The entire effect of open-market operations, changes in rediscount rates and reserve requirements, and the like will be produced in this way, and it seems likely that these effects would take the longest to make themselves felt.

The automatic reactions embodied in the proposal here advanced operate in part like tax changes—in so far as tax receipts vary—and in part like expenditure changes—in so far as transfer payments vary; and, like both of these, some part of their effect is through changes in the quantity of money. One might expect, therefore, that the lag between action and its effects would be roughly the same for automatic reactions as for discretionary tax changes, a good deal shorter for automatic reactions than for discretionary monetary changes, and somewhat longer for automatic reactions than for discretionary changes in government expenditures on goods and services.

This analysis, much of which is admittedly highly conjectural, suggests that the total lag is definitely longer for discretionary monetary or tax changes than for automatic reactions, since each of the three parts into which the total lag has been subdivided is longer. There is doubt about the relative length of the total lag only for discretionary expenditure changes. Even for these, however, it seems doubtful that the shorter lag between action and its effects can more than offset the longer lag between the need for action and the taking of action.

Given less extreme conditions than those required to convert the present proposal into a destabilizing influence, the reduction achieved in the severity of fluctuations would depend on the extent and rapidity of price adjustments, the nature of the responses of individuals to these price changes and to the changes in their incomes and asset holdings resulting from the induced surpluses or deficits, and the lags in such responses. If these were such as to make the system operate reasonably well, the improvement would tend to be cumulative, since the experience of damped fluctuations would lead to patterns of expectations on the part of both businessmen and consumers that would make it rational for them to take action that would damp fluctuations still more. This favorable result would occur, however, only if the proposed system operated reasonably well without such aid; hence, in my view, this proposal, and all others as well, should be judged primarily on their direct effects, not on their indirect effects in stimulating a psychological climate favorable to stability. It must be granted however, that the present proposal is less likely to stimulate such a favorable psychological climate than a proposal which has a simpler and more easily understood goal, for example, a proposal which sets a stable price level as its announced goal. *If the business world were sufficiently confident of the ability of the government to achieve the goal,* it would have a strong incentive to behave in such a way as greatly to simplify the government's task.

IV. Implications of the Proposal if Prices Are Flexible and Lags in Response Minor

The ideal possibilities of the monetary and fiscal framework proposed in this paper, and the stabilizing economic forces on which these possibilities depend, can be seen best if we put aside the difficulties that have been detaining us and examine the implications of the proposal in an economy in which prices of both products and factors of production are flexible[17] and lags in other types of response are minor. In such an economy the monetary and fiscal system described above would tend toward an equilibrium characterized by reasonably full employment.

To describe the forces at work, let us suppose that the economy is initially in a position of reasonably full employment with a balanced actual budget and is subjected to a disturbance producing a decline in aggregate money demand that would be permanent if no other changes occurred.[18] The initial effect of the decline in aggregate demand will be a decline in sales and the piling-up of inventories in at least some parts of the economy, followed shortly by unemployment and price declines caused by the attempt to reduce inventories to the desired level. The lengthening of the list of unemployed will increase government transfer payments; the loss of income by the unemployed will reduce government tax receipts. The deficit created in this way is a net contribution by the government to the income stream which directly offsets some of the decline in aggregate demand, thereby preventing unemployment from becoming as large as it

17. The concept of flexible prices, though one we use continually and can hardly avoid using, is extremely difficult to define precisely. Fortunately, a precise definition is not required for the argument that follows. All that is necessary for the argument is that there be a "substantial" range of prices that are not "rigid" because of long-term contracts or organized noncontractual agreements to maintain price and that these prices should react reasonably quickly to changes in long-run conditions of demand or supply. It is not necessary that there be "perfect" flexibility of prices, however that might be defined, or that contracts involving prices be subject to change at will, or that every change in long-run conditions of demand or supply be reflected instantaneously in market price.

18. The same analysis would apply to disturbances producing only a temporary decline. The reason for assuming a permanent decline is to trace through the entire process of adjustment to a new equilibrium position.

otherwise would and serving as a shock absorber while more fundamental correctives come into play.

These more fundamental correctives, aside from changes in relative prices and interest rates, are (1) a decline in the general level of prices which affects (*a*) the real value of the community's assets and (*b*) the government contribution to the income stream and (2) an increase in the stock of money.

The decline in the general level of prices that follows the initial decline in aggregate demand will clearly raise the real value of the community's stock of money and government bonds, since the nominal value of these assets will not decrease. The real value of the remainder of the community's assets may be expected to remain roughly the same, so the real value of the total stock of assets will rise.[19] The rise in the real value of assets will lessen the need for additional saving and hence increase the fraction of any given level of real income that the community will wish to consume. This force, in principle, would alone be sufficient to assure full employment even if the government maintained a rigidly balanced actual budget and kept the quantity of money constant, since there would presumably always be some price level at which the community could be made to feel rich enough to spend on consumption whatever fraction or multiple of its current income is required to yield an aggregate demand sufficient to permit full employment.

This effect of a lower price level in increasing the fraction of current private (disposable) income devoted to consumption is reinforced by its effect on the government's contribution to the

19. If the real value of other assets of the community should fall, this would simply mean that the price level would have to fall farther in order to raise the real value of the community's total stock of assets. Note that, under the proposed framework, all money in the community either is a direct government obligation (nondeposit currency) or is backed 100 per cent by a direct government obligation (deposits in the central bank). If this analysis were to be applied to a fractional reserve system, the assets whose aggregate real value could be guaranteed to rise with no directly offsetting fall in the real value of private assets would be the total amount of government obligations (currency and bonds) held outside the treasury and central bank. On this and what follows see A. C. Pigou, "The Classical Stationary State," *Economic Journal,* LIII (December, 1943), 342–51, and "Economic Progress in a Stable Environment," *Economica,* XIV (new ser.; August, 1947), 180–90; and Don Patinkin, "Price Flexibility and Full Employment," *American Economic Review,* XXXVIII (September, 1948), 543–64.

income stream. So long as the price level, and with it money income, is below its initial level, the government will continue to run a deficit. This will be true even if employment is restored to its initial level, so that transfer payments and loss in tax receipts on account of unemployment are eliminated. The tax structure is progressive, and exemptions, rates, etc., are expressed in absolute dollar amounts. Receipts will therefore fall more than in proportion to the fall in the price level; expenditures, at most, proportionately.[20] Because of the emergence of such a deficit, the price decline required to restore employment will be smaller than if the government were to maintain a rigidly balanced actual budget, and this will be true even aside from the influence of the deficit on the stock of money. The reason is that the price level will have to fall only to the point at which the amount the community desires to add to its hoards equals the government deficit rather than to the point at which the community desires to add nothing to its hoards.[21]

20. The effect of the lower price level on expenditures depends somewhat on the precise expenditure and transfer policy adopted. If, as is called for by the principle of determining the expenditure program by the community's objectives, the real volume of government expenditures on goods and services is kept cyclically stable and if the program of transfer payments is also stated in real terms, expenditures will decline proportionately. If government expenditures on goods and services are kept cyclically stable in dollar terms, or the program of transfer expenditures is stated in dollar terms, expenditures will decline less than proportionately.

21. If the real volume of government expenditures on goods and services is kept cyclically stable and the transfer program is also stated in real terms, the aggregate expenditures of government under fixed expenditure and transfer programs would tend to be the same fraction of the full-employment income of society no matter what the price level. This fraction would be the maximum net contribution the government could make to the income stream no matter how low prices, and with them money income and government receipts, fell. Consequently, this force alone would be limited in magnitude and might not, even in principle, be able to offset every disturbance. If either program is in absolute terms, there would be no limit to the fraction that the government contribution could constitute of the total income stream.

An alternative way to describe this effect is in terms of the relation between the expected expenditures and receipts of consumers, business, and government. It is a condition of equilibrium that the sum of the desired expenditures of these groups equal the sum of their receipts. If the government maintains a rigidly balanced budget, equilibrium requires that consumers and business together plan to spend what they receive (i.e., not seek to add to their money hoards). If the government runs a deficit, consumers and business together need not plan to spend all they re-

The decline in the price level may restore the initial level of employment through the combined effects of the increased average propensity to consume and the government deficit. But, so long as a deficit exists, the position attained is not an equilibrium position. The deficit is financed by the issue of money. The resultant increase in the aggregate stock of money must further raise the real value of the community's stock of assets and hence the average propensity to consume. This is the same effect as that discussed above except that it is brought about by an increase in the absolute stock of money rather than by a decline in prices. Like the corresponding effect produced by a decline in prices, the magnitude of this effect is, in principle, unlimited. The rise in the stock of money and hence in the average propensity to consume will tend to raise prices and reduce the deficit. If we suppose no change to occur other than the one introduced to start the analysis going, the final adjustment would be attained when prices had risen sufficiently to yield a roughly balanced actual budget.

A disturbance increasing aggregate money demand would bring into play the same forces operating in the reverse direction: the increase in employment would reduce transfer payments and raise tax receipts, thus creating a surplus to offset part of the increase in aggregate demand; the rise in prices would decrease the real value of the community's stock of money and hence the fraction of current income spent on consumption; the rise in prices would also mean that, even after "overemployment" was eliminated, the government would run a surplus that would tend to offset further the initial increase in aggregate demand;[22] and, finally, the surplus would reduce the stock of money.

As this analysis indicates, the proposed fiscal and monetary framework provides defense in depth against changes in aggre-

---

ceive; equilibrium requires that their planned expenditures fall short of their receipts by the amount of the deficit (i.e., that they seek to add to their hoards per period the amount of the deficit).

22. The limit to the possible effect of the surplus on the current income stream would be set by the character of the tax structure, since there would probably be some maximum percentage of the aggregate income that could be taken by taxes no matter how high the price level and the aggregate income.

gate demand. The first line of defense is the adjustment of transfer payments and tax receipts to changes in employment.[23] This eases the shock while the defense is taken over by changes in prices. These raise or lower the real value of the community's assets and thereby raise or lower the fraction of income consumed. They also produce a government deficit or surplus in addition to the initial deficit or surplus resulting from the effect of changes in employment on transfer payments and tax receipts. The final line of defense is the cumulative effect of the deficits or surpluses on the stock of money. These changes in the stock of money tend to restore prices to their initial level. In some measure, of course, these defenses all operate simultaneously; yet their main effects are likely to occur in the temporal order suggested in the preceding discussion.

Even given flexible prices, the existence of the equilibrating mechanism described does not of course mean that the economy will in fact achieve relative stability. This depends, in addition, on the number and magnitude of the disturbances to which the economy is subject, the speed with which the equilibrating forces operate, and the importance of such disequilibrating forces as adverse price expectations. If the lags of response are minor, and initial perverse reactions unimportant, adjustments would be completed rapidly, and there would be no opportunity for disequilibria to cumulate, so that relative stability would be attained. Even in this most favorable case, however, the equilibrating mechanism does not prevent disturbances from arising and does not counteract their effects instantaneously—as, indeed, no system can in the absence of ability to predict everything in advance with perfect accuracy. What the equilibrating mechanism does accomplish is, first, to keep governmental monetary and fiscal

23. It should be noted that this is the only effect taken into account by Musgrave and Miller in their calculations of the possible magnitude of the effect of automatic variations in government receipts and expenditures (R. A. Musgrave and M. H. Miller, "Built-in Flexibility," *American Economic Review*, XXXVIII [March, 1948], 122–28). They conclude that "the analysis here provided lends no justification to the view now growing in popularity that 'built-in flexibility' can do the job alone and that deliberate countercyclical fiscal policy can be dispensed with." While this is a valid conclusion, it does not justify rejecting the view that "built-in flexibility" can do the job alone, since the "analysis here provided" takes no account of what have been termed above the "more fundamental correctives."

operations from themselves contributing disturbances and, second, to provide an automatic mechanism for adapting the system to the disturbances that occur.

Given flexible prices, there would be a tendency for automatic neutralization of any errors in the hypothetical income level assumed or in the calculations of the volume of expenditures and revenues at the hypothetical income level. Further, it would ultimately be of no great importance exactly what decision was reached about the relation to establish between expenditures and revenue at the hypothetical income level (i.e., whether exactly to balance, to strive for a deficit sufficient to provide a predetermined secular increase in the quantity of money, etc.). Suppose, for example, that errors in the assumed income level, the calculated volume of expenditures and receipts, and the relation established between expenditures and receipts combined to produce a deficit larger than was consistent with stable prices. The resulting inflationary pressure would be analogous to that produced by an external disturbance, and the same forces would come into play to counteract it. The result would be that prices would rise and the level of income tend to stabilize at a higher level than the hypothetical level initially assumed.

Similarly, the monetary and fiscal framework described above provides for adjustment not only to cyclical changes but also to secular changes. I do not put much credence in the doctrine of secular stagnation or economic maturity that is now so widely held. But let us assume for the sake of argument that this doctrine is correct, that there has been such a sharp secular decline in the demand for capital that the volume of investment at a full-employment level of income and at the minimum rate of interest technically feasible would be very much less than the volume of savings that would be forthcoming at this level of income and at the current price level.[24] The result would simply

24. Because of the effect discussed above of price changes on the real value of assets, and in this way on the average propensity to consume, it seems to me that such a state of affairs would not lead to secular unemployment even if the quantity of money were kept constant, provided that prices are flexible (which is the reason for including the qualification "at the current price level" in the sentence to which this footnote is attached). But I am for the moment accepting the point of view of those who deny the existence or importance of this equilibrating force.

be that the equilibrium position would involve a recurrent deficit sufficient to provide the hoards being demanded by savers. Of course, this would not really be a long-run equilibrium position, since the gradual increase in the quantity of money would increase the aggregate real value of the community's stock of money and thereby of assets, and this would tend to increase the fraction of any given level of real income consumed. As a result, there would tend to be a gradual rise in prices and the level of money income and a gradual reduction in the deficit.[25]

V. Conclusion

In conclusion, I should like to emphasize the modest aim of the proposal. It does not claim to provide full employment in the absence of successful measures to make prices of final goods and of factors of production flexible. It does not claim to eliminate entirely cyclical fluctuations in output and employment. Its claim to serious consideration is that it provides a stable framework of fiscal and monetary action; that it largely eliminates the uncertainty and undesirable political implications of discretionary action by governmental authorities; that it provides for adaptation of the governmental sector to changes occurring in other sectors of the economy of a kind designed to offset the effects of these changes; and that the proposed fiscal and monetary frame-

---

Moreover, if the quantity of money were constant, the adjustment would be made entirely through a secular decline in prices, admittedly a difficult adjustment. Once again changes in the government contribution to the income stream and through this in the quantity of money can reduce the extent of the required price change.

25. This and the preceding paragraph, in particular, and this entire section, in general, suggest a problem that deserves investigation and to which I have no satisfactory answer, namely, the characteristics of the system of equations implicit in the proposal and of their equilibrium solution. It is obvious that under strictly stationary conditions, including a stationary population, the equilibrium solution would involve constancy of prices, income per head, etc., and a balanced actual budget. The interesting question is whether there is any simple description of the equilibrium solution under specified dynamic situations. For example, are there circumstances, and, if so, what are they, under which the equilibrium solution will tend to involve constant money income per head with declining prices, or constant prices with rising money income per head, etc? It is obvious that no such simple description will suffice in general, but there may well be broad classes of circumstances under which one or another will.

work is consistent with the long-run considerations stated at the outset of this paper. It is not perhaps a proposal that one would consider at all optimum if our knowledge of the fundamental causes of cyclical fluctuations were considerably greater than I, for one, think it to be; it is a proposal that involves minimum reliance on uncertain and untested knowledge.

The proposal has of course its dangers. Explicit control of the quantity of money by government and explicit creation of money to meet actual government deficits may establish a climate favorable to irresponsible government action and to inflation. The principle of a balanced stable budget may not be strong enough to offset these tendencies. This danger may well be greater for this proposal than for some others, yet in some measure it is common to most proposals to mitigate cyclical fluctuations. It can probably be avoided only by moving in a completely different direction, namely, toward an entirely metallic currency, elimination of any governmental control of the quantity of money, and the re-enthronement of the principle of a balanced actual budget.

The proposal may not succeed in reducing cyclical fluctuations to tolerable proportions. The forces making for cyclical fluctuations may be so stubborn and strong that the kind of automatic adaptations contained in the proposal are insufficient to offset them to a tolerable degree. I do not see how it is possible to know now whether this is the case. But, even if it should prove to be, the changes suggested are almost certain to be in the right direction and, in addition, to provide a more satisfactory framework on which to build further action.

A proposal like the present one, which is concerned not with short-run policy but with structural reform, should not be urged on the public unless and until it has withstood the test of professional criticism. It is in this spirit that the present paper is published.

The Case for Flexible Exchange Rates*

THE Western nations seem committed to a system of international payments based on exchange rates between their national currencies fixed by governments and maintained rigid except for occasional changes to new levels. This system is embodied in the statutes of the International Monetary Fund, which provides for changes in exchange rates of less than 10 per cent by individual governments without approval of the Fund and for larger changes only with approval; it is implicit in the European Payments Union; and it is taken for granted in almost all discussions of international economic policy.

Whatever may have been the merits of this system for another day, it is ill suited to current economic and political conditions. These conditions make a system of flexible or floating exchange rates—exchange rates freely determined in an open market primarily by private dealings and, like other market prices, varying from day to day—absolutely essential for the fulfilment of our basic economic objective: the achievement and maintenance of a free and prosperous world community engaging in unrestricted multilateral trade. There is scarcely a facet of international economic policy for which the implicit acceptance of a system of rigid exchange rates does not create serious and unnecessary difficulties. Promotion of rearmament, liberalization of trade, avoidance of allocations and other direct controls both internal and external, harmonization of internal monetary and fiscal policies— all these problems take on a different cast and become far easier

* This paper had its origin in a memorandum written in the fall of 1950 when I was a consultant to the Finance and Trade Division of the Office of Special Representative for Europe, United States Economic Cooperation Administration. Needless to say, the views it expresses are entirely my own. I am grateful to Joel Bernstein and Maxwell Obst for criticism of the original memorandum and to Earl J. Hamilton and Lloyd A. Metzler for criticism of a subsequent draft. The paper owes much, also, to extensive discussion of the general problem with a number of friends, particularly Aaron Director, James Meade, Lloyd Mints, and Lionel Robbins. Unfortunately, these discussions failed to produce sufficient agreement to make a disclaimer of their responsibility unnecessary.

to solve in a world of flexible exchange rates and its corollary, free convertibility of currencies. The sooner a system of flexible exchange rates is established, the sooner unrestricted multilateral trade will become a real possibility. And it will become one without in any way interfering with the pursuit by each nation of domestic economic stability according to its own lights.[1]

Before proceeding to defend this thesis in detail, I should perhaps emphasize two points to avoid misunderstanding. First, advocacy of flexible exchange rates is *not* equivalent to advocacy of unstable exchange rates. The ultimate objective is a world in which exchange rates, while *free* to vary, are in fact highly stable. Instability of exchange rates is a symptom of instability in the underlying economic structure. Elimination of this symptom by administrative freezing of exchange rates cures none of the underlying difficulties and only makes adjustment to them more painful. Second, by unrestricted multilateral trade, I shall mean a system in which there are no direct quantitative controls over imports or exports, in which any tariffs or export bounties are reasonably stable and nondiscriminatory and are not subject to manipulation to affect the balance of payments, and in which a substantial fraction of international trade is in private (nongovernmental) hands. Though admittedly vague and subject to considerable ambiguity, this definition will do for our purposes. I shall take for granted without detailed examination that unrestricted multilateral trade in this sense[2] is a desirable objective of economic policy.[3] However, many of the arguments for flexible exchange rates remain valid even if this premise is not accepted.

1. Indeed, I have elsewhere argued that flexible exchange rates are the logical international counterpart of the monetary and fiscal framework for economic stability that seems to me the most promising. See "A Monetary and Fiscal Framework for Economic Stability," *supra,* pp. 133–56.

2. And indeed in the even more extreme sense of trade free from all barriers, including tariffs and export bounties.

3. In brief, it is desirable in its own right as one of the basic freedoms we cherish; it promotes the efficient use of resources through an appropriate international division of labor and increases consumer welfare by maximizing the range of alternatives on which consumers can spend their incomes; it facilitates international political amity by removing potent sources of conflict between governments.

I. Alternative Methods of Adjusting to Changes Affecting International Payments

Changes affecting the international trade and the balance of payments of various countries are always occurring. Some are in the "real" conditions determining international trade, such as the weather, technical conditions of production, consumer tastes, and the like. Some are in monetary conditions, such as divergent degrees of inflation or deflation in various countries.

These changes affect some commodities more than others and so tend to produce changes in the structure of relative prices—for example, rearmament by the United States impinges particularly on selected raw materials and tends to raise their prices relatively to other prices. Such effects on the relative price structure are likely to be much the same whether exchange rates are rigid or flexible and to raise much the same problem of adjustment in either case and so will receive little attention in what follows.

But, over and above these effects on particular commodities and prices, the changes in question affect each country's balance of payments, taken as a whole. Holders of foreign currencies want to exchange them for the currency of a particular country in order to purchase commodities produced in that country, or to purchase securities or other capital assets in that country, or to pay interest on or repay debts to that country, or to make gifts to citizens of that country, or simply to hold for one of these uses or for resale. The amount of currency of a particular country that is demanded per unit of time for each of these purposes will, of course, depend in the first instance on the exchange rate—the number of units of a foreign currency that must be paid to acquire one unit of the domestic currency. Other things the same, the more expensive a given currency, that is, the higher the exchange rate, the less of that currency will in general be demanded for each of these purposes. Similarly, holders of the currency of the country in question want to exchange that currency for foreign currencies for the corresponding purposes; and, again, the amount they want to exchange depends, in the first instance, on the price which they can get. The changes continuously taking place in the conditions of international trade alter the "other things" and so the desirability of using the currencies of various countries for each of the purposes listed. The aggregate effect is at one time to increase, at another to decrease, the amount of a country's currency demanded at any given rate of exchange relative to the amount offered for sale at that rate. Of course, after the event, the amount of a particular currency purchased must equal the amount sold—this is a question simply of double-entry bookkeeping. But, in advance, the amount people want to buy need not equal the amount people want to sell. The *ex post* equality involves a reconciliation of these divergent desires, either through changes in the desires themselves or through their frustration.

There is no way of avoiding this reconciliation; inconsistent desires cannot simultaneously be satisfied. The crucial question of policy is the mechanism whereby this reconciliation is brought about. Suppose the aggregate effect of changes in the conditions affecting international payments has been to increase the amount of a country's currency people want to buy with foreign currency relatively to the amount other people want to sell for foreign currency at the pre-existing exchange rate—to create an incipient surplus in the balance of payments. How can these inconsistent desires be reconciled? (1) The country's currency may be bid up, or put up, in price. This increase in the exchange rate will tend to make the currency less desirable relative to the currency of other countries and so eliminate the excess demand at the pre-existing rate.[4] (2) Prices within the country may rise, thus making its

4. It is conceivable that, under some conditions and for some range of exchange rates, a rise in exchange rates would increase the excess demand. Though this possibility has received considerable attention, it will be neglected in what follows as of little practical relevance. As a purely theoretical matter, there will always be some set or sets of rates that will clear the market, and, in the neighborhood of at least one of these sets of rates a rise in the rate will mean a decline in excess demand (i.e., a negative excess demand) ; a fall, a rise in excess demand. Exchange rates can remain in a region in which this is not true only if they are not free to move and if some nonprice mechanism is used to ration domestic or foreign currency. As a practical matter, the conditions necessary for any relevant range of rates to have the property that a rise increases excess demand seem to me highly unlikely to occur. But, if they should occur, it would merely mean that there might be two possible positions of equilibrium, one above, the other below, the existing controlled rate. If the higher is regarded as preferable, the implication for policy would be first to appreciate the controlled rate and then to set it free.

goods less desirable relative to goods in other countries, or incomes within the country may rise, thus increasing the demand for foreign currencies. (3) Direct controls over transactions involving foreign exchange may prevent holders of foreign balances from acquiring as much domestic exchange as they would otherwise like to; for example, they may be prevented from buying domestic goods by the inability to get a required export license. (4) The excess amount of domestic currency desired may be provided out of monetary reserves, the foreign currency acquired being added to reserves of foreign currencies—the monetary authorities (or exchange equalization fund or the like) may step in with a "desire" to buy or sell the difference between the amounts demanded and supplied by others.

Each of these four methods has its obvious counterpart if the effect of the changes is to create an incipient deficit. Aside from purely frictional frustrations of desires (the inability of a buyer to find a seller because of imperfections of the market), these are fundamentally the only four ways in which an *ex ante* divergence between the amount of a country's currency demanded and the amount supplied can be converted into the *ex post* equality that necessarily prevails. Let us consider each in turn.

A. CHANGES IN EXCHANGE RATES

Two different mechanisms whereby exchange-rate changes may be used to maintain equilibrium in the balance of payments must be sharply distinguished: (1) flexible exchange rates as defined above and (2) official changes in temporarily rigid rates.

1. *Flexible exchange rates.*—Under flexible exchange rates freely determined in open markets, the first impact of any tendency toward a surplus or deficit in the balance of payments is on the exchange rate. If a country has an incipient surplus of receipts over payments—an excess demand for its currency—the exchange rate will tend to rise. If it has an incipient deficit, the exchange rate will tend to fall. If the conditions responsible for the rise or the fall in the exchange rate are generally regarded as temporary, actual or potential holders of the country's currency will tend to change their holdings in such a way as to moderate the movement in the exchange rate. If a rise in the exchange rate,

for example, is expected to be temporary, there is an incentive for holders of the country's currency to sell some of their holdings for foreign currency in order to buy the currency back later on at a lower price. By doing so, they provide the additional domestic currency to meet part of the excess demand responsible for the initial rise in the exchange rate; that is, they absorb some of what would have been surplus receipts of foreign currency at the former exchange rate. Conversely, if a decline is expected to be temporary, there is an incentive to buy domestic currency for resale at a higher price. Such purchases of domestic currency provide the foreign currency to meet some of what would have been a deficit of foreign currency at the former exchange rate. In this way, such "speculative" transactions in effect provide the country with reserves to absorb temporary surpluses or to meet temporary deficits. On the other hand, if the change in the exchange rate is generally regarded as produced by fundamental factors that are likely to be permanent, the incentives are the reverse of those listed above, and speculative transactions will speed up the rise or decline in the exchange rate and thus hasten its approach to its final position.

This final position depends on the effect that changes in exchange rates have on the demand for and supply of a country's currency, not to hold as balances, but for other purposes. A rise in the exchange rate produced by a tendency toward a surplus makes foreign goods cheaper in terms of domestic currency, even though their prices are unchanged in terms of their own currency, and domestic goods more expensive in terms of foreign currency, even though their prices are unchanged in terms of domestic currency. This tends to increase imports, reduce exports, and so offset the incipient surplus. Conversely, a decline in the exchange rate produced by a tendency toward a deficit makes imports more expensive to home consumers, and exports less expensive to foreigners, and so tends to offset the incipient deficit.

Because money imparts general purchasing power and is used for such a wide variety of purposes abroad as well as at home, the demand for and supply of any one country's currency is widely spread and comes from many sources. In consequence, broad, active, and nearly perfect markets have developed in foreign exchange whenever they have been permitted—and usually even when they have not been. The exchange rate is therefore potentially an extremely sensitive price. Changes in it occur rapidly, automatically, and continuously and so tend to produce corrective movements before tensions can accumulate and a crisis develop. For example, if Germany had had a flexible exchange rate in 1950, the crisis in the fall of that year would never have followed the course it did. The exchange rate would have been affected not later than July and would have started to produce corrective adaptations at once. The whole affair would never have assumed large proportions and would have shown up as a relatively minor ripple in exchange rates. As it was, with a rigid exchange rate, the warning of impending trouble was indirect and delayed, and the government took no action until three months later, by which time the disequilibrium had grown to crisis dimensions, requiring drastic action at home, international consultation, and help from abroad.

The recurrent foreign-exchange crises of the United Kingdom in the postwar period are perhaps an even more dramatic example of the kind of crises that could not develop under a system of flexible exchange rates. In each case no significant corrective action was taken until large disequilibriums had been allowed to cumulate, and then the action had to be drastic. The rigidities and discontinuities introduced by substituting administrative action for automatic market forces have seldom been demonstrated so clearly or more impressively.

2. *Official changes in exchange rates.*—These examples suggest the sharp difference between flexible exchange rates and exchange rates held temporarily rigid but subject to change by government action to meet substantial difficulties. While these exchange-rate changes have the same kind of effect on commodity trade and the like as those produced automatically under a system of flexible exchange rates, they have very different effects on speculative transactions. Partly for this reason, partly because of their innate discontinuity, each exchange-rate change tends to become the occasion for a crisis. There is no mechanism for producing changes in exchange rates of the required magnitude or for correcting mistakes, and some other mechanism must be used

to maintain equilibrium during the period between exchange-rate changes—either internal price or income changes, direct controls, or monetary reserves.

Even though an exchange-rate change would not otherwise be the occasion for a crisis, speculative movements are highly likely to convert it into one, for this system practically insures a maximum of destabilizing speculation. Because the exchange rate is changed infrequently and only to meet substantial difficulties, a change tends to come well after the onset of difficulty, to be postponed as long as possible, and to be made only after substantial pressure on the exchange rate has accumulated. In consequence, there is seldom any doubt about the direction in which an exchange rate will be changed, if it is changed. In the interim between the suspicion of a possible change in the rate and the actual change, there is every incentive to sell the country's currency if devaluation is expected (to export "capital" from the country) or to buy it if an appreciation is expected (to bring in "capital"); either can be done without an exchange loss and will mean an exchange gain when and if the rate is changed. This is in sharp contrast with the situation under flexible exchange rates when the decline in the exchange rate takes place along with, and as a consequence of, the sales of a currency and so discourages or penalizes sales, and conversely for purchases. With rigid rates, if the exchange rate is not changed, the only cost to the speculators is a possible loss of interest earnings from an interest-rate differential. It is no answer to this argument to say that capital flows can be restricted by direct controls, since our ultimate objective in using this method is precisely to avoid such restrictions.

In short, the system of occasional changes in temporarily rigid exchange rates seems to me the worst of two worlds: it provides neither the stability of expectations that a genuinely rigid and stable exchange rate could provide in a world of unrestricted trade and willingness and ability to adjust the internal price structure to external conditions nor the continuous sensitivity of a flexible exchange rate.

B. CHANGES IN INTERNAL PRICES OR INCOME

In principle, changes in internal prices could produce the same effects on trade as changes in the exchange rate. For example, a decline of 10 per cent in every internal price in Germany (including wages, rents, etc.) with an unchanged dollar price of the mark would clearly have identically the same effects on the relative costs of domestic and foreign goods as a decline of 10 per cent in the dollar price of the mark, with all internal prices unchanged. Similarly, such price changes could have the same effects on speculative transactions. If expected to be temporary, a decline in prices would stimulate speculative purchases of goods to avoid future higher prices, thus moderating the price movement.

If internal prices were as flexible as exchange rates, it would make little economic difference whether adjustments were brought about by changes in exchange rates or by equivalent changes in internal prices. But this condition is clearly not fulfilled. The exchange rate is potentially flexible in the absence of administrative action to freeze it. At least in the modern world, internal prices are highly inflexible. They are more flexible upward than downward, but even on the upswing all prices are not equally flexible. The inflexibility of prices, or different degrees of flexibility, means a distortion of adjustments in response to changes in external conditions. The adjustment takes the form primarily of price changes in some sectors, primarily of output changes in others.

Wage rates tend to be among the less flexible prices. In consequence, an incipient deficit that is countered by a policy of permitting or forcing prices to decline is likely to produce unemployment rather than, or in addition to, wage decreases. The consequent decline in real income reduces the domestic demand for foreign goods and thus the demand for foreign currency with which to purchase these goods. In this way, it offsets the incipient deficit. But this is clearly a highly inefficient method of adjusting to external changes. If the external changes are deep-seated and persistent, the unemployment produces steady downward pressure on prices and wages, and the adjustment will not have been completed until the deflation has run its sorry course.

Despite these difficulties, the use of changes in internal prices might not be undesirable if they were called for only rarely and only as a result of changes in the real underlying conditions of trade. Such changes in underlying conditions are likely in any event to require considerable changes in relative prices of particular goods and services and only changes of a much smaller order of magnitude in the general level of internal prices. But neither condition is likely to be satisfied in the modern world. Adjustments are required continuously, and many are called for by essentially monetary phenomena, which, if promptly offset by a movement in the exchange rate, would require no change in the actual allocation of resources.

Changes in interest rates are perhaps best classified under this heading of changes in internal prices. Interest-rate changes have in the past played a particularly important role in adjustment to external changes, partly because they have been susceptible to direct influence by the monetary authorities, and partly because, under a gold standard, the initial impact of a tendency toward a deficit or surplus was a loss or gain of gold and a consequent tightening or ease in the money market. The rise in the interest rate produced in this way by an incipient deficit increased the demand for the currency for capital purposes and so offset part or all of the deficit. This reduced the rate at which the deficit had to be met by a decline in internal prices, which was itself set in motion by the loss of gold and associated decrease in the stock of money responsible for the rise in interest rates. Conversely, an incipient surplus increased the stock of gold and eased the money market. The resulting decline in the interest rate reduced the demand for the currency for capital purposes and so offset part or all of the surplus, reducing the rate at which the surplus had to be met by the rise in internal prices set in motion by the gain of gold and associated rise in the stock of money.

These interest-induced capital movements are a desirable part of a system relying primarily on changes in internal prices, since they tend to smooth out the adjustment process. They cannot, however, be relied on alone, since they come into operation only incidentally to the adjustment of internal prices.

Primary reliance on changes in internal prices and incomes was tolerable in the nineteenth century partly because the key countries of the Western world placed much heavier emphasis on freedom from government interference at home and unrestricted multilateral trade abroad than on domestic stability; thus they were willing to allow domestic economic policy to be dominated by the requirements of fixed exchange rates and free convertibility of currencies. But, equally important, this very emphasis gave holders of balances confidence in the maintenance of the system and so made them willing to let small differences in interest rates determine the currency in which they held their balances. Furthermore, the emphasis on freedom from government interference at home gave less scope to internal monetary management and so meant that most changes affecting international trade reflected real changes in underlying conditions, or else monetary changes, such as gold discoveries, more or less common to the major nations. Modern conditions, with the widespread emphasis on full employment at home and the extensive intervention of government into economic affairs, are clearly very different and much less favorable to this method of adjustment.

C. DIRECT CONTROLS

In principle, direct controls on imports, exports, and capital movements could bring about the same effects on trade and the balance of payments as changes in exchange rates or in internal prices and incomes. The final adjustment will, after all, involve a change in the composition of imports and exports, along with specifiable capital transactions. If these could be predicted in advance, and if it were technically possible to control selectively each category of imports, exports, and capital transactions, direct controls could be used to produce the required adjustment.

It is clear, however, that the changes in imports and exports and the required capital transactions cannot be predicted; the fact that each new foreign-exchange crisis in a country like Britain is officially regarded as a bolt from the blue is ample evidence for this proposition. Even if they could be predicted, direct control of imports, exports, and capital transactions by techniques other than the price system[5] necessarily means ex-

---

5. Note that a tariff of a uniform percentage on all imports used to pay a subsidy of a uniform percentage on all exports is equivalent to a depreciation in the exchange rate by the corresponding percentage; and, similarly, a subsidy of a uniform percentage on all imports financed by a tax of a uniform percentage on all exports is equivalent to an appreciation in the exchange rate by the corresponding percentage. Thus devices such as these should be classified under exchange-rate changes rather than direct controls.

tending such control to many internal matters and interfering with the efficiency of the distribution and production of goods— some means must be found for rationing imports that are being held down in amount or disposing of increased imports and for allocating reduced exports or getting increased exports.

Aside from the many unfortunate results of such a process which are by now abundantly clear, it has a perverse effect on the foreign-payments problem itself, particularly when direct controls are used, as they have been primarily, to counter an actual or incipient deficit. The apparent deficit that has to be closed by direct controls is larger than the deficit that would emerge at the same exchange rate without the direct controls and, indeed, might be eliminated entirely or converted into a surplus if the direct controls on imports and exports and their inevitable domestic accompaniments were removed. The mere existence of the direct controls makes the currency less desirable for many purposes because of the limitations it places on what holders of the currency may do with it, and this is likely to reduce the demand for the currency more than it would be reduced by the fluctuations in exchange rates or other adaptive mechanisms substituted for the direct controls. In addition, permitted imports are generally distributed at prices lower than those that would clear the market and so are used wastefully and in the wrong places, increasing apparent import "requirements"; similarly, the composition of imports is determined by administrative decisions that tend to have the same effect. Both of these are particularly important in hindering exports, because export industries are not likely to get so large a fraction of the imports as they would bid away in a free market, even if the government supposedly favors export industries, and cannot make their influence fully felt in determining the composition of imports; and the direct controls have a tendency to make the incentive to export lower than it would otherwise be.[6]

6. Selling import licenses at a price that would clear the market would eliminate the first effect; it would not eliminate the second and third unless the permits were not for specific commodities but for foreign exchange to be used in any way desired. Even this would not eliminate the fourth unless the proceeds were used to pay a percentage subsidy to exports and other transactions leading to the acquisi-

The considerations mentioned in the preceding paragraph may help to reconcile—and, indeed, their elaboration was stimulated by my own need to reconcile—the impression of casual visitors to England, and the conclusions of some careful students of the subject, that the pound is currently (1952) undervalued in purchasing power terms with the recurrent pressures on the pound and the restrictive measures that seem to be required to maintain the pound at its present rate. They show that there is no necessary inconsistency between the following two assertions: (1) the market value of the pound would be higher than $2.80 if all exchange restrictions and associated controls were removed and the exchange rate were allowed to be determined by primarily private dealings in a free market; (2) given the retention of an official exchange rate and of the existing *system* of exchange restrictions and associated internal controls, an *easing* of restrictions would produce pressure on the exchange rate and require a rate lower than $2.80 to keep exchange reserves from being depleted. Both statements may not, in fact, be correct; but there is no such obvious contradiction between them as there appears to be at first sight.

Finally, whatever the desirability of direct controls, there are political and administrative limits to the extent to which it is possible to impose and enforce such controls. These limits are narrower in some countries than in others, but they are present in all. Given sufficient incentive to do so, ways will be found to evade or avoid the controls. A race develops between officials seeking to plug legal loopholes and to discover and punish illegal evasions of the controls and the ever numerous individuals whose inventive talents are directed toward discovering or opening up new loopholes by the opportunities for large returns or whose respect for law and fear of punishment are overcome by the same opportunities. And the race is by no means always to the officials, even when they are honest and able. In particular, it has

---

tion of foreign exchange. This final system is, as indicated in the preceding note, identical with a change in the exchange rate. If the price of permits to use foreign exchange and the subsidy for acquiring it were determined in a free market so as to make total receipts equal total payments, the result is equivalent to or identical with a system of flexible exchange rates.

proved extremely difficult in all countries to prevent capital movements by direct controls.

D. USE OF MONETARY RESERVES

Given adequate reserves, tendencies toward a surplus or a deficit can be allowed to produce an actual surplus or deficit in transactions other than those of the monetary authority (or exchange equalization fund, or whatever the name may be) without a change in exchange rates, internal prices or incomes, or direct controls, the additional domestic or foreign currency demanded being supplied by the monetary authority. This device is feasible and not undesirable for movements that are small and temporary, though, if it is clear that the movements are small and temporary, it is largely unnecessary, since, with flexible exchange rates, private speculative transactions will provide the additional domestic or foreign currency demanded with only minor movements in exchange rates.

The exclusive use of reserves is much less desirable, if possible at all, for movements of large magnitude and long duration. If the problem is a deficit, the ability of the monetary authorities to meet the deficit is immediately limited by the size of their reserves of foreign currency or the equivalent plus whatever additional sums they can or are willing to borrow or acquire in other ways from holders of foreign currency. Moreover, if the internal price level (or level of employment) is to be kept stable, the proceeds from the sales of foreign-exchange reserves must not be impounded or used in other deflationary ways. This assumes, of course, that the deficit is not itself produced by internal inflationary policies but occurs despite a stable internal price level. The proceeds must be used to retire debt or to finance a deficit in the budget to whatever extent is necessary to prevent a price decline.

If the problem is a surplus, the monetary authorities must be prepared to accumulate foreign exchange indefinitely, providing all the domestic currency that is demanded. Moreover, if the internal price level is to be maintained constant, it must obtain the domestic currency it sells for foreign currency in noninflationary ways. It can print or create the currency only to the extent that is consistent with stable prices. For the rest it must get the amount required by borrowing at whatever interest rates are necessary to keep domestic prices stable or from a surplus of the appropriate amount in the government budget. Entirely aside from the technical problems of monetary management involved, the community is unlikely to be willing to exchange indefinitely part of its product for unproductive currency hoards, particularly if the source of the surplus is monetary inflation abroad, and thus the foreign currency is decreasing in real value.

Traditionally, of course, monetary reserves have not been used as the primary method of adjusting to changes in external conditions but as a shock absorber pending changes in internal prices and incomes. A deficit has been met out of monetary reserves in the first instance, but the proceeds or even a multiple of the proceeds have been, as it were, impounded; that is, the stock of money has been allowed or made to decrease as a result of the decline of monetary reserves, with a consequent rise in interest rates and downward pressure on internal prices. Similarly, the domestic currency exchanged for a surplus of foreign currency has, as it were, been created and allowed to or made to increase the stock of money by the same amount or a multiple of that amount, with a consequent decline in interest rates and upward pressure on internal prices.[7]

Since the end of the first World War, nations have become increasingly unwilling to use reserves in this way and to allow the effect to be transmitted directly and immediately to internal monetary conditions and prices. Already during the 1920's, the United States, to cite one outstanding and critical example, refused to allow its surplus, which took the form of gold imports, to raise domestic prices in the way the supposed rules of the gold standard demanded; instead, it "sterilized" gold imports. Especially after the Great Depression completed the elevation of full employment to the primary goal of economic policy, nations have been unwilling to allow deficits to exert any deflationary effect.

7. Under a pure gold standard, these effects follow automatically, since any international claims not settled otherwise are settled by gold, which, in case of a deficit, is bodily extracted from the monetary stock and, in case of a surplus, bodily added to it.

The use of monetary reserves as the sole reliance to meet small and temporary strains on balances of payments and of other devices to meet larger and more extended or more basic strains is an understandable objective of economic policy and comes close to summarizing the philosophy underlying the International Monetary Fund. Unfortunately, it is not a realistic, feasible, or desirable policy. It is seldom possible to know in advance or even soon after the event whether any given strain in the balance of payments is likely to be reversed rapidly or not; that is, whether it is a result of temporary or permanent factors. Reserves must be very large indeed if they are to be the sole reliance in meeting changes in external conditions until the magnitude and probable duration of the changes can be diagnosed with confidence and more fundamental correctives undertaken in light of the diagnosis, far larger than if they serve the function they did under the classical gold standard. Except perhaps for the United States, and even for the United States only so long as gold is freely acceptable as an international currency, reserves are nothing like this large. Under the circumstances there is a strong tendency to rely on reserves too long for comfort yet not long enough for confident diagnosis and reasoned action. Corrective steps are postponed in the hope that things will right themselves until the state of the reserves forces drastic and frequently ill-advised action.

E. A COMPARISON

One or another of the methods of adjustment just described must in fact be used to meet changes in conditions affecting external trade; there is no avoiding this necessity short of the complete elimination of external trade, and even this would be an extreme form of direct controls over imports and exports. On the basis of the analysis so far, flexible exchange rates seem clearly the technique of adjustment best suited to current conditions: the use of reserves is not by itself a feasible device; direct controls are cumbrous and inefficient and, I venture to predict, will ultimately prove ineffective in a free society; changes in internal prices and incomes are undesirable because of rigidities in internal prices, especially wages, and the emergence of full employment—or independence of internal monetary policy—as a major goal of policy.

The argument for flexible exchange rates is, strange to say, very nearly identical with the argument for daylight saving time. Isn't it absurd to change the clock in summer when exactly the same result could be achieved by having each individual change his habits? All that is required is that everyone decide to come to his office an hour earlier, have lunch an hour earlier, etc. But obviously it is much simpler to change the clock that guides all than to have each individual separately change his pattern of reaction to the clock, even though all want to do so. The situation is exactly the same in the exchange market. It is far simpler to allow one price to change, namely, the price of foreign exchange, than to rely upon changes in the multitude of prices that together constitute the internal price structure.

II. Objections to Flexible Exchange Rates

Three major criticisms have been made of the proposal to establish a system of flexible exchange rates: first, that flexible exchange rates may increase the degree of uncertainty in the economic scene; second, that flexible exchange rates will not work because they will produce offsetting changes in domestic prices; and, third, that flexible exchange rates will not produce the best attainable timing or pace of adjustment. The first objection takes many different forms, and it will promote clarity to deal with some of these separately, even though this means considerable overlapping.

A. FLEXIBLE EXCHANGE RATES AND UNCERTAINTY

1. *Flexible exchange rates mean instability rather than stability.*—On the naïve level on which this objection is frequently made, it involves the already-mentioned mistake of confusing the symptom of difficulties with the difficulties themselves. A flexible exchange rate need not be an unstable exchange rate. If it is, it is primarily because there is underlying instability in the economic conditions governing international trade. And a rigid exchange rate may, while itself nominally stable, perpetuate and accentuate other elements of instability in the economy. The

mere fact that a rigid official exchange rate does not change while a flexible rate does is no evidence that the former means greater stability in any more fundamental sense. If it does, it is for one or more of the reasons considered in the points that follow.

2. *Flexible exchange rates make it impossible for exporters and importers to be certain about the price they will have to pay or receive for foreign exchange.*—Under flexible exchange rates traders can almost always protect themselves against changes in the rate by hedging in a futures market. Such futures markets in foreign currency readily develop when exchange rates are flexible. Any uncertainty about returns will then be borne by speculators. The most that can be said for this argument, therefore, is that flexible exchange rates impose a cost of hedging on traders, namely, the price that must be paid to speculators for assuming the risk of future changes in exchange rates. But this is saying too much. The substitution of flexible for rigid exchange rates changes the form in which uncertainty in the foreign-exchange market is manifested; it may not change the extent of uncertainty at all and, indeed, may even decrease uncertainty. For example, conditions that would tend to produce a decline in a flexible exchange rate will produce a shortage of exchange with a rigid exchange rate. This in turn will produce either internal adjustments of uncertain character or administrative allocation of exchange. Traders will then be certain about the rate but uncertain about either internal conditions or the availability of exchange. The uncertainty can be removed for some transactions by advance commitments by the authorities dispensing exchange; it clearly cannot be removed for all transactions in view of the uncertainty about the total amount of exchange available; the reduction in uncertainty for some transactions therefore involves increased uncertainty for others, since all the risk is now concentrated on them. Further, such administrative allocation of exchange is always surrounded by uncertainty about the policy that will be followed. It is by no means clear whether the uncertainty associated with a flexible rate or the uncertainty associated with a rigid rate is likely to be more disruptive to trade.

3. *Speculation in foreign-exchange markets tends to be de-*

stabilizing.—This point is, of course, closely related to the preceding one. It is said that speculators will take a decline in the exchange rate as a signal for a further decline and will thus tend to make the movements in the exchange rate sharper than they would be in the absence of speculation. The special fear in this connection is of capital flight in response to political uncertainty or simply to movements in the exchange rate. Despite the prevailing opinion to the contrary, I am very dubious that in fact speculation in foreign exchange would be destabilizing. Evidence from some earlier experiences and from current free markets in currency in Switzerland, Tangiers, and elsewhere seems to me to suggest that, in general, speculation is stabilizing rather than the reverse, though the evidence has not yet been analyzed in sufficient detail to establish this conclusion with any confidence. People who argue that speculation is generally destabilizing seldom realize that this is largely equivalent to saying that speculators lose money, since speculation can be destabilizing in general only if speculators on the average sell when the currency is low in price and buy when it is high.[8] It does not, of course, follow that speculation is not destabilizing; professional speculators might on the average make money while a changing body of amateurs regularly lost larger sums. But, while this may happen, it is hard to see why there is any presumption that it will; the presumption is rather the opposite. To put the same point differently, if speculation were persistently destabilizing, a government body like the Exchange Equalization Fund in England in the 1930's could make a good deal of money by speculating in exchange and in the process almost certainly eliminate the destabilizing speculation. But to suppose that speculation by governments would generally be profitable is in most cases equivalent to supposing that government officials risking funds that they do not themselves own are better judges of the likely move-

8. A warning is perhaps in order that this is a simplified generalization on a complex problem. A full analysis encounters difficulties in separating "speculative" from other transactions, defining precisely and satisfactorily "destabilizing speculation," and taking account of the effects of the mere existence of a system of flexible rates as contrasted with the effects of actual speculative transactions under such a system.

ments in foreign-exchange markets than private individuals risking their own funds.

The widespread belief that speculation is likely to be destabilizing is doubtless a major factor accounting for the cavalier rejection of a system of flexible exchange rates in the immediate postwar period. Yet this belief does not seem to be founded on any systematic analysis of the available empirical evidence.[9] It rests rather, I believe, primarily on an oversimplified interpretation of the movements of so-called "hot" money during the 1930's. At the time, any speculative movements which threatened a depreciation of a currency (i.e., which threatened a *change* in an exchange rate) were regarded as destabilizing, and hence these movements were so considered. In retrospect, it is clear that the speculators were "right"; that forces were at work making for depreciation in the value of most European currencies relative to the dollar independently of speculative activity; that the speculative movements were anticipating this change; and,

9. Perhaps the most ambitious attempt to summarize the evidence is that by Ragnar Nurkse, *International Currency Experience* (Geneva: League of Nations, 1944), pp. 117–22. Nurkse concludes from interwar experience that speculation can be expected in general to be destabilizing. However, the evidence he cites is by itself inadequate to justify any conclusion. Nurkse examines only one episode in anything approaching the required detail, the depreciation of the French franc from 1922 to 1926. For the rest, he simply lists episodes during which exchange rates were flexible and asserts that in each case speculation was destabilizing. These episodes may or may not support his conclusion; it is impossible to tell from his discussion of them; and the list is clearly highly selective, excluding some cases that seem prima facie to point in the opposite direction.

Even for the French episode, the evidence given by Nurkse does not justify any firm conclusion. Indeed, so far as it goes, it seems to me clearly less favorable to the conclusion Nurkse draws, that speculation was destabilizing, than to the opposite conclusion, that speculation was stabilizing.

In general, Nurkse's discussion of the effects of speculation is thoroughly unsatisfactory. At times, he seems to regard any transactions which threaten the existing value of a currency as destabilizing even if underlying forces would produce a changed value in the absence of speculation. At another point, he asserts that destabilizing transactions may occur on *both* capital and current account simultaneously, in a context in which these two accounts exhaust the balance of payments, so that his statement is an arithmetical impossibility (pp. 210–11). It is a sorry reflection on the scientific basis for generally held economic beliefs that Nurkse's analysis is so often cited as "the" basis or "proof" of the belief in destabilizing speculation.

hence, that there is at least as much reason to call them "stabilizing" as to call them "destabilizing."

In addition, the interpretation of this evidence has been marred by a failure to distinguish between a system of exchange rates held temporarily rigid but subject to change from time to time by government action and a system of flexible exchange rates. Many of the capital movements regarded as demonstrating that foreign-exchange speculation is destabilizing were stimulated by the existence of rigid rates subject to change by government action and are to be attributed primarily to the absence of flexibility of rates and hence of any incentive to avoid the capital movements. This is equally true of post–World War II experience with wide swings in foreign-payments positions. For reasons noted earlier, this experience has little direct bearing on the character of the speculative movements to be expected under a regime of genuinely flexible exchange rates.

4. *Flexible exchange rates involve increased uncertainty in the internal economy.*—It is argued that in many countries there is a great fear of inflation and that people have come to regard the exchange rate as an indicator of inflation and are highly sensitive to variations in it. Exchange crises, such as would tend to occur under rigid exchange rates, will pass unnoticed, it is argued, except by people directly connected with international trade, whereas a decline in the exchange rate would attract much attention, be taken as a signal of a future inflation, and produce anticipatory movements by the public at large. In this way a flexible exchange rate might produce additional uncertainty rather than merely change the form in which uncertainty is manifested. There is some merit to this argument, but it does not seem to me to be a substantial reason for avoiding a flexible exchange rate. Its implication is rather that it would be desirable, if possible, to make the transition to a flexible rate at a time when exchange rates of European countries relative to the dollar would be likely to move moderately and some to rise. It further would be desirable to accompany the transition by willingness to take prompt monetary action to counter any internal reactions. A fear of inflation has little or no chance of producing inflation, except in a favorable monetary environment. A demonstration

that fears of inflation are groundless, and some experience with the absence of any direct and immediate connection between the day-to-day movements in the exchange rate and internal prices would very shortly reduce to negligible proportions any increase in uncertainty on purely domestic markets, as a result of flexible yet not highly unstable exchange rates. Further, public recognition that a substantial decline in the exchange rate is a symptom of or portends internal inflation is by no means an unmixed evil. It means that a flexible exchange rate would provide something of a barrier to a highly inflationary domestic policy.

Very nearly the opposite of this argument is also sometimes made against flexible exchange rates. It is said that, with a flexible exchange rate, governments will have less incentive and be in a less strong position to take firm internal action to prevent inflation. A rigid exchange rate, it is said, gives the government a symbol to fight for—it can nail its flag to the mast of a specified exchange rate and resist political pressure to take action that would be inflationary in the name of defending the exchange rate. Dramatic foreign-exchange crises establish an atmosphere in which drastic if unpopular action is possible. On the other hand, it is said, with a flexible exchange rate, there is no definite sticking point; inflationary action will simply mean a decline in the exchange rate but no dramatic crisis, and people are little affected by a change in a price, the exchange rate, in a market in which relatively few have direct dealings.

Of course, it is not impossible for both these arguments to be valid—the first in countries like Germany, which have recently experienced hyperinflations and violently fluctuating exchange rates, the second in countries like Great Britain, which have not. But, even in countries like Britain, it is far from clear that a rigid exchange rate is more conducive under present conditions to noninflationary internal economic policy than a flexible exchange rate. A rigid exchange rate thwarts any immediate manifestation of a deterioration in the foreign-payments position as a result of inflationary internal policy. With an independent monetary standard, the loss of exchange reserves does not automatically reduce the stock of money or prevent its continued increase; yet it does temporarily reduce domestic inflationary pressure by providing goods in return for the foreign-exchange reserves without any simultaneous creation of domestic income. The deterioration shows up only sometime later, in the dull tables of statistics summarizing the state of foreign-exchange reserves. Even then, the authorities in the modern world have the alternative—or think they have—of suppressing a deficit by more stringent direct controls and thus postponing still longer the necessity for taking the appropriate internal measures; and they can always find any number of special reasons for the particular deterioration other than their internal policy. While the possibilities of using direct controls and of finding plausible excuses are present equally with flexible exchange rates, at least the deterioration in the foreign-payments position shows up promptly in the more readily understandable and simpler form of a decline in the exchange rates, and there is no emergency, no suddenly discovered decline in monetary reserves to dangerous levels, to force the imposition of supposedly unavoidable direct controls.

These arguments are modern versions of an argument that no longer has much merit but was at one time a valid and potent objection to flexible exchange rates, namely, the greater scope they give for government "tampering" with the currency. When rigid exchange rates were taken seriously, and when the armory of direct controls over international trade had not yet been resurrected, the maintenance of rigid rates left little scope for independent domestic monetary policy. This was the great virtue of the gold standard and the basic, albeit hidden, source of its emotional appeal; it provided an effective defense against hyperinflation, against government intervention of a kind that had time and again led to the debasement and depreciation of once-proud currencies. This argument may still be a source of emotional resistance to flexible exchange rates; it is clear that it does not deserve to be. Governments of "advanced" nations are no longer willing to submit themselves to the harsh discipline of the gold standard or any other standard involving rigid exchange rates. They will evade its discipline by direct controls over trade if that will suffice and will change exchange rates before they will surrender control over domestic monetary policy. Perhaps a few modern inflations will establish a climate in which such behavior does not qualify as "advanced"; in the meantime we had best recognize the necessity of allowing exchange rates to adjust to internal policies rather than the reverse.

B. FLEXIBLE EXCHANGE RATES AND INTERNAL PRICES

While I have just used the primacy of internal policy as an argument for flexible exchange rates, it has also been used as an argument against flexible exchange rates. As we have seen, flexible exchange rates promote adjustments to changes in external circumstances by producing changes in the relation between the prices of foreign and domestic goods. A decline in an exchange rate produced by a tendency toward a deficit in the balance of payments tends to make the prices of foreign goods higher in terms of domestic currency than they would otherwise have been. If domestic prices are unaffected—or affected less— this means a higher price of foreign goods relative to domestic goods, which stimulates exports and discourages imports.

The rise in prices of foreign goods will, it is argued, mean a rise in the cost of living, and this, in turn, will give rise to a demand for wage increases, setting off what is typically referred to as a "wage-price spiral"—a term that is impressive enough to conceal the emptiness of the argument that it generally adorns. In consequence, so the argument continues, prices of domestic goods rise as much as prices of foreign goods, relative prices remain unchanged, there are no market forces working toward the elimination of the deficit that initially caused the decline in the exchange rate, and so further declines in the exchange rate are inevitable until nonmarket forces are brought into play. But these might as well have been used before as after the decline in the exchange rate.

This argument clearly applies only to rather special circumstances. At most, it may be an objection to a particular country at a particular time allowing its currency to go free; it is not a general objection to a *system* of flexible exchange rates as a long-run structure. It does not apply to circumstances making for the appreciation of a currency and applies only to some circumstances making for depreciation. Suppose, for example, that the tendency toward a deficit were produced by monetary deflations in other countries. The depreciation of the currency would then prevent the fall in external prices from being transmitted to the country in question; it would prevent prices of foreign goods from being forced down in terms of domestic currency. There is no way of eliminating the effect of the lowered "real" income of other countries; flexible exchange rates prevent this effect from being magnified by monetary disturbances. Similarly, the argument has little relevance if the decline in exchange rates reflects an open inflationary movement at home; the depreciation is then an obvious result of inflation rather than a cause. The argument has perhaps most relevance in either of two cases: an inflationary situation being repressed by direct controls or a depreciation produced by a change in the "real" conditions of trade.

Even in these cases, however, the argument cannot be fully granted. The crucial fallacy is the so-called "wage-price spiral." The rise in prices of foreign goods may add to the always plentiful list of excuses for wage increases; it does not in and of itself provide the economic conditions for a wage rise—or, at any rate, for a wage rise without unemployment. A general wage rise—or a general rise in domestic prices—becomes possible only if the monetary authorities create the additional money to finance the higher level of prices.[10] But if the monetary authorities are ready to do so to validate any rise in particular prices or wages, then the situation is fundamentally unstable without a change in the exchange rate, since a wage rise for any other excuse would lead to similar consequences. The assumption is that to him who asks will be given, and there is never a shortage of willingness to ask under such circumstances.

It will be answered that this innate instability is held in check by some sort of political compromise and that this compromise would be disturbed by the change in the exchange rate. This is a special case of the general argument considered earlier that

10. In principle, there are other possibilities related to the "velocity of circulation" of money that I neglect to simplify the argument; they do not change its essence.

the government is more likely to resist political pressure to take inflationary action if it nails its flag to the mast of a rigid exchange rate than if it lets the exchange rate fluctuate. But note that the forces leading to a changed exchange rate are not eliminated by freezing the rate; foreign exchange will have to be acquired or economized somehow. The "real" adjustment must be made in one way or another; the question is only how. Why should this way of making the adjustment destroy the compromise while other ways do not? Or, if this is true for a time, can it be expected to continue to be true? If, as we have argued, flexible exchange rates are the least costly way of making the adjustment, will not other methods be even more likely to destroy a tenuous political compromise?

C. FLEXIBLE EXCHANGE RATES AND THE TIMING OF ADJUSTMENT

The ultimate adjustment to a change in external circumstances will consist of a change in the allocation of productive resources and in the composition of the goods available for consumption and investment. But this ultimate change will not be achieved immediately. It takes time to shift from the production of goods for domestic consumption to the production of goods for export, or conversely; it takes time to establish new markets abroad or to persuade consumers to substitute a foreign for a domestic good to which they have been accustomed; and so on in endless variety. The time required will vary widely: some types of adaptations can take place instantaneously (e.g., curtailment by a high price of the purchase of imported cheese, though even here the price rise required to achieve a given curtailment will be higher at first than after a time when people have had a chance to adapt their habitual pattern of consumption to the new price); other types of adaptation may take a generation (e.g., the development of a new domestic industry to produce goods formerly imported).

Suppose a substantial change in (real) external circumstances to occur and, to keep matters simple, circumstances thereafter to remain essentially unchanged for a lengthy period, so that we can (conceptually) isolate the adaptation to this one change.

Suppose, further, that exchange rates are flexible and that international "capital" or "speculative" transactions are impossible, so that payments on current account must balance—a condition it is admittedly difficult to define precisely in any way susceptible to observation. It is clear that the initial change in exchange rates will be greater than the ultimate change required, for, to begin with, all the adjustment will have to be borne in those directions in which prompt adjustment is possible and relatively easy. As time passes, the slower-moving adjustments will take over part of the burden, permitting exchange rates to rebound toward a final position which is between the position prior to the external change and the position shortly thereafter. This is, of course, a highly oversimplified picture: the actual path of adjustment may involve repeated overshooting and undershooting of the final position, giving rise to a series of cycles around it or to a variety of other patterns. We are here entering into an area of economics about which we know very little, so it is fortunate that a precise discussion of the path is not essential for our purposes.

Under these circumstances it clearly might be in the interests of the community to pay something to avoid some of the initial temporary adjustments: if the exchange rate depreciates, to borrow from abroad at the going interest rate to pay for an excess of imports while the slower-moving adjustments take place rather than making the full immediate adjustment by curtailing those imports that can be readily curtailed and forcing out those exports that can be readily increased; if the exchange rate appreciates, to lend abroad at the going interest rate to finance an excess of exports while the slower-moving adjustments take place rather than making the full immediate adjustment by expanding those imports that can be readily expanded and curtailing those exports that can be readily curtailed. It would not, however, be worth doing this indefinitely, even if it were possible. For, if it were carried to the point at which the exchange rate remained unchanged, no other adjustments at all would take place. Yet the change in external circumstances makes a new allocation of resources and composition of goods optimal for the country concerned. That is, there is some optimum pace and timing of adjustment through exchange-rate-induced changes in the allocation of resources which is neither at the extreme of full immediate adjustment in this way alone nor at the other extreme of complete avoidance of adjustment.

Under a flexible exchange-rate system with a reasonably broad and free market in foreign exchange and with correct foresight on the part of speculators, just such an intermediate pace and timing of adjustment is produced even if there is no explicit negotiation of foreign loans. If the exchange rate depreciates, for example, the tendency for the exchange rate to fall further initially than ultimately offers an opportunity to make a profit by buying the currency now and reselling it later at a higher price. But this is precisely equivalent to lending by speculators to the country whose currency has depreciated. The return to the speculators is equal to the rate at which the currency they hold appreciates. In a free market with correct foresight, this will tend, aside from the minor costs of buying or selling the foreign exchange, to approach the interest rate that speculators could earn in other ways. If the currency appreciates at more than this rate, speculators still have an incentive to add to their holdings; if it appreciates at less than this rate, it is costing the speculators more in foregone interest to hold the balances than they are gaining in the appreciation of the exchange rate. In this way, speculation with a flexible exchange rate produces the same effect as explicit borrowing by a country whose currency has depreciated or explicit lending by one whose currency has appreciated. In practice, of course, there will be both explicit lending or borrowing and implicit lending or borrowing through exchange speculation. Moreover, the prospect of appreciation of a currency is equivalent to a higher interest rate for loans to the country and thus serves the same function in attracting capital to that country as the rises in interest rate that took place under the gold standard when a country was losing gold. There is, however, this important difference: under flexible exchange rates the inducement to foreign lenders need involve no change in the interest rate on domestic loans; under the gold standard, it did—a particular example of the independence of domestic monetary policy under flexible exchange rates.

But is the pace and timing of adjustment achieved in this way under flexible exchange rates an approximation to the optimum? This is an exceedingly difficult question to answer, depending as it does on whether the interest rate implicitly paid in the form of the appreciation or depreciation of the currency reflects the full relevant costs of too rapid or too slow adjustment. About all one can say without much more extensive analysis, and perhaps even with such analysis, is that there seems no reason to expect the timing or pace of adjustment under the assumed conditions to be systematically biased in one direction or the other from the optimum or to expect that other techniques of adaptation—through internal price changes, direct controls, and the use of monetary reserves with rigid exchange rates— would lead to a more nearly optimum pace and timing of adjustment.

This much would probably be granted by most persons who argue that flexible exchange rates lead to an undesirable pace and timing of adjustment. But, they would maintain, the foreign-exchange market is not nearly so perfect, or the foresight of speculators so good, as has been assumed to this point. The argument already considered, that speculation in foreign exchanges is destabilizing, is an extreme form of this objection. For, in that case, the immediate change in the foreign-exchange rate must go far enough to produce an immediate adaptation sufficient not only to balance current transactions but also to provide payment in foreign currencies for the balances of domestic currency that speculators perversely insist on liquidating when the exchange rate falls, or to provide the domestic currency for the balances speculators perversely insist on accumulating when the exchange rate rises. The country lends, as it were, when it should be borrowing and borrows when it should be lending.

But one need not go this far. Speculation may be stabilizing on balance, yet the market for foreign exchange, it can be said, is so narrow, foresight so imperfect, and private speculation so dominated by socially irrelevant political considerations that there is an insufficient smoothing-out of the adjustment process. For this to be a valid argument against flexible exchange rates, even if true, there must be some alternative that promises a better pace and timing of adjustment. We have already considered several other possibilities. We have seen that direct controls with a rigid exchange rate and the official use of monetary reserves have striking defects of their own, at least under modern conditions; they are likely to produce a highly erratic pace and timing of adjustment with alternate fits of unduly slow and unduly rapid adjustments, and direct controls are besides likely to produce the wrong kind of adjustments. Private capital movements in response to interest-rate differentials were at one time a real alternative but have been rendered largely unavailable by the unwillingness of monetary authorities to permit the required changes in interest rates, by the loss of confidence in the indefinite maintenance of the fixed exchange rates, and by the fear of restrictions on the use of exchange. In any event, such capital movements are, as we have seen, available and at least as likely to take place under flexible exchange rates.

The plausibility of the view that private exchange speculation produces too little smoothing of exchange-rate fluctuations derives, I believe, primarily from an implicit tendency to regard any slowing-down of the adjustment process as an improvement; that is, implicitly to regard no adjustment at all or an indefinitely prolonged one as the ideal.[11] This is the counterpart of the tendency to believe that internal monetary policy can and should avoid all internal adjustments in the level of income.[12] And both,

11. An interesting example is provided by an argument for 100 per cent banking reserves under a gold standard given by James E. Meade, *The Balance of Payments,* Vol. I of *The Theory of International Economic Policy* (Oxford: Oxford University Press, 1951), p. 185. Meade argues correctly that with 100 per cent reserves the internal adaptations consequent on an external change of any given size will be at a slower rate than with a lower reserve ratio. On this ground, he says, 100 per cent reserves are better than fractional reserves. But this conclusion follows only if any slowing-down in the rate of internal adaptation is an improvement, in which case 200 per cent reserves or their equivalent ("sterilization" of gold imports and exports) would be better than 100 per cent, and so on indefinitely. Given that there is some optimum rate of adjustment, all one can say is that there exists some reserve ratio that would tend to produce this rate of adjustment and so be optimal on these grounds alone; I see no way of knowing on the basis of the considerations Meade presents whether this ratio would be 5 per cent or 500 per cent.

12. See "The Effects of a Full-Employment Policy on Economic Stability: A Formal Analysis," *supra,* pp. 117–32, for a more detailed consideration of the for-

I suspect, are a manifestation of the urge for security that is so outstanding a feature of the modern world and that is itself a major source of insecurity by promoting measures that reduce the adaptability of our economic systems to change without eliminating the changes themselves.

III. SPECIAL PROBLEMS IN THE ESTABLISHMENT AND OPERATION OF A FLEXIBLE EXCHANGE-RATE SYSTEM
A. ROLE OF GOVERNMENTS IN THE EXCHANGE MARKET

The argument that private exchange speculation will not produce a sufficient smoothing of exchange fluctuations is sometimes used to justify, not rigid exchange rates, but extensive intervention by individual governments or international agencies in the exchange market to even out minor fluctuations in exchange rates and to counter capital flights.[13] Such intervention, it should be noted, is in no way necessary for the operation of a flexible exchange-rate system; the issue is solely whether it is desirable. Private traders could buy and sell exchange at prices determined entirely by private demands and offers. Arbitrageurs would keep cross-rates in line. Futures markets would exist—and should be encouraged—to provide facilities for hedging. Markets like these now exist wherever they are permitted, and there is ample experience to demonstrate that they would expand rapidly and efficiently as the area in which they were permitted to operate widened.

Two separate issues are involved in judging the desirability of governmental intervention:[14] first, what, if any, restrictions on governments are desirable as part of an international agreement for establishing a system of flexible exchange rates; second, what behavior is desirable for an individual nation in its own interests.

From the international point of view, the fundamental requirement is that governments not use restrictions on trade of any kind to protect exchange rates. If they wish to use their reserves

---

mal problem involved in both internal and external policy and for some examples of this tendency.

13. See Meade, *op. cit.,* pp. 218–31.

14. I owe this distinction to Robert Triffin.

to speculate in exchange markets, that is primarily their business, provided they do not use the weapons of exchange controls, trade restrictions, and the like to protect their speculations. If they make money in exchange speculations without using such weapons, they perform the useful social function of smoothing out temporary fluctuations. If they lose money, they make gifts to other speculators or traders, and the primary cost—though not quite the whole cost—is borne by them.

From the national point of view, on balance it seems to me undesirable for a country to engage in transactions on the exchange market for the purpose of affecting the rate of exchange. I see no reason to expect that government officials will be better judges than private speculators of the likely movements in underlying conditions of trade and, hence, no reason to expect that government speculation will be more successful than private speculation in promoting a desirable pace and timing of adjustment. There is every reason to expect an extensive exchange market to develop and, hence, no need for government participation to assure sufficient speculation. A positive disadvantage of government speculation is the danger that government authorities operating under strong political pressures will try to peg the exchange rate, thereby converting a flexible exchange-rate system into a system of rigid rates subject to change from time to time by official action. Even if this does not occur, the continuous possibility that it may is likely to hinder the fullest development of a private market.

At the same time one cannot be dogmatic about this issue. It may be that private speculation is at times destabilizing for reasons that would not lead government speculation to be destabilizing; for example, government officials may have access to information that cannot readily be made available, for security or similar reasons, to private speculators. In any event, it would do little harm for a government agency to speculate in the exchange market provided it held to the objective of smoothing out temporary fluctuations and not interfering with fundamental adjustments. And there should be a simple criterion of success —whether the agency makes or loses money.

There is one qualification that needs to be made to this generally negative conclusion about the desirability of government intervention: a case can be made for government speculation in response to a capital flight produced by a threat of successful invasion of one country by another, and this even if private individuals correctly assess the threat. Suppose everybody agrees that there is, say, one chance in four of a successful invasion. Private individuals will have a strong incentive separately to get capital out of the country. They cannot, of course, in the aggregate do so except in so far as they can literally ship physical goods out of the country into storage elsewhere or can induce foreigners to purchase from them physical capital (or claims to it) in the country. In the attempt to do the latter, they would drive down the rate of exchange. Suppose now that the government has reserves of foreign exchange. It can transfer these to its citizens by buying its own currency and thereby keep up the rate of exchange. If the invasion does not occur, the foreign-exchange reserves will tend to be repatriated, and the government will make money. On the other hand, if the invasion does occur and is successful, the government will lose, in a bookkeeping sense, and the expected loss will be greater than the expected gain. However, in this case the government may figure that all is lost anyway and that, if it had not transferred its reserves to its citizens, it would be forced to transfer them to the enemy. The incentives may therefore be different to the government than to its private citizens considered separately. Even this case, however, is not thoroughly clear. If there is hope of resistance, the government will want to mobilize all the foreign exchange it can to use in promoting the military effort.

B. ROLE OF EUROPEAN PAYMENTS UNION AND INTERNATIONAL MONETARY FUND IN A SYSTEM OF FLEXIBLE EXCHANGE RATES

The transition to flexible exchange rates might be organized in stages involving, first, the introduction of flexible exchange rates and free convertibility within Europe with a continuance of discrimination against the dollar and, as a later stage, free convertibility with the dollar. If this were done, the European Payments Union would retain the extremely important function of policing such a separation. When the separation was removed, EPU would lose its special functions. If it were continued at all, its only remaining functions would be as a check-clearing institution and as a body able to give advice to individual countries and to facilitate international consultation.

On the other hand, it is worth emphasizing that there is nothing essential in EPU arrangements that would be an obstacle to flexible exchange rates. The debits and credits could perfectly well be calculated in terms of an exchange rate changing from day to day. The only cost would be complication of the arithmetical calculations.

These comments apply equally to the International Monetary Fund, with, however, one important difference. The statutes of the IMF are designed for a world of exchange rates determined by government action and subject to major change only after consultation and discussion (changes of 10 per cent are permitted without consultation); indeed, the decision to adopt this technique of exchange-rate determination is, I believe, the major mistake made in postwar international economic policy. The explicit adoption of a system of flexible exchange rates might therefore require a major rewriting of the statutes of the IMF.

There is some evidence, however, that the IMF is giving way on its former insistence on announced parities. Most recently, it has acceded to the Canadian decision to have a floating rate for the Canadian dollar—with, it is true, the qualification that the floating rate is to be regarded as a temporary expedient until a satisfactory parity rate can be determined. Given the will, it may well be that some means could be found of interpreting the present statutes so that they would offer no effective obstacle to a system of flexible rates. And the apparent success of the Canadian experiment may help to produce the will.

There remains the question what, if any, functions the IMF would have in a world of flexible rates. As implied earlier, some proponents of flexible rates would have the IMF act as an international exchange equalization fund, speculating in exchange markets under instructions to make as much money as possible. This seems to me highly undesirable; any doubts about the advisability of national equalization funds are multiplied many fold for an international fund subject to political pressures from many governments. Could it, for example, really be in a position to sell a depreciating currency of a major country because of a belief that unwise internal policy would lead to still further depreciation?

If it is not given this function, the ones that might remain are to serve as a short-term international lender of funds along commercial lines, though I see no particular need for such an institution in a world of fully convertible currencies; to provide advice about internal monetary and fiscal policy; and possibly to serve as some kind of clearing agency.

C. ROLE OF GOLD IN A SYSTEM OF FLEXIBLE EXCHANGE RATES

A system of flexible exchange rates is incompatible with the existence in more than one country of a fixed nominal price of gold and free convertibility of currency into gold and gold into currency. The logical domestic counterpart of flexible exchange rates is a strict fiduciary currency changed in quantity in accordance with rules designed to promote domestic stability.[15] Gold could be used as part of the "backing" for such a currency, provided it was not bought and sold at a fixed price; its monetary role would then be purely fictional and psychological, designed to promote "confidence."

A fixed price for gold could, however, be maintained in one country without interfering with flexible exchange rates. The United States now has such a fixed price, and it could retain it. If it did so, other countries could use gold for the settlement of international payments, since this would be equivalent to using dollars. In so far as the United States bought gold net, it would be providing dollars to other countries, getting in return gold to be added to its hoards in Fort Knox; and, conversely, if it sold gold. There seems no reason why the United States should follow this policy. It seems better that any dollar aid that it gives should be given directly and openly on the basis of explicit legislative authorization, without requiring other countries to use resources

15. See "A Monetary and Fiscal Framework for Economic Stability," *supra,* pp. 133–56, and "Commodity-Reserve Currency," *infra,* pp. 204–50.

in acquiring gold, ultimately in digging it out of the ground so that it can be reburied in Fort Knox.

A much better alternative is to have a free gold market. There is no reason why people who want to hold gold should not be permitted to do so and no reason why speculation in gold should be discouraged. In this case, gold would lose its place in official monetary systems and become a commodity like all others. For a long time, however, it would be a rather special commodity, widely regarded as a highly safe means of keeping a liquid reserve—safer than most domestic currencies in terms of real value. Its availability for this purpose would serve the useful function of inhibiting inflationary currency issue, at the cost, however, of introducing an additional element of instability. Any fear of inflation would lead to widespread substitution of gold for currency, thereby speeding up the inflation but also reducing the resources capable of being acquired by inflationary currency issue and hence the pressure to resort to it.

These are highly dogmatic statements on an exceedingly complex issue. They are included here primarily to indicate the range of problems involved rather than as a comprehensive analysis of them.

D. THE STERLING AREA

The sterling area raises a rather special problem in connection with the establishment of flexible exchange rates, since the sterling area includes a number of different currencies linked by fixed exchange rates and convertible one into the other. Sterling could be integrated into a world of flexible exchange rates in either of two ways: (1) flexible exchange rates could be instituted within the sterling area as well as between sterling and other currencies or (2) fixed exchange rates could be retained within the sterling area.

The above analysis of a world of flexible exchange rates applies in full to the first method of handling the sterling area. However, for both financial and political reasons there is likely to be a strong and entirely understandable preference on the part of the British for the second method. As the center of the sterling area, Britain can make the most out of its banking facilities and experience, command relatively cheap credit, and exercise a considerable degree of commercial and political influence, to mention only the most obvious reasons.

In principle there is no objection to a mixed system of fixed exchange rates within the sterling area and freely flexible rates between sterling and other countries, *provided* that the fixed rates within the sterling area can be maintained without trade restrictions. There are numerous examples of such mixed systems in the past.[16] And it may well be desirable to take the attainment of such a mixed system as the immediate goal of policy. Its attainment would remove the obstacle presented by fixed exchange rates to the liberalization of trade by continental European countries and would permit observation of the operation of the two different systems side by side.

At the same time the dangers inherent in such a policy objective should be clearly recognized. These are of two kinds: (1) such a mixed system may not be viable under current political and economic conditions and (2) Britain may be unwilling to accept such a mixed system, since it may feel that freeing the exchange rate of the pound sterling would increase the difficulty of maintaining the sterling area.

The problem of maintaining fixed exchange rates within the sterling area without restrictions on trade differs only in degree

16. In a sense, any flexible exchange system is such a mixed system, since there are rigid rates between the different sections of one nation—between, say, the different states of the United States. The key difference for present purposes between the different states of the United States, on the one hand, and the different members of the sterling area, on the other, is that the former are, while the latter are not, all effectively subject to a single central fiscal and monetary authority—the federal government—having ultimate fiscal and monetary powers. In addition, the former have, while the latter have not, effectively surrendered the right to impose restrictions on the movements of goods, people, or capital between one another. This is a major factor explaining why a central monetary authority is able to operate without producing serious sectional strains. Of course, these are questions of economic fact, not of political form, and of degree, not of kind. A group of politically independent nations all of which firmly adhered to, say, the gold standard would thereby in effect submit themselves to a central monetary authority, albeit an impersonal one. If, in addition, they firmly adhered to the free movement of goods, people, and capital without restrictions, and economic conditions rendered such movement easy, they would, in effect, be an economic unit for which a single currency—which is the equivalent of rigid exchange rates—would be appropriate.

from the corresponding problem for the world as a whole. In both cases the area includes a number of sovereign political units with independent final monetary and fiscal authority. In consequence, in both cases, the permanent maintenance of a system of fixed rates without trade restrictions requires the harmonization of internal monetary and fiscal policies and a willingness and ability to meet at least substantial changes in external conditions by adjustments in the internal price and wage structure.

The differences in degree are, of course, important. The smaller extent of the area involved has somewhat divergent effects. On the one hand, it reduces the problem of harmonizing potentially divergent policies; on the other, it means that the area is subjected to larger strains from outside. The composition of the area is perhaps more important than its mere extent. It includes political units that have a long tradition of close co-operation and of mutual confidence, many of the areas are dependencies whose internal policies can be fairly well controlled from the center, and the financial relations among the members of the area are of long standing and have withstood severe strain. The preservation of these relations is considered extremely important, and, in consequence, there is a very real willingness on the part of its members to go a long way in adapting internal policies to common needs. Finally, the area has relatively large currency reserves that can be used to meet temporary strains, and its members have shown considerable willingness to accumulate balances in the currencies of other members.

Many of these differences are, of course, themselves the product of the prior existence of fixed and stable exchange rates. Whatever their cause, there can, I think, be little doubt that on balance they mean that a system of fixed exchange rates has more chance of surviving without trade restrictions in the sterling area than in the world as a whole. But, granted that the prospects are better for the sterling area than for the world as a whole, it does not follow that they are very good. There have already been substantial strains within the sterling area, most notably the drain of supposedly frozen balances and the strains within the sterling area that were among the immmediate reasons for devaluation in 1949. Direct quantitative restrictions on trade have been imposed by some members on imports from others, and indirect restrictions have arisen, through some aspects of state trading and of other selective policies aimed at the foreign balance.

It is hard to see how further serious strains can be avoided in the future. Members of the sterling area are clearly not going to be willing to accumulate indefinitely balances in the currencies of other members. Reserves, no matter how large, cannot eliminate the necessity of adapting to fundamental changes in external conditions. Yet the United Kingdom and most other members of the sterling area are strongly committed to a full-employment policy which greatly limits the possibility of using changes in the internal price and wage structure as a means of adjusting to changes in external conditions. Thus within the sterling area, as in the rest of the world, if exchange-rate adjustments are ruled out, substantial strains are likely to be met sooner or later by direct controls over international trade. In consequence, I am inclined to be pessimistic about the long-run viability without trade restrictions of a sterling area with fixed exchange rates.

There remains the question whether the freeing of the pound would on balance make it more or less difficult to maintain the sterling area. The answer to this question reached in Britain is certain to be a major factor in Britain's willingness to free the pound.

The freeing of the rate for the pound, together with the removal of exchange restrictions and accompanying internal direct controls, would relieve the stress on the sterling area in some ways; in others, increase it. It would relieve the stress by insulating the sterling area as a whole from outside disturbances, and the experience of the 1930's shows how important this can be; by producing a more efficient use of imports and a better allocation of resources between the production of goods for export and for domestic use; and by making sterling a more desirable and useful currency and so increasing the willingness to hold sterling balances. On the other hand, it might increase the stress, at least initially, because of the danger that holders of the present large sterling balances would seek to convert them into dollars or other currencies and because the substitution of a flexible for a nominally fixed rate might reduce the willingness to hold balances more than the elimination of restrictions on use of balances increased the willingness to hold them. If there were any immediate, widespread attempt to shift out of sterling, the rate for the pound might fall drastically unless Britain were willing to use a large part of its reserves to prevent the pound from falling.

This is an exceedingly complex problem that deserves much better-informed and more extensive analysis. The above highly tentative remarks on it are, however, perhaps sufficient to justify the qualified conclusion that, if the immediate problem of the transition could be surmounted, the longer-run effect of a floating pound would be to reduce the stress on the sterling area and thereby increase the chance that it could be viable without trade restrictions—though, even so, the chances do not seem to me to be high.

IV. Some Examples of the Importance of a System of Flexible Exchange Rates

It cannot be too strongly emphasized that the structure and method of determining exchange rates have a vital bearing on almost every problem of international economic relations. It will illustrate this basic proposition and at the same time help to bring out some of the implications of the preceding analysis if we consider the relation of flexible exchange rates to three specific problems of great current importance: (*a*) the promotion of unrestricted multilateral trade; (*b*) the harmonization of internal monetary and fiscal policies; and (*c*) the rearmament drive.

A. UNRESTRICTED INTERNATIONAL TRADE

We have seen that flexible exchange rates are entirely consistent with unrestricted multilateral trade. On the other hand, the absence of flexible exchange rates is almost certain to be incompatible with unrestricted multilateral trade. With rigid exchange rates, any changes in conditions of trade can be met only by changes in reserves, internal prices and monetary conditions, or direct controls over imports, exports, and other exchange transactions. With few exceptions, reserves of European countries are small, and, in any event, the use of reserves is a feasible device only for mild and temporary movements. Primary reliance on changes in the internal price level is undesirable, and, largely for this reason, there is great political reluctance to rely on such changes. Germany, Belgium, and Italy might perhaps be willing to go some way in this direction. England, France, Norway, and some other countries would almost certainly be completely unwilling to allow the level of prices and employment at home to be determined primarily by the vagaries of foreign trade.

The only other alternative to movements in exchange rates is direct control of foreign trade. Such control is therefore almost certain to be the primary technique adopted to meet substantial movements in conditions of international trade so long as exchange rates are maintained rigid. The implicit or explicit recognition of this fact is clearly one of the chief sources of difficulty in attempts to achieve a greater degree of liberalization of trade in Europe; it is reflected in the extensive escape clauses of all recent international agreements; it is dramatically demonstrated by the ultimately successful pressure on the Germans to use direct controls in the exchange crisis of the fall of 1950, despite the general belief that the crisis was temporary and would be over in a matter of months. It is part of the explanation of the pressures for direct controls produced by the rearmament drive.

Suppose that, by some fortunate turn of events, complete liberalization of trade and convertibility of currencies were achieved tomorrow and resulted in equilibrium in the balance of payments of all European countries at existing exchange rates without American aid. Suppose, in consequence, American aid and pressure were permanently removed. I have no hesitancy in predicting that, given the existing system of determination of exchange rates and the present general political and economic environment, direct controls over exports and imports would be reimposed on a large scale within two or three years at the most.

But even this understates the problem raised by fixed exchange rates. Not only is ultimate liberalization of trade almost certain to be inconsistent with rigid and fixed exchange rates in the present state of the world; equally important, the process of moving toward this objective is rendered unduly difficult. There is no way of predicting in advance the precise economic effects of meaningful reductions of trade barriers. All that is clear is that the impact of such reductions will vary from country to country and industry to industry and that many of the impacts will be highly indirect and not at all in the particular areas liberalized. The very process of liberalization will therefore add substantial and unpredictable pressures on balances of payments over and above those that would occur in any event. These pressures would make any system of rigid exchange rates appropriate to the initial position almost certainly inappropriate to the final position and to intermediate positions. And there seems no way to decide on the appropriate final exchange rates in advance; they must be reached by trial and error. Thus, even if the ultimate goal were a new system of rigid exchange rates, it seems almost essential to have flexibility in the interim period. In the absence of such flexibility, liberalization is likely to be brought to an untimely end by the very consequences of any initial successes.

The current political reluctance to use changes in internal price levels and employment to meet external changes is matched by a political reluctance to use changes in exchange rates. But I submit that the reluctance to use changes in exchange rates is on a different level and has a different basis than the reluctance to use internal changes. The reluctance to use changes in exchange rates reflects a cultural lag, the survival of a belief the bases for which have disappeared; it is a consequence of tradition and lack of understanding. The reluctance to use changes in internal price levels and employment, on the other hand, is a new development, a product of harsh experience of the recent past and, for the moment at least, in tune with current economic conditions.

B. HARMONIZATION OF INTERNAL MONETARY AND FISCAL POLICIES

The positive side of the reluctance to use changes in internal price levels and employment to meet external changes is the promotion of internal monetary stability—the avoidance of either inflation or deflation. This is clearly a highly desirable objective for each country separately. But, under a system of rigid exchange rates and unrestricted trade, no country can attain this objective unless *every* other important country with which it is linked directly or indirectly by trade does so as well. If any one country inflates, for example, this tends to increase its imports and reduce its exports. Other countries now start to accumulate currency balances of the inflating country. They must either be willing to accumulate such balances indefinitely—which means they must be willing to continue shipping out goods without a return flow and thus in effect subsidize the inflating country—or they must follow the inflation themselves (or impose import controls). Hence the strong pressure to achieve harmonization of internal monetary policies.

But this pressure has understandably not been matched by a willingness of all countries to submit their internal policy to external control. Why should a country do so when the failure of any one country to co-operate or to behave "properly" would destroy the whole structure and permit it to transmit its difficulties to its neighbors? Really effective "co-ordination" would require essentially either that nations adopt a common commodity monetary standard like gold and agree to submit unwaveringly to its discipline or that some international body control the supply of money in each country, which in turn implies control over at least interest-rate policy and budgetary policy. The first alternative is neither currently feasible nor particularly desirable in the light of our past experience with the gold standard.[17] As to the second alternative, whether feasible or not, is it desirable that such far-reaching powers be surrendered to any authority other than an effective federal government democratically elected and responsible to the electorate?

A system of flexible exchange rates eliminates the necessity for such far-reaching co-ordination of internal monetary and fiscal policy in order for any country separately to follow a stable internal monetary policy. If, under such a system, any one country inflates, the primary effect is a depreciation in its exchange rate. This offsets the effect of internal inflation on its international trade position and weakens or eliminates the tendency for the inflation to be transmitted to its neighbors; and conversely with deflation. Inflation and deflation in any one country will then affect other countries primarily in so far as it affects the real income

17. See "Commodity-Reserve Currency," *infra,* pp. 204–50, for a more extensive discussion of the advantages and disadvantages of a commodity standard.

position of the initial country; there will be little or no effect through purely monetary channels.

In effect, flexible exchange rates are a means of combining interdependence among countries through trade with a maximum of internal monetary independence; they are a means of permitting each country to seek for monetary stability according to its own lights, without either imposing its mistakes on its neighbors or having their mistakes imposed on it. If all countries succeeded, the result would be a system of reasonably stable exchange rates; the substance of effective harmonization would be attained without the risks of formal but ineffective harmonization.

The chance that all countries would succeed is far greater with flexible exchange rates than with a system of rigid exchange rates that is not also a strict commodity standard. For not only do the laggards tend to call the tune under rigid exchange rates by infecting the other countries with which they are linked but also the very existence of this link gives each country an incentive to engage in inflationary action that it would not otherwise have. For, at least in the initial stages, inflationary currency issue enables the issuers to acquire resources not only from within the country but also from without: the rigid rates mean, as we have seen, that other countries accumulate balances of the currency of the inflating country. Under reasonably stable but not rigid rates, this incentive is largely removed, since the rates will remain stable only so long as countries avoid inflationary action. Once they embark on it, a decline in the exchange rates for their currency will replace the accumulation of balances that would have to take place to keep the rates rigid.

C. THE CURRENT REARMAMENT DRIVE

A particular example of the preceding problem is provided by the present rearmament drive. A really serious rearmament drive is almost certain to produce inflationary pressure, differing in degree from country to country because of differences in fiscal structures, monetary systems, temper of the people, the size of the rearmament effort, etc. With rigid exchange rates, these divergent pressures introduce strains and stresses that are likely to interfere with the armament effort. Country *A*, let us say, has more inflationary pressure than *B,* and *B* more than *C. B* will tend to find its exports to *A* expanding at the same time that its exports to *C* are falling and its imports from *C* expanding. Over all it may be in balance, but it is not in particular industries. It will be under strong pressure to impose export controls on products that it tends to export to *A* and at the same time import controls on products it imports from *C.* Under flexible exchange rates neither might have been necessary; its currency would appreciate relative to *A*'s currency and depreciate relative to *B*'s, thus offsetting both distortions in its trade patterns—distortions because by assumption the changes were produced primarily by differences in the rate of monetary expansion.

This kind of phenomenon is, I believe, one of the important factors that has made for resistance to the removal of import controls and for renewed pressure for export controls, though clearly there are other factors involved as well.

Of course, the rearmament drive will require changes in the structure of trade for technical and physical reasons and not merely for monetary reasons. It is essential for the efficiency of the armament effort that such changes be permitted. Under flexible exchange rates they would tend to be the primary ones. Monetary expansion in any country produces a general increase in demand for imports and a general reduction in supply of exports and so, with flexible exchange rates, is reflected primarily in exchange rates. On the other hand, the rearmament effort involves a shift of demand from some products to others and need involve no change in aggregate money demand. In consequence, particular prices rise relative to other prices, thereby providing the incentive for the required changes in production and trade. Even if the rearmament effort is financed by means that involve an increased aggregate money demand, it will mean a much greater increase in demand for some products than others and so can still lead to the required changes in *relative* prices.

V. Conclusion

The nations of the world cannot prevent changes from occurring in the circumstances affecting international transactions. And they would not if they could. For many changes reflect natural changes in weather conditions and the like; others arise from the freedom of countless individuals to order their lives as they will, which it is our ultimate goal to preserve and widen; and yet others contain the seeds of progress and development. The prison and the graveyard alone provide even a close approximation to certainty.

The major aim of policy is not to prevent such changes from occurring but to develop an efficient system of adapting to them—of using their potentialities for good while minimizing their disruptive effects. There is widespread agreement, at least in the Western world, that relatively free and unrestricted multilateral trade is a major component of such a system, besides having political advantages of a rather different kind. Yet resounding failure has so far marked repeated attempts to eliminate or reduce the extensive and complex restrictions on international trade that proliferated during and immediately after World War II. Failure will continue to mark such attempts so long as we allow implicit acceptance of an essentially minor goal—rigid exchange rates—to prevent simultaneous attainment of two major goals: unrestricted multilateral trade and freedom of each country to pursue internal stability after its own lights.

There are, after all, only four ways in which the pressures on balances of payments produced by changes in the circumstances affecting international transactions can be met: (1) by counterbalancing changes in currency reserves; (2) by adjustments in the general level of internal prices and incomes; (3) by adjustments in exchange rates; and (4) by direct controls over transactions involving foreign exchange.

The paucity of existing currency reserves makes the first impractical for all but very minor changes unless some means can be found to increase the currency reserves of the world enormously. The failure of several noble experiments in this direction is testimony to the difficulty of this solution.

The primacy everywhere attached to internal stability makes the second method one that would not be permitted to operate; the institutional rigidities in internal price structures make it undesirable that it should be the major means of adjustment.

The third—at least in the form of a thoroughgoing system of

flexible rates—has been ruled out in recent years without extensive explicit consideration, partly because of a questionable interpretation of limited historical evidence; partly, I believe, because it was condemned alike by traditionalists, whose ideal was a gold standard that either ran itself or was run by international central bankers but in either case determined internal policy, and by the dominant strain of reformers, who distrusted the price system in all its manifestations—a curious coalition of the most unreconstructed believers in the price system, in all its other roles, and its most extreme opponents.

The fourth method—direct controls over transactions involving foreign exchange—has in this way, by default rather than intention, been left the only avenue whereby pressures on balances of payments can be met. Little wonder that these controls have so stubbornly resisted elimination despite the repeated protestations that they would be eliminated. Yet this method is, in my view, by all odds the least desirable of the four.

There are no major economic difficulties to prevent the prompt establishment by countries separately or jointly of a system of exchange rates freely determined in open markets, primarily by private transactions, and the simultaneous abandonment of direct controls over exchange transactions. A move in this direction is the fundamental prerequisite for the economic integration of the free world through multilateral trade.

Commodity-Reserve Currency[*]

CURRENCY arrangements have frequently been in a state of confusion and change, but seldom to so great an extent as in the period since the end of World War II. On the one hand, the Western nations have agreed, through the International Monetary Fund, to erect an international currency by maintaining essentially rigid exchange rates between national currencies; on the other hand, they have refused to make their national currencies fully convertible into some common medium such as gold at fixed rates and on demand. They have insisted on maintaining a considerable amount of freedom in national monetary policy. The resulting system of currency standards—if, indeed, it can be called a "system"—has provided neither the favorable environment for international trade offered by a truly international currency nor the freedom from external monetary disturbances of truly national currencies. It has rather combined the worst features of the two standards—the rigidity of an international standard and the caprice and uncertainty of national standards. The absence of satisfactory currency standards has been an important—indeed, in my view, the most important —obstacle to the elimination of direct controls over international trade and to the growth of multilateral trade, free from government control and intervention.

The alternatives available include, at the one extreme, restoration of a "real" gold standard; at the other, national fiat currencies linked by flexible exchange rates freely determined in private markets. The first extreme has been widely regarded as "outmoded"; yet, paradoxically, the prestige of gold has seldom, if ever, been as high as it is currently, despite—or, perhaps, because of —the almost complete disappearance of free convertibility of currencies into gold. The second extreme runs directly counter to the agreements under the International Monetary Fund and, far more important, bears the odium of repeated

* Reprinted from *Journal of Political Economy*, LIX (June, 1951), 203–32.

experiences of currency depreciation under fiat standards. These circumstances help explain both the existing hybrid standards and the attention that has been devoted to attempts to construct satisfactory currency arrangements that would avoid both extremes.

One such arrangement that has received significant intellectual support is the commodity-reserve monetary standard proposed and championed by Benjamin Graham and by Frank D. Graham.[1] This standard is a member of the same broad species of monetary systems as the gold standard (Sec. I) but has characteristics of its own that deserve special attention (Sec. II). It is doubtful, however, that these characteristics make it preferable either to the gold standard or to the particular fiat standard with which it is compared in Section III below.

I. COMMODITY STANDARDS IN GENERAL

The central feature of a commodity standard is that the medium of exchange consists either of a commodity (or group of commodities) in physical form—full-bodied "coins"— or of titles to designated physical quantities of a commodity (or group of commodities). The standard may be said to be a *strict*

1. See Benjamin Graham, *Storage and Stability* (New York: McGraw-Hill Book Co., 1937), and *World Commodities and World Currency* (New York: McGraw-Hill Book Co., 1944) ; Frank D. Graham, *Social Goals and Economic Institutions* (Princeton, N.J.: Princeton University Press, 1942), pp. 94–119.

It should be noted that the two Grahams espoused the proposal for somewhat different reasons. To Benjamin Graham the monetary aspects of commodity reserves were secondary; his primary interest was in its contribution to the "problem of raw materials" and of "burdensome surpluses," whatever they may be. To Frank Graham the monetary aspects were primary.

A recent study by the Stanford Food Research Institute examines Benjamin Graham's proposal in great detail and contains two chapters by Edward S. Shaw on the method of financing commodity purchases (M. K. Bennett and associates, *International Commodity Stockpiling as an Economic Stabilizer* [Stanford, Calif.: Stanford University Press, 1949]). However, Bennett and his associates restrict themselves entirely to the stock-piling aspects of the proposal. They view it as simply added to existing monetary arrangements and explicitly eschew analysis of the proposal as a basic monetary reform. The present paper, on the other hand, is devoted almost entirely to the latter aspect of the proposal. In consequence, although initially written without knowledge of or reference to the Stanford study, the present paper turned out neither to duplicate nor to conflict with it but rather to be entirely complementary.

commodity standard if either no titles are used or any that are used are literal warehouse certificates for the designated quantities of the monetary commodity. It is a *partial commodity standard* if titles are used that are not literal warehouse certificates. In general, such titles take the form of claims to the monetary commodity issued by public or private institutions that attempt to insure redemption by holding "reserve" stocks of the monetary commodity smaller in amount than the total of outstanding claims.

Monetary history records a bewildering variety of commodities that have served as mediums of exchange—from the wampum beads used by American Indians to the cigarettes and cognac used in Germany after World War II. At the same time, strict commodity standards have been rare in modern times; the major part of the circulating medium typically has been evidences of debt, generally in the form of claims to nonexistent stocks of the monetary commodity or commodities.

A. STRICT COMMODITY STANDARDS

Under a strict commodity standard the supply of currency and the prices of other goods in terms of the currency commodity are determined entirely in the market by the demand for the commodity for monetary and other uses and by the supply of the commodity, which is ultimately governed by costs of production. Government action is not required, though government may provide the service of certifying the quality and quantity of the currency commodity or of issuing or certifying warehouse receipts, or may designate the commodity or commodities to be used as currency. Indeed, strict commodity currencies have sometimes arisen because of the collapse of the official currency (e.g., German postwar cigarette currency).

In equilibrium, the cost of producing a unit of the currency commodity is equal at the margin to a unit of the commodity. This equilibrium will be disturbed by anything that changes the cost (in terms of the currency commodity) of producing the currency commodity. For our purposes, such changes can be divided into those that arise from changes in technological conditions of production and all others.

Changes in technological conditions of production will tend to produce permanent changes in the price level of final products if they change the cost of producing the currency commodity relative to the cost of producing other commodities. For example, if discovery or invention makes the production of the currency commodity relatively cheap, its cost of production will fall below its price, output will be stimulated, and the supply of the currency will tend to increase at a greater rate than that required to keep prices stable. Equilibrium will be restored when the increased supply of currency has raised the prices of other commodities, and hence the cost of production of the currency commodity, sufficiently to reduce the output of the currency commodity to its normal level. Technological change will leave the equilibrium price level of final products unchanged only if it affects the cost of production of the currency and of other commodities alike and so does not affect their relative cost. For example, if the costs of both groups of commodities decline, prices of other commodities will initially decline; and the output of the currency commodity will expand to a level above normal. Equilibrium will be restored when the increase in the supply of currency has brought prices back to their original level.

Changes in the cost of producing the currency commodity that arise from changes in prices in response to shifts in demand, the velocity of circulation of money, and the like set in motion corrective, countercyclical forces. A rise in the prices of other goods increases the cost of producing the currency commodity and so tends to reduce the current rate of production; it also makes the currency commodity relatively cheap for nonmonetary uses and thus tends to reduce the fraction of the existing stock used for monetary purposes. Both effects tend to halt and reverse the rise in prices. Similarly, a fall in the prices of other goods tends to increase the current rate of production of the currency commodity and to increase the fraction of the existing stock used for monetary purposes, and both effects tend to halt or reverse the fall in prices.[2]

2. The statements in this and the preceding paragraph are exact only if the industry producing the currency commodity is a (long-run) constant-cost industry. Otherwise, changes in demand would tend also to change the price level by chang-

Because current output of the currency commodity is generally a small fraction of the existing stock, deviations from equilibrium can be substantial; and a relatively long time may be required to correct them. Considerable movements in the price level can thus take place even in the absence of any changes in technological conditions. The equilibrating forces will clearly be stronger, the higher the short-run elasticity of supply of the currency commodity and the greater the sensitivity of expenditures to changes in the quantity of currency.

The offsetting or countercyclical effects of a strict commodity currency are of two kinds: direct effects on the income stream and indirect effects through the monetary stock. A decline in other prices not originating from changes in technological conditions will mean or reflect a reduced flow of income. The hiring of resources to produce the currency commodity means a direct addition to the income stream, offsetting in some measure the initial reduction. Conversely, a rise in other prices means an increased flow of income, which is directly offset in some measure by reduced payments to factors of production in the industry producing the currency commodity. Indirect effects flow from the changes in the monetary stock produced by changes in both the fraction of the existing stock used for monetary purposes and the current rate of production. Expenditures are doubtless related to the stock of currency, if only because the currency is regarded as part of the real wealth of the community. A rise in the stock of the currency commodity will stimulate expenditures and so indirectly add to the flow of income, and vice versa.

Under a strict commodity currency, the government obviously cannot finance any expenditures by currency creation. It must balance its budget continuously or else finance any deficit with funds borrowed in the market or taken from previously accumulated hoards of currency and use any surpluses to repay debt or to accumulate hoards of currency. Similarly, the only monetary policy available to the government is the sale of securities for currency and the use of accumulated hoards of

ing the location of the "margin." These complications would not alter the substance of the argument and so are omitted.

currency to buy securities. Such sales or purchases might have considerable effects over short periods. In so far as they did, they would tend to alter prices and thereby induce expansion or contraction in the production of the currency commodity, so that their major effect in the long run would be on the supply of the currency commodity. The freedom of the government would be still further limited if more than one political unit adopted the same commodity or commodities as the standard. The relevant economic unit is then the group of countries, and the above analysis applies to that economic unit as a whole. Exchange rates between countries or, for that matter, within countries can fluctuate within limits determined by the cost of transporting the medium of circulation; wider movements are impossible so long as the countries remain on the identical standard.

In the older literature, discussion of the relative merits of alternative currency commodities largely emphasized the physical characteristics required of a literal medium of circulation—in White's words, "The requisites of a good kind of money are portability, homogeneity, durability, divisibility, cognizability, and stability of value."[3] Today, in judging a monetary standard, we pay little attention to any but the last of these features; we pay primary attention to broader economic consequences—probable movements in the level of prices, the implications of the standard for cyclical behavior, and the like. From this point of view, all strict commodity standards have common virtues and common vices. Perhaps their most important virtue is automaticity and impersonality: they require no forecasting and no administrative or legislative policy decisions. They automatically tend to operate countercyclically—to add to income when it is relatively low and to subtract from income when it is relatively high. The existence of physical costs of production sets limits to the quantity of currency, and so runaway inflation is impossible so long as a commodity standard is adhered to.

The vices of strict commodity standards are the other side of their virtues. Being automatic, they may not provide sufficient flexibility or adaptability to prevent substantial swings in prices or in income. The physical cost of production of currency does

3. Horace White, *Money and Banking* (3d ed.; Boston: Ginn & Co., 1908), p. 15.

not make either moderate inflation or substantial deflation impossible; it means that price movements may be produced by technological changes in the relative cost of production of the currency commodity and that some resources are devoted to the creation of money. This last is doubtless the major reason why strict commodity standards have tended to disappear. The prospect of saving the resources they require is no mean incentive for the invention of less costly methods of providing a circulating medium. For example, it would have required about a 3 per cent per year addition to the circulating medium of the United States over the last fifty years or so to have kept prices stable if the velocity of circulation had remained unchanged. In fact, the velocity of circulation has apparently been declining at the rate of something over 1 per cent per year, which would mean that something over a 4 per cent per year addition to the circulating medium would have been required for stable prices.[4] The circulating medium proper (currency plus demand deposits) is currently about half the national income. It follows that, even if we neglect changes in velocity, something like $1\frac{1}{2}$ per cent of the national income would have had to be devoted to the production of the currency commodities in order for prices to have remained stable under a strict commodity standard. Note that this figure is the same regardless of the commodity or commodities used as the monetary standard. The limitation that a strict commodity standard imposes on national monetary or economic policies is a feature that some will regard as an advantage, others as a disadvantage.

B. ALTERNATIVE STRICT COMMODITY STANDARDS

The relative desirability of different commodities or groups of commodities as currency standards depends in part on the price-level behavior accepted as desirable and in part on the relative importance attached to the various countercyclical reactions under a strict commodity currency.

If a stable price level of final products is taken as the objective—as, for convenience, we shall assume—a desirable com-

4. See Clark Warburton, "The Secular Trend in Monetary Velocity," *Quarterly Journal of Economics*, LXIII (February, 1949), 68–91.

modity or group of commodities would be one that was affected by technological change to the same extent as other commodities, so that it was immune from any technologically induced changes in relative costs of production. Even so, technological or other changes in underlying conditions affecting the demand for, or supply of, the monetary commodity could produce substantial transitional departures from the equilibrium price level unless the monetary supply of the currency commodity or commodities were highly elastic, because of either a large nonmonetary supply that shifted readily into monetary uses or an elastic supply schedule of current output.

The effectiveness of the standard in countering cyclical movements in income depends on the importance of the various countercyclical effects automatically produced by such changes in the level of income. If changes in the fraction of total assets in the form of money have alone a powerful effect on expenditures, then a standard will be highly stabilizing so long as there is a large stock that will readily shift into or out of monetary channels in response to small changes in the prices of other commodities; a highly elastic supply schedule of current output is unnecessary. If changes in the fraction of total assets in the form of money do not have a powerful effect on expenditures but changes in the total volume of assets do, then a large shiftable stock is of little value, and a highly elastic supply schedule of current output is required. Finally, if asset changes are not very powerful, the stabilizing effect of the standard will have to come primarily through its direct contribution to the income stream. This will require that the supply schedule of current output be highly elastic and that the industries producing the currency commodities account for a sizable fraction of the economy's output, so that the volume of resources employed in producing the currency commodities and the corresponding flow of income payments can vary substantially. Over the past few decades increasing importance has been assigned in economic theory—whether rightly or wrongly—to the direct income effect relative to the effect of changes in total assets, and to the effect of changes in the total volume of assets relative to the effect of changes in the composition of assets. In consequence, economists would currently stress the need for a highly elastic current supply produced by sizable industries.

In terms of these criteria, gold and silver—the commodities most widely used as currency—do not rank very well. The discovery of new mines and the special impact of technological change have caused their relative cost of production to shift frequently and sometimes quite drastically. The elasticity of their current supply, while not negligible, is not substantial, at any rate in the short run and over a wide range. A substantial fraction of the output of the industries producing them is devoted to monetary uses, so these industries account for only a small fraction of the economy's total output. They rank reasonably well only in terms of the size of the stock that shifts fairly readily between monetary and nonmonetary uses. They achieved their dominant position primarily, one suspects, because of their more homely virtues—"portability, homogeneity, durability, divisibility, and cognizability." In terms of broader economic criteria they will appear reasonably satisfactory only to one who stresses very highly the effect on expenditures of the fraction of total assets held in the form of money. Their chief recommendation, beyond this, is the symbolism that has been attached to them, which has made it possible for them to afford a real bulwark against government "tinkering."

By contrast, the late Charles O. Hardy always cited common building bricks as perhaps the best available single monetary commodity. The absence of the homely virtues required for the physical use of bricks as a medium of circulation could be remedied by the use of warehouse certificates, which possess these virtues in high measure. Bricks possess the minor virtues required of a commodity to be used as a currency—they can be reasonably well defined and checked for quality, they can be stored, etc. And they have the major virtue of an exceedingly elastic supply. They can be made practically everywhere—Hardy claimed that bricks are made in each of the over three thousand counties in the United States—and require little capital investment or specialized skill. In consequence, the rate of output can be stepped up or down rapidly. There is a large stock—some, indeed, incorporated in buildings—that could be shifted readily from nonmonetary to monetary use and conversely. It follows that, under a brick standard, any decline in the prices of other goods that would tend to make it profitable to produce bricks for monetary use would have a rapid, widespread, and substantial effect on the rate of output and employment in the brick industry. This would provide a powerful offset to any decline in income. Any tendency for prices to rise would similarly tend to be offset by a prompt decline in the rate of output and employment in the brick industry. There is real merit in Hardy's contention that the chief defect of the brick standard is simply the impossibility of getting anyone to think seriously of bricks as money.

Impressed with the deficiencies of gold or silver separately, a number of economists, including Marshall, proposed toward the end of the nineteenth century that the two be wedded in what was called "symmetallism."[5] Under this proposal the currency unit would have been a specified weight of silver plus a specified weight of gold—one can, if one wishes, think of a physical combination of the two in a single bar. The price of silver relative to gold could vary to any extent at all; the price of a particular combination of the two not at all.[6] The broadening of the monetary base achieved under symmetallism would tend to lessen the influence of inventions or discoveries affecting one metal alone and thus would give a less variable price level.

In principle, the ultimate extension of the idea of symmetallism is to include in the standard every commodity and service produced in the economy roughly in proportion to the amounts produced (presumably as measured by "value-added" in their production). This could not be done physically because of problems of storage; but if for a moment we suppose it could, the unit would be a market basket of commodities and services

5. See Alfred Marshall, "Remedies for Fluctuations of General Prices" (1887), reprinted in *Memorials of Alfred Marshall,* ed. A. C. Pigou (London: Macmillan & Co., 1925), pp. 188–211, esp. pp. 204–6. It should be noted that Marshall recommended symmetallism only as superior to either gold or silver alone or to bimetallism; he did not think it much superior to them and preferred other devices, like the tabular standard, to any commodity standard.

6. This scheme should be sharply distinguished from bimetallism—the use as a currency unit of a specified weight of silver *or* a specified weight of gold.

representing in microcosm the total national basket and would provide an almost ideal commodity currency standard. Since the price of this same market basket would be the price index, stability of the price index would be immediately and perfectly attained, though, given the general index number problem, perhaps not stability of the "price level." Technological change could not, at least initially, affect the currency unit differently from aggregate output. The elasticity of current supply of currency would, again at least initially, be essentially infinite in response to any putative change in money income, since any proportionate reduction in output for nonmonetary uses would be in the form required for addition to the money stock, so that the major impact of any change would be on the destination of production rather than its amount or composition. But, even at this obviously impossible extreme, there are difficulties suggested by the phrase "at least initially." The composition of total output would change over time. A currency unit fixed in composition would no longer appropriately represent total output; the fraction of the output devoted to monetary use would vary from commodity to commodity so that technological change could have differential effects on the currency unit; and the elasticity of current supply would be reduced. In view of the small fraction of the current output of each product that would have to be devoted to monetary use, none of these effects would be serious until a very considerable period had elapsed. What they illustrate is simply the impossibility of a complete solution of the index-number problem.

I have cited this extreme primarily because it is the ideal that animates the commodity-reserve scheme and gives it its real appeal. The commodity-reserve scheme is essentially an attempt to go as far in the direction of this ideal as the hard facts of life will permit. Its value and adequacy in large measure hinge on how far in this direction it is possible to go.

C. PARTIAL COMMODITY STANDARDS

As we have seen, in a world in which total output is growing in response to technological and other changes and in which the velocity of circulation is fairly constant, a strict commodity standard requires the regular use of a considerable volume of resources for additions to the monetary stock in order to keep prices stable. To use the example given above, something like $1\frac{1}{2}$ per cent of the resources of the United States would have had to be devoted to the production of currency commodities for monetary use.

It is not surprising, therefore, that the countries of the Western world have not used strict commodity standards. Nominal gold or silver standards have contained a large admixture of fiat elements.[7] In the main, gold (or other currency commodity) has been "economized" through the use of fractional reserves for mediums of circulation in the form of hand-to-hand currency and, even more widely, in the form of demand deposits. That is, convention or law has permitted the issuance of claims to an amount of gold a more or less definite number of times the amount actually available for monetary use. More rarely, notably in the English Banking Act of 1844, gold has been "economized" by providing for a fixed fiduciary issue and requiring that all nominal claims to the currency commodity in excess of that issue be literal warehouse certificates. The conditions under which either of these procedures will in any relevant sense "economize" gold and the senses in which this phrase can be interpreted are subjects that have not yet been adequately explored or analyzed; but we shall pass these fascinating questions by and, instead, examine the consequences of the use of a partial commodity currency.[8]

7. I shall use the term "fiat" to refer both to inconvertible government-issued currency (to which alone the dictionary restricts the term) and to other types of currency that have one essential feature in common with the former, namely, that they are evidences of debt rather than of the existence of specified physical amounts of the currency commodity. In this sense we may regard the "fiat" element in a partial commodity currency as the difference between the total amount of currency outstanding and the monetary value of the reserve stocks of the currency commodity.

8. The naïve notion that there is an immediate and direct "economy" in the use of gold achieved by making gold only a fraction of the total circulating medium is obviously wrong. Assume a fixed initial amount of gold in the monetary stock of a closed economy. Then the only effect of a smaller fractional reserve is a larger quantity of money and a higher price level. Next, suppose the total volume of money must rise by, say, 3 per cent per year to keep prices stable; then, whatever

The introduction of fiat elements into the monetary stock immediately raises the question, Who is to create the fiat currency and control its issuance? Fiat currency is practically costless, whereas commodity currency is not. Under competition there will be a tendency for each kind to be produced up to the point at which its value equals its costs. This sets definite limits to the quantity of a commodity currency; it means indefinite increase in the quantity of a fiat currency and indefinite decrease in its value. There is no stable competitive equilibrium except when the fiat currency declines so much in value that it becomes a commodity currency, the commodity being the paper and services used in producing the currency. Competition is therefore inappropriate for determining the amount of a fiat currency. The production of fiat currency is, as it were, a natural monopoly, which explains why a measure of control has typically been exercised by government, why the privilege of issuing currency has been fought for so vigorously, and why proponents of a private competitive order, like Henry Simons, have held the view—

---

the fractional reserve, so long as the fraction does not change, the gold stock, too, must rise by 3 per cent a year to keep prices steady. Hence, if the initial monetary gold stock were the same, there would be no direct economy here, either, if enough gold were added to keep prices constant. But this needs to be complicated to take account of the forces determining the output of gold. Assume a 100 per cent gold currency in equilibrium in the sense that the annual output of gold is just sufficient to provide for the annual increase in the monetary stock needed to maintain stable prices—say, 3 per cent per year. Let the reserve ratio be changed to 50 per cent. If we temporarily suppose no shifts in the monetary stock of gold to nonmonetary uses, the nominal quantity of money would double, and we may suppose prices to double too. This will decrease the production of gold. The annual output of gold will therefore be less than 3 per cent of the stock; hence gold will be "economized" in the sense that fewer resources will be devoted to its production, but at the expense of instituting a decline in prices. As prices decline, gold production is encouraged, and a new equilibrium will emerge. How gold production in the new position compares with initial gold production depends on the long-run supply conditions in the gold industry. For example, if the supply curve were horizontal, the ultimate equilibrium would involve the production of half as much gold as the initial equilibrium. Further complications arise from shifts in the stock of gold between monetary and nonmonetary uses, as well as from the introduction of a number of national units and the possibility of different fractional reserves in different countries. As even this superficial analysis suggests, the most efficient "economizing" technique is the one that was actually used historically, namely, a steady decline in the fraction of reserves required.

which I share—that the creation of fiat currency should be a government monopoly. This problem of control is seen clearly and faced openly when the fiat element is introduced through a fiduciary issue, as in Peel's Act of 1844. It is less obvious under a fractional reserve system when the fiat elements are produced continuously, in conjunction with changes in the currency commodity, and as part of other activities.

Almost uniformly the provision of the fiat element in the monetary system has been taken over by "banks" as an indistinguishable part of their lending and investing activities. Such a connection is clearly not inevitable. Under a strict commodity currency, there could and would still be lending and borrowing. At the same time, it is no accident that financial institutions have provided at least part of the circulating medium of all advanced countries in the course of performing what they regarded as their primary function of serving as an intermediary between lenders and borrowers. Lenders differ in the kind of security or claim they prefer. Some will wish to keep part or all of their assets in a form immediately available for emergencies and subject to little or no risk of (nominal) capital loss. Borrowers seldom wish to provide securities or claims of this form; they typically require some assurance that repayment will not be demanded before a specified time. Accordingly, there is room for profit for an institution that will borrow on demand and lend on time. It can successfully borrow on demand, however, only if it can convince a class of lenders that it will be able to meet their demands when they occur. If it succeeds in so convincing a fairly large class of lenders, the institution, as an indirect consequence of seeking to meet the desires of lenders, will have created an evidence of debt that is almost ideally suited to serve as a medium of circulation. In the absence of any equally satisfactory alternative or of direct statutory prohibition, it is almost inevitable that the next step will be taken and that the financial institution will seek to make the claims it offers to lenders even more attractive by facilitating their use as a medium of circulation.

The tendency for part of the circulating medium to be created as an incident of the lending and investing activities of "banks" has meant government intervention into these activities in the course of attempts to control the circulating medium. Thus it has meant extension of government control to activities that could appropriately be left to competition if they were not intertwined with the creation of currency.

The introduction of fiat elements into the monetary system, especially through the medium of private financial institutions, almost necessarily means the existence of different kinds of circulating media. This raises a problem of maintaining interconvertibility. The chief device that has been used for this purpose is the attempted provision of two-way convertibility of all other types of currency into the commodity that is ostensibly the currency standard. Thus, under the nineteenth- and early twentieth-century gold standard, the government or one of its agencies offered to buy or sell gold in unlimited amounts at a fixed price in terms of a particular category of currency (usually warehouse certificates or government fiat money), and financial institutions issuing circulating mediums were required to make them convertible into either gold itself or that category of currency. Under this system the potential volume of claims to the currency commodity so created was many times the physical volume available for meeting the claims. As Bagehot pointed out so well, maintenance of the system requires some agency that will not act in its immediate private interest but will maintain an emergency "reserve." This must be the government or an agent of the government, and it must inevitably exercise control over the institutions that create currency.

The existence of several types of currency under a fractional reserve system, together with the maintenance of convertibility into the currency commodity, necessarily spells "inherent instability" in the total volume of currency: a change in the *form* in which the public wishes to keep its currency tends to change the total volume of currency. The reason is that a unit of the currency commodity in "reserve" tends to "support" several units of circulating medium; the same unit in circulation, only a single unit of circulating medium. Put differently, for the type of currency consisting of the physical currency commodity itself or a literal warehouse certificate a 100 per cent reserve is required; for other currency, only a fractional reserve; and typically there have been several classes of currency with different fractional reserve requirements. An attempted shift among any of these classes obviously changes the total volume of circulating medium that can be outstanding, given the total available volume of the currency commodity. Such shifts will certainly take place. When they do, the monetary system is itself converted into a source of instability.

One way to eliminate this inherent instability is to prohibit the use of the currency commodity as a circulating medium, restrict its use to reserves, and make the reserve requirements uniform for all types of currency. The first two steps were taken with gold in the United States after 1933, though without elimination of inherent instability because of failure to take the third step.[9] Essentially, this action involved the abandonment of even a partial commodity currency and the substitution of a strictly fiat currency, along with a buying program for a particular commodity and some fairly loose rules connecting the total amount of fiat currency with the amount of that commodity in storage.

Partial commodity standards thus lead to two major evils: government intervention into lending and investing activities that can appropriately be left to the market and inherent instability in the monetary system. These evils can be eliminated by acceptance of either of two extreme monetary standards: (1) a circulating medium composed entirely of the physical currency commodity or literal warehouse certificates (i.e., a strict commodity currency) or (2) a circulating medium composed entirely of a single kind, or essentially equivalent kinds, of fiat currency. The second would eliminate both evils only if the government monopolized the creation of the fiat currency. If the government did not do so but allowed private banks to create the currency under strict rules that kept the circulating medium uniform, the evil of inherent instability would be eliminated but not the evil of government intervention into lending and investing activities.

9. United States action still left different kinds of circulating mediums with different reserve requirements (in particular, Federal Reserve notes and demand deposits in commercial banks). This was unnecessary. It would have been far better if the ultimate reserve requirements had been made uniform.

Under either a strict commodity standard or a strict fiat standard, the elimination of the twin evils involves essentially the separation of the depositary and check-clearance function of existing banks from their lending and investing activities, that is, what has come to be known as the "100 per cent reserve proposal." This is the only proposal that would permit the lending and investing activities of banks to be left free from government control; and, though it is not the only way to eliminate the inherent instability of the monetary system, it is a satisfactory way. And, it may be added, the most attractive alternative way to eliminate inherent instability—allowing banks to issue both hand-to-hand currency and deposits under the same fractional reserve requirements—has little or no support among economists, bankers, or the public.

Like a strict commodity standard, a partial commodity standard limits the freedom of government with respect to economic and monetary policy. The government can finance some of its expenditures by currency creation and has some measure of freedom with respect to economic and monetary policy, especially if reserves of the currency commodity are fairly large. Ultimately, however, its freedom is limited by the necessity of maintaining convertibility into the commodity used as the currency standard. The range of freedom will be smaller if the same standard prevails in several countries than if it prevails in one country alone, and it may be negligible if the country in question has a small fraction of the economic resources of the currency area and engages in extensive international trade.

II. COMMODITY-RESERVE STANDARD[10]

A. GENERAL CHARACTERISTICS

As already noted, the proposal for a commodity-reserve currency is an attempt to carry the principle of symmetallism as

10. See W. T. M. Beale, Jr., M. T. Kennedy, and W. J. Winn, "Commodity Reserve Currency: A Critique," *Journal of Political Economy*, L (August, 1942), 578–94, for a careful, critical examination of the proposal. This article is reprinted in B. Graham, *World Commodities*, pp. 151–63, along with his answer to it in the *Journal of Political Economy*, February, 1943, pp. 66–69; F. D. Graham also wrote an answer in *Journal of Political Economy*, February, 1943. See also Lloyd

far as is feasible. The basic currency unit would be a market basket of commodities: so many units of commodity X, so many units of commodity Y, etc. To put it differently, the monetary authorities would offer to buy and sell unlimited quantities of a specified bundle of commodities (or perhaps literal warehouse receipts for the specified quantities of the commodities) at fixed prices in terms of nominal currency units—say, to buy the specified bundle at \$95,000 and sell at \$105,000, the difference representing a seignorage charge. While the total price of the commodity bundle would in this way be held within narrow limits, the prices of individual items in the bundle would be free to vary, and, with any large number of items in the bundle, to vary enormously. Any one item or group of items could rise or fall in price so long as other items fell or rose.

The necessity of accumulating bundles of commodities in specified proportions—or bundles of warehouse receipts—would raise no special problem so long as the commodities were openly traded in fairly broadly based markets. Under such circumstances specialists would develop who would act as arbitragers, putting together bundles for sale to the monetary authorities when the total market value of the bundle fell below the official buying price and buying bundles from the monetary authority when the total market value of the bundle rose above the official selling price.

In order to keep the coverage of the commodity bundle as broad and representative as possible, it would probably be desirable to provide for periodic revisions. Since it would be hard to introduce any rigid principle for such revisions, the necessity for them would detract from the automaticity of the scheme and its freedom from political interference. In addition, the adjustments required in reserve stocks to bring their composition in line with the revised commodity bundle might at times involve substantial disturbances in particular markets.

Commodity-reserve currency can be assigned different roles in the currency system as a whole; and any judgment of its

---

W. Mints, *Monetary Policy for a Competitive Society* (New York: McGraw-Hill Book Co., 1950), pp. 159–67; Bennett and associates, *op. cit.*

merits hinges critically on the role it is assigned. At one extreme, commodity-reserve currency could simply be added to existing monetary systems. It would then be primarily a device for supporting the average price of a group of commodities and for providing the equivalent of deficits and surpluses in the government budget at different stages of the business cycle. Any discussion of its operation would have to take account of the character of the associated monetary structure and of the monetary policy of the government in question. In this form the commodity-reserve scheme is better analyzed as a particular countercyclical gadget or as a device for providing government assistance to a particular group of producers than as a basic monetary reform. Therefore, we shall omit any further discussion of it.[11]

An intermediate possibility is the substitution of commodity-reserve currency for what has sometimes been called "high-powered" money—the kinds of currency eligible for use as reserves behind the circulating medium. In the United States this would mean its substitution for Federal Reserve notes and deposits and Treasury currency or perhaps for gold and Treasury currency alone, or, more generally, for the fiat currency issued by the central bank or government or the commodity reserves ostensibly backing them. This would mean a partial commodity standard and, presumably, the retention of existing fractional reserve banking. It follows from our earlier analysis that it could cure neither widespread government intervention into and control over lending and investing activity nor the inherent instability of the monetary system. To get some idea of the quantities involved, it may be noted that "high-powered" money in the United States is currently between one-third and one-half of total currency and demand deposits, or between one-sixth and one-quarter of the annual national income.

At the other extreme, commodity-reserve currency could be adopted as a strict commodity standard. In this form, commod-

11. It should be noted that this is the role envisaged and favored by Benjamin Graham, which explains why the bulk of his writings on commodity reserves is irrelevant for our present purpose. It is also the role examined in detail by Bennett and associates, *op. cit.*

ity-reserve currency would replace all existing currency (including demand deposits). It would be combined with 100 per cent reserve banking so that the twin evils of government intervention into lending and investing activity and of inherent instability would simultaneously be eliminated. This is the most radical use of the scheme and would involve the most fundamental reconstruction of the monetary system.[12]

Whether commodity-reserve currency is designed to replace present reserve currency, or all existing currency, its introduction would be complicated by the presence of currency in the system of the kind it is desired to replace. It is undesirable to wipe out the existing currency and start afresh; yet, if the commodity-reserve system had been in effect all along, this currency would have been matched by stocks of the commodity-reserve bundles. The obvious solution is the principle of Peel's Act—a fixed fiduciary issue equal in amount to the initial amount of currency in the system of the kind it is desired to replace. If, to begin with, the commodity-reserve bundle were slightly overpriced, a reserve would quickly be accumulated and, in a growing economy, would continue to accumulate.

B. COMPOSITION OF THE CURRENCY BUNDLE

To qualify for inclusion in the bundle, commodities would have to admit of precise price quotation—which means that they must be capable of accurate specification and standardization. It would be highly desirable, if not essential, that they be traded in fairly broad markets, so that trading in the commodity bundles could be carried on readily and inexpensively. They should be supplied under reasonably competitive conditions, since otherwise any downward pressure on the price of the bundle could be absorbed by rises in the prices of the monopolized items instead of by sales to the monetary agency from increased output. They would obviously have to be storable in both a physical and an economic sense; that is, it would have to be possible to preserve relatively inexpensively not only their physical characteristics but

12. Frank D. Graham would apparently have preferred this use of the plan, though he supported its less extensive use as preferable to its abandonment (see *Social Goals and Economic Institutions*).

also their economic value. For example, it probably is technically feasible to preserve new 1951 automobiles from physical deterioration for a long period; yet 1951 automobiles could hardly be considered "storable" for our purposes, since their value is highly perishable in a world of changing models.

These elementary requirements rule out all services except in so far as they are incorporated in the value of storable goods, practically all manufactured goods, many products of mining (coal, especially bituminous coal, deteriorates rapidly outside the mine; petroleum and natural gas would be inordinately, if not prohibitively, expensive to store),[13] and many agricultural products (e.g., perishable foods and livestock). There remain primarily storable agricultural products, such as corn, wheat, and cotton, metallic mineral products, and some highly standardized manufactured products such as standard cotton textiles, steel rails, newsprint, standard storable chemicals, and similar items.

But not even all these could be included. Other requirements connected with conditions of supply rule out essentially all agricultural products. The output of agricultural crops is not subject to much deliberate control in short periods. The growing season is relatively long, and vagaries of weather play a substantial role. The consequent inelasticity of current supply would greatly reduce the short-run countercyclical effectiveness of the commodity-reserve standard. In addition, it would raise other difficulties for the commodity-reserve scheme that can be brought out best by an example. Suppose the commodity-reserve scheme were in opera-

13. Benjamin Graham includes both petroleum and coal in his most recent illustrative commodity unit. Indeed, the two together account for 21.5 per cent of the total value of the unit and over half the nonagricultural component (see *World Commodities*, pp. 43–45). Petroleum but not coal was included in his earlier unit (*Storage and Stability*, p. 57). Yet in the earlier volume he estimated the cost of storing petroleum at 22 per cent of its average price per year (*ibid.*, p. 108). In the later volume the only justification for including coal is a reference to an article, "Super-normal Granary," by Dr. Frank Thorne, in *Science News Letter*, January 21, 1939, which, according to B. Graham, "indicates . . . that both coal and lumber may be stored under water with a minimum of deterioration" (*World Commodities*, p. 148).

Bennett and associates (*op. cit.*, pp. 106–7) exclude both petroleum and coal from their suggested unit as inordinately expensive to store. They also exclude on the same grounds pig iron, which is included by B. Graham.

tion, that wheat were one of the commodities in the currency unit, and that a general deflationary movement happened to coincide with an abnormally short crop of wheat. The deflation would tend to make it profitable to sell commodity bundles to the monetary agency for commodity-reserve currency. Each bundle would have to include a specified amount of wheat. Since wheat would be only one of many items in the bundle, even a small decline in the prices of the other commodities might justify the payment of extremely high prices for wheat for inclusion in commodity bundles. The demand for wheat from this source might be sizable relative to the total supply and so might raise its price substantially above the level that would otherwise prevail.[14] When a basic foodstuff is already in abnormally short supply, would or should the community tolerate the extraction of a large amount and the associated bidding-up of its price, in order to add it to stocks unavailable for consumption? Indeed, would it not instead demand, and quite properly, the use of the previously accumulated stocks of the commodity?[15] It may be argued in answer

14. E.g., suppose that there is a strict commodity-reserve standard, that the commodity bundle covers 10–20 per cent of total output (which it might if agricultural commodities could be included), and that the deflation causes double the usual increase in currency. The increase in currency would then amount to about 3 per cent of the national income, or to 15–30 per cent of the usual nonmonetary supply of the commodities in the bundle, or to 14–26 per cent of the usual total supply of the commodities in the bundle. With a short wheat crop this might easily call for 20–35 per cent of the crop.

15. An ingenious device has been proposed by Benjamin Graham to make possible the use of the accumulated stocks of the commodity under such circumstances. This consists in permitting (or requiring) any commodity in either the reserves or units sold to the monetary agency to be replaced by futures contracts for that commodity whenever the futures price bears a specified relation to the spot price—in Graham's concrete proposal, whenever the futures price is below the spot price. In general, of course, the futures price will exceed the spot price by costs of storage. The reverse relation is a reasonably clear indication that the current supply and private stocks are abnormally low and hence a good signal to justify the release of commodities from the reserve. F. A. Hayek emphasizes this feature of the plan in his article supporting the plan ("A Commodity Reserve Currency," *Economic Journal*, June–September, 1943, pp. 176–84).

On the whole, this device is about as close to an impersonal and foolproof mechanism for the purpose as could be expected and might well be a desirable feature of a commodity-reserve system not intended as a fundamental monetary reform. I do not consider it a desirable expedient for a commodity-reserve currency primarily because it changes the fundamental character of the currency from a warehouse

that, while the output of individual crops varies substantially because of the weather, statistical averaging-out yields a relatively
stable total agricultural output. But it is the individual crop that
is relevant to the commodity-reserve scheme.[16] These considera-

---

certificate to an evidence of debt. A currency unit represented in part by a futures
contract is logically equivalent to a note promising to pay gold, say, issued under
fractional gold reserves. In both cases a fraction of the currency is essentially fiat
currency, constituting a claim to nonexistent stocks and depending upon confidence
and good faith for convertibility. Further, the fiat element would be "created" by
the private individuals who sell the futures. Inability to redeem strict commodity
currency cannot occur except as a result of direct fraud or embezzlement; inability
to redeem a commodity currency in which futures could replace the commodities is
possible. In one version B. Graham suggests that a fraction of the currency corresponding to that nominally backed by the futures contract should not be issued
until delivery of the commodity as a means of guaranteeing performance (*Storage
and Stability*, p. 70). This would be logically equivalent to eliminating the commodity in question from the unit and later restoring it and so would mean repeated
changes in the number of commodities in the unit and its composition.

A number of other considerations also argue against the incorporation of this
device in a commodity-reserve currency: (1) Next year's wheat is not the same as
this year's; so, no matter how treated, the substitution of futures involves repeated
changes in the composition of the bundle. (2) The price relation suggested to determine when futures may be substituted is essentially arbitrary. It would make
equally good sense to permit substitution whenever the spot price is below the future by less than some estimated cost of storage. Hence this device introduces precisely the kind of arbitrary and discretionary element that it is of the greatest importance to exclude from a currency scheme whose major virtue is its automaticity
and impersonality. (3) It further follows that the device involves interference with
a specific price relationship, namely, that between the future and spot price of a
particular commodity, thus undermining one of the possible attractions of the plan,
that it need involve no interference with relative prices.

It should be noted that the issue is not quantitatively insignificant. Very substantial substitutions of futures could be required at times to keep the futures price
equal to the spot price, and there is nothing to prevent the need for such substitutions from occurring in several commodities at the same time.

More generally, proponents of commodity-reserve currency are somewhat dis-
ingenuous when they claim the availability of commodity stocks to meet special
needs as an advantage of the plan. Either the plan is an essential part of a monetary system designed to be stable and to operate under definite rules, in which case
the commodity-reserve stocks must be determined by monetary considerations
alone, or it is purely an excuse for *ad hoc* government intervention. One cannot
serve two masters at the same time.

16. The principle of bimetallism could conceivably be used for some group of
crops to avoid the problem discussed above. But this would mean a fundamental
change in the scheme, involving essentially the fixing of prices, or limits to prices,
of individual commodities.

tions clearly call for the exclusion of foodstuffs, and probably justify as well the exclusion of agricultural products like cotton and flax used for purposes other than food.[17]

These considerations apply, it should be noted, only to short-run fluctuations in output, not to the secular absorption of a fraction of output in order to provide a secular addition to the stock of money. For, over the long run, agriculture, like the other industries involved, would expand to a larger size than in the absence of the monetary demand.

The elimination of agricultural products for these technical reasons not only greatly reduces the potential breadth of coverage of the currency unit but also has important political implications. Producers of agricultural commodities are a vocal and powerful political pressure group. They might be highly favorable to commodity-reserve currency if agricultural products were included in the currency unit; they would probably be indifferent or hostile otherwise. In consequence, their political strength, instead of being an asset, would be a liability, since it would be exercised primarily to have the commodity-reserve scheme take a technically undesirable form. Political support for the scheme is important, it should be noted, not only to have it initially adopted but perhaps even more to prevent "tinkering" with it thereafter.

The elimination of agricultural products leaves only metallic mineral products and standardized products of manufacturing. I know of no detailed study of the value of the annual output of goods in these categories that would be eligible for inclusion in the commodity-reserve bundle, so anything more than a very rough estimate to indicate orders of magnitude is out of the question.[18] The value of metallic mineral products produced in the

---

17. Over 60 per cent of the value of the two illustrative commodity units proposed by B. Graham and over 80 per cent of the value of the unit proposed by Bennett and associates consists of agricultural products. But it must be recalled that their viewpoint is not mine. To quote one comment from B. Graham's earlier book: "The Reservoir plan may be viewed, in large measure, as a proposal for the support and relief of agriculture" (*Storage and Stability,* p. 169).

18. The data and calculations in B. Graham, *World Commodities,* and in Bennett and associates, *op. cit.,* do not satisfy our needs because they are concerned exclusively with importance of commodities in international trade and because they are compiled for a different objective.

United States in 1947 was approximately $3 billion, or about $1\frac{1}{2}$ per cent of the national income.[19] Even some of these might have to be excluded because they are not traded in sufficiently broad and free markets (e.g., aluminum). It is considerably more difficult to make a reasonable estimate for manufacturing; extremely rough and unsatisfactory evidence suggests that the value of eligible manufactured products was probably less than $10 billion in 1947, or about 5 per cent of national income, and possibly very much less.[20]

19. U.S. Department of Commerce, *Statistical Abstract of the United States, 1949*, p. 759.

20. To get a rough idea of the magnitude involved, I summed the value added by manufacturing in 1947 for those census industries any substantial fraction of whose products might—so far as an untrained layman could judge—be eligible for inclusion. I included the following industries: sugar, woolen and worsted manufactures; yarn and thread mills, except wool; cotton and rayon broad woven fabrics; narrow fabric mills; lumber and timber basic products; pulp, paper, and paperboard; leather tanning and finishing; cement, hydraulic; structural clay products; and primary metal industries (which includes blast furnaces and steel mills, iron and steel foundries, primary nonferrous metals, secondary nonferrous metals, nonferrous metal rolling and drawing, and miscellaneous primary metal industries). The total value added in 1947 in these industries was $13.4 billion (*ibid.*, pp. 933–43).

1. This is obviously an overestimate of the value added in producing eligible products in the indicated industries, since probably well over half their products would be ineligible for inclusion. For example, $2 billion of the total is for cotton and rayon broad woven fabrics. Much of this must be for style goods of a kind not easily standardized or stored. Further, the reasons justifying the exclusion of cotton from the eligible list would also call for the exclusion of cotton products. Another $6 billion is for primary metal industries. But a large fraction of the output of these industries is in special shapes and other unstandardized products. In addition, even many standardized products might have to be excluded because not traded in sufficiently broad and free markets.

2. On the other hand, there must be many detailed products in other manufacturing industries that would be eligible for inclusion. Examination of the remaining industries suggests, however, that this underestimate is much less than the overestimate under 1, since I have included all moderately doubtful cases in my list.

3. Another source of error is that value added is not the figure relevant for our purposes. What we want is rather (*a*) the total value of product less (*b*) the value of any part used in producing metallic mineral products—since these have already been counted in the total value of metallic mineral products—and less (*c*) the value of any metallic mineral products used in producing the listed manufactured products—since this, too, has already been counted. It would take an extensive study to get accurate and detailed estimates of these items. However, we

It seems reasonable, therefore, that commodities in the currency unit would represent something like 3–6 per cent of the current output of the nation for other uses. By including petroleum and coal and making a generous allowance for the inclusion of imported products, this could be stretched to something like 6–11 per cent, but this is certainly an outside figure.[21]

C. PRICE BEHAVIOR OF THE CURRENCY BUNDLE

This breadth of coverage achievable under a commodity-reserve standard is substantial, certainly many times greater than under a gold or silver or symmetallic standard. At the same time it is disappointingly far from the ideal of 100 per cent coverage. Moreover, the commodities readily capable of being included in the currency bundle are highly special and not at all representative of the great bulk of economic activity. For the most part, they are metallic minerals and manufactured products made from metallic minerals. In consequence, there is every reason to expect their relative cost of production to be subject to special influences and to be capable of changing drastically. Stability in the nominal price of the commodity bundle could mean substantial instability in the prices of other commodities.

---

know that total value generally runs slightly more than twice value-added. Item *b* would be small and can be neglected. Item *c,* however, would be substantial for the selected industries: most of the $3 billion assigned to metallic mineral products would be used in the primary metal industries included in our selected list.

Eliminating cotton products from the value-added figure, doubling the result to allow for 3*a,* and correcting for 3*b* and 3*c* would yield a total unduplicated value under $20 billion. The $10 billion cited includes a crude allowance for the excess of the overestimate under 1 over the underestimate under 2.

21. 1. The addition of coal and petroleum, included by B. Graham in his illustrative commodity unit, would add 2–3 percentage points.

2. The items in the unit could, of course, include imported goods. The domestic commodities exported to purchase the imports eligible for the commodity-reserve bundle are then the domestic equivalent for them and should be added. This has implicitly been done already, in so far as the exports would consist of items judged eligible for the commodity-reserve bundle. The order of magnitude of maximum additional allowance on this score is suggested by the fact that imports of crude materials have amounted to something like 1–2 per cent of national income in the last few decades (the excluded categories of imports are crude foodstuffs, manufactured foodstuffs, semimanufactures, finished manufactures) (*Statistical Abstract of the United States,* 1948, p. 909).

This expectation can be tested, at least roughly, with existing index numbers of wholesale prices for the United States. Index numbers are available for a long period that purport to describe the price behavior both of "all commodities" and of various subgroups. One subgroup, "metals and metal products," covers a bundle of commodities that overlaps substantially with a feasible commodity-reserve bundle. Perhaps the most important difference in coverage for recent decades is the inclusion of motor vehicles in the "metals and metal products" subgroup. This and other differences in coverage make it impossible to derive accurate estimates of the price behavior that might have been expected under an actual commodity-reserve standard. But they in no way vitiate the use of the index for this subgroup to suggest the kind of variation in price level that could reasonably be expected to arise under a commodity-reserve currency. A feasible currency bundle would neither be significantly more representative nor cover a much broader segment of economic activity than the metals and metal products subgroup, and the elements common to the two would probably account for the greater part of each.

The metals and metal products category has shown a tendency to decline substantially in price over the last century and a half relative to other commodities. A commodity-reserve scheme with a similar currency bundle would have produced stability in its nominal price and hence substantial inflation in other prices. Table 1 illustrates the possible magnitude of the resulting instability in the general price level. For every tenth year from 1800 through 1940 and every year from 1940 through 1949, it gives an index of the ratio of the wholesale prices of all commodities to the wholesale prices of metals and metal products. The hypothetical index so computed approximates the actual wholesale price index that would have prevailed if the commodity-reserve scheme had been in operation during this period, the commodity-reserve bundle had been identical with that covered by the "metals and metal products" index, and the movements in the relative price of metals and metal products had not been substantially affected by the additional monetary demand for them.

According to this table, prices under such a commodity-reserve currency would have risen by 75 per cent from 1800 to 1870, fallen by over 10 per cent in the next decade, more than doubled from then to 1920, and fallen by more than a fifth from 1920 to 1940. During the decade ending in 1949 prices would have first risen by almost a third and then have fallen by almost a seventh. Indeed, for the period as a whole, the range of price fluctuations would have been greater under the commodity-reserve scheme

TABLE 1*

INDEX NUMBERS OF WHOLESALE PRICES (1910–14 = 100): HYPOTHETICAL
INDEX UNDER COMMODITY-RESERVE STANDARD AND ACTUAL
INDEX, SELECTED YEARS, 1800–1949
(Commodity Reserve Unit Assumed Composed of Metals and Metal Products)

Year	Hypothetical Wholesale Price Index	Actual BLS Wholesale Price Index	Year	Hypothetical Wholesale Price Index	Actual BLS Wholesale Price Index
1800........	40	129	1930.......	117	126
1810........	40	131	1940.......	102	115
1820........	39	106			
1830........	44	91	1941.......	109	128
1840........	47	95	1942.......	119	144
1850........	57	84	1943.......	124	151
1860........	62	93	1944	125	152
1870........	68	135	1945.......	126	155
1880........	60	100	1946.......	131	177
1890........	67	82	1947.......	131	222
1900........	71	80	1948.......	126	241
1910........	103	103	1949.......	113	226
1920........	129	226			

* Source and derivation of table: From 1800 through 1880, based on Warren and Pearson Wholesale Price Index numbers; from 1890 on, based on Bureau of Labor Statistics Wholesale Price Index numbers. The Warren and Pearson indexes are on a 1910–14 base; therefore, the figures in the table for the hypothetical index through 1880 are 100 times the ratio of their index for "all commodities" to their index for "metals and metal products." The BLS index numbers are on a 1926 base; so the figures in the table for the hypothetical index for 1890 and subsequent years are 100 times the ratio of the BLS index for "all commodities" to the BLS index for "metals and metal products" times a factor to shift the base to 1910–14. This factor is equal to the reciprocal of the ratio of the average value of the BLS index for "all commodities" for the years 1910 through 1914 to the corresponding average value for "metals and metal products." The actual index is taken directly from the indicated sources except that the base of the BLS index was shifted from 1926 to 1910–14. For the basic data see U.S. Department of Commerce, *Historical Statistics of the United States*, 1789–1945, Ser. L-2, L-9, L-15, and L-21; *Federal Reserve Bulletin*, May, 1950, p. 577.

than it actually was. Over shorter periods, the hypothetical index shows consistently smaller fluctuations than the actual index only during wartime inflations, when the standard would almost certainly have been departed from. If these are omitted, the hypothetical index shows no greater stability than the actual index even over short periods and considerably less secular stability.

The statistical evidence thus confirms general reasoning. A

commodity-reserve currency cannot be expected to give price stability because the currency unit can at best cover only a small and atypical fraction of the economy's output.

D. ELASTICITY OF SUPPLY

The elasticity of supply of the monetary stock under a commodity-reserve currency depends on (1) the possible shifts between monetary and nonmonetary stocks and (2) the elasticity of current supply of the commodity-reserve bundle.

1. *Possible shifts between monetary and nonmonetary stocks.* —The total stocks of metallic mineral and manufactured products held for nonmonetary purposes is, in the ordinary course of events, a small fraction of annual output—costs of storage make larger stocks undesirable, and the elasticity of current output makes them unnecessary. To get an extreme picture, suppose them to be a half-year's output and the total money supply to be equal to a half-year's national income as it currently is in the United States. The nonmonetary stocks of the commodities in the currency unit would then be the same fraction of the money supply as their output for nonmonetary uses was of the nation's output. We have set the latter at 3–6 per cent, so that this would also be an estimate of the maximum normal nonmonetary stocks as a percentage of the total amount of money. This is the relevant figure under a strict commodity standard or a partial commodity standard with a fixed fiduciary issue. Under a fractional reserve standard the relevant figure is larger by a factor equal to the ratio of the total money supply to the "high-powered" money. This is currently less than 3 in the United States, so even in this case the maximum possible expansion in the money supply capable of being produced by the use of nonmonetary stocks would be from 9 to 18 per cent.

These figures are exaggerations not only because we have probably overestimated the size of the stocks in the aggregate but also because we have taken no account of their composition. The nonmonetary stocks can be converted into monetary stocks only in bundles of the proper composition; hence the limit is set by that commodity the stocks of which would make the fewest commodity bundles. It is clear, therefore, that the possible changes in the supply of money via shifts between monetary and nonmonetary stocks are extremely limited.

The limited possibility of changing the monetary supply by diversion to or from nonmonetary stocks means that any change in the desired ratio of the volume of money to the flow of income or to the total stock of wealth would be reflected in the short run primarily in the level of prices and income; it could be satisfied by a change in the stock of money only in the longer run as the rate of current additions to the stock was speeded up or slowed down in response to the changes in prices. The automatic countercyclical reaction under a commodity standard produced by shifts between monetary and nonmonetary stocks would be largely ineffective under a commodity-reserve standard—a defect the importance of which obviously depends on the sensitivity of expenditures to the fraction of total assets in the form of money.

Under a strict commodity standard there is no compensation for this defect, since shifts into or out of nonmonetary stocks have no indirect consequences for monetary stability. Under a fractional reserve commodity standard, the limited possibility of shifts between monetary and nonmonetary stocks is by no means an unmixed evil, since each unit shifted may require the destruction or creation of several units of money to maintain the same fractional reserve and may thereby threaten the entire monetary structure. Put differently, one source of inherent instability in a fractional reserve system is removed if the basic reserve currency cannot be diverted to nonmonetary use.

2. *The elasticity of current supply.*—The metallic mineral products and manufactured products that would be the major components of the commodity-reserve bundle could be expected to have a fairly high elasticity of current supply. The physical volume of output of metallic mineral products fell by three-quarters in the United States from 1929 to 1932, quadrupled from 1932 to 1937, fell by one-third from 1937 to 1938, and more than doubled from 1938 to 1947. Similarly, the physical volume of output in manufacturing as a whole was halved from 1929 to 1932 and more than doubled from 1932 to 1937 and again from

1938 to 1947.[22] Of course, these changes were associated with, or were induced by, substantial price changes; moreover, the larger changes were over considerable periods; year-to-year changes are much more moderate. Nevertheless, it seems clear that changes in the flow of income that tended to change the relative value of the commodity-reserve bundle could produce sizable percentage changes in the aggregate output of the industries producing commodities in the bundle.

Once again, account must be taken not only of the aggregate output but also of its composition, since the bundle would have to be available in the right proportions. If the possible flows into the commodity reserve were a small fraction of the aggregate output of each commodity separately, this qualification would be unimportant. Any items whose aggregate supply was fairly inelastic could be obtained without raising their prices substantially, and so without reducing substantially the incentive to expansion, by bidding the requisite quantities away from other uses. But this condition is not likely to be satisfied for a commodity bundle the nonmonetary output of which accounts for only 3–6 per cent of aggregate output—at least not if any significant income effects are to be produced. The flow into commodity reserves would on occasion amount to a large fraction of the total output of individual commodities, and hence the necessity of producing the bundle in the right proportion might reduce substantially the elasticity of its current supply.

The direct countercyclical contribution to income of a commodity-reserve currency depends not only on the elasticity of its current supply but also on the importance of the industries producing the commodities in the bundle. These industries would, of course, be somewhat more important under a commodity-reserve standard than otherwise, since they would expand to provide any secular increase in commodity-reserve stocks. Even so, they would hardly account for more than 4–8 per cent of aggregate output. The significance of this fact can be shown best by an

22. These statements are based on rough deflations of total value of metallic mineral products and income originating in manufacturing. For figures used see *Statistical Abstract of the United States, 1949,* pp. 283, 302, 304, and 759; *National Income Supplement to the Survey of Current Business,* July, 1947, p. 26.

example. Suppose that, under a condition of reasonably full employment, money income and hence the prices of other commodities rise rapidly by 10 per cent, so that the relative price of the commodity-reserve bundle declines by 10 per cent. Suppose that this decline produces a reduction in the output of the bundle of one-quarter (i.e., an elasticity of supply of approximately 2.5) and a corresponding withdrawal from monetary stocks. This would mean a decline in income flows equal to about 1–2 per cent of aggregate income. That is, reductions in the commodity-reserve industries would offset some 10–20 per cent of the assumed initial rise in income. Similarly, under the assumed conditions, additional income flows in the commodity-reserve industries would offset the same percentage of any decline in aggregate income that was reflected primarily in prices (including, of course, wages) rather than in employment.

A countercyclical income offset of 10–20 per cent of the initial movement in income is substantial and suggests that a commodity-reserve currency could conceivably be a fairly powerful stabilizing factor. However, this conclusion may well overestimate the size of the offset, since we have probably used too high a value for both the elasticity of current supply and the fraction of output accounted for by the commodity-reserve industries. Further, the specialized character of the commodities in the currency bundle would make the offsetting variations in income highly localized, both industrially and geographically.

E. PROVISION FOR SECULAR GROWTH

A secular increase in the quantity of money is required in a growing economy if a secularly falling price level is to be avoided. Under a strict commodity-reserve standard or one with a fixed fiduciary issue, that is, one that involved 100 per cent reserves behind all additions to the circulating medium, the corresponding secular growth in the commodity-reserve stocks would equal the whole increase in the quantity of money. It has already been pointed out that, for the United States during the last half-century or so, this would have required the use of something over $1\frac{1}{2}$ per cent of aggregate resources for the production of commodities to be added to the reserve.[23] In absolute magnitudes, at current levels of national income in the United States, the required average annual addition to commodity stocks would be about $3.5 billion, aside from any costs of storage. If the currency-reserve industries expanded to provide this additional annual amount, their share in aggregate output would rise from the 3–6 per cent estimated above to about 4–8 per cent, and something like one-fifth to one-third of their total output would, on the average, be destined for addition to commodity reserve.

As noted earlier, the cost of providing for secular growth would be essentially the same under any strict commodity standard; hence the necessity of paying such a price is no argument against commodity-reserve currency as compared with other strict commodity standards. And, indeed, it would be a small price to pay if it would, in fact, purchase monetary stability, and if this were the only, or even a markedly superior, way of doing so. But even if the first condition were satisfied, which is by no means clear, the second is not. There are—or seem to be—less costly alternatives. In consequence, it is hard to believe that any nation would deliberately decide to devote so large an amount of its resources to the accumulation of stocks of useful commodities with the definite expectation that they would never be used. This one consideration by itself is almost enough to rule out a strict commodity-reserve standard or one with a fixed fiduciary issue.

Various devices could be used to avoid so large a secular accumulation of reserves. Perhaps the most attractive would be to provide for a regular annual increase in the fiduciary issue by an amount or percentage fixed in advance and rigidly adhered to. It would, however, have to be subject to at least periodic revision to correct errors in its determination. The increase in the fiduciary issue could be used to retire government debt or to pay some part

23. The total volume of money might bear a smaller ratio to the national income under a strict commodity standard than at present because it would be more expensive to hold circulating medium in view of the service charges that depositary institutions would have to make under a 100 per cent reserve system. However, the figure of $1\frac{1}{2}$ per cent makes no allowance for the observed secular decline in velocity of circulation, which itself would raise the figure to over 2 per cent. A decline of about one-quarter in the ratio of the stock of money to national income would be required to offset this factor.

of the government's running expenses. For the rest, the system would be identical with a strict commodity standard. This device could prevent substantial secular increases in the stocks of reserve commodities and so reduce the average annual cost to a moderate figure. It would do so, however, only by sacrificing the possibility of complete automaticity and freedom from political control that in many ways is the greatest—if not the only—advantage of a strict commodity standard over a pure fiat standard.

The annual cost would be greatly reduced if the commodity-reserve currency were used to replace only the existing reserve or high-powered currency and if the present system of fractional reserves were continued. But, even so, it would be significant. As noted, total high-powered money in the United States is currently between one-third and one-half of total currency and demand deposits; therefore, the required secular increase would call for the use of one-half to three-quarters of 1 per cent of national income, or between $1 billion and $2 billion a year in the United States at current levels of national income. Even this cost could be avoided by providing for a regular increase in the fiduciary issue. Either technique would mean political intervention into lending and investing activities and inherent instability in the monetary system.

F. INTERNATIONAL TRADE

Commodity-reserve currency could be adopted by a single country or by several. If adopted by a single country, the rate of exchange between the currency of that country and other currencies could vary. It would be determined in the market or, under present circumstances, more probably by a combination of market forces and government intervention. For the commodity-reserve scheme to be adopted by several countries, the initial bundle and subsequent revisions would have to be agreed upon either through negotiation or by the adoption by other countries of a bundle initially decided upon by one. The composition of the bundle would be a matter of great importance to the various countries, and considerable disagreement could be expected to arise over the proportions in which the commodities should be combined, as well as over the commodities to be included.

An even more important problem would be the integration of the monetary system with trade policy. The allegedly common monetary standard would be a pure fiction if the various countries impeded the free movement of commodities in the bundle by tariffs, export bounties or taxes, or quantitative controls. Completely free trade in the commodities in the bundle among the countries involved is a prime requisite for the effective international operation of the system. This is a highly congenial and desirable requirement to liberals and would be a strong recommendation for the commodity-reserve scheme if it seemed likely that urgent pressure for commodity-reserve currency would overcome reluctance to abolish trade barriers. It seems reasonably obvious, however, that the situation is more nearly the reverse—unwillingness to submit to complete free trade would prevent serious consideration of commodity-reserve currency as an international monetary standard.

Much the same problem would arise with respect to other monetary and economic policies. The commodity-reserve scheme, like any other commodity standard, would impose its discipline on the entire economic and monetary policy of the countries that adopted it; and it would work well only if all accepted this discipline. In consequence, it seems best to think in terms of the adoption of the scheme by a single large country. Other countries could then adhere to it if they wished.

If the scheme were adopted by several countries along with free trade among them in the commodities in the bundle, exchange rates among the currencies of the various countries could fluctuate only within limits set by the cost of transporting the bundle. This stability of exchange rates would certainly stimulate and facilitate international trade. It is, however, somewhat misleading to regard the stimulation of international trade as a special virtue of the commodity-reserve scheme in any other than a purely political sense. The stimulation of international trade would be a consequence of the adoption of internal policies by the various countries of a kind required to prevent the breakdown of the commodity-reserve standard; the same policies would have the same results even if the various countries were on independent fiat standards (see Sec. III, B, below).

If effectively adopted by several countries, the actual provision of currency in return for commodity bundles or of bundles for currency could be by each country separately or by an international authority. The plan followed would matter only in the event of the ultimate breakdown of the standard, in which case the physical location of the reserves or the locus of legal title to them might determine who got the use of them for other purposes.

III. COMPARISON OF COMMODITY RESERVE WITH ALTERNATIVE STANDARDS

A final judgment about the commodity-reserve standard cannot be reached except by comparison with feasible alternative standards. To bring out the issues involved, I shall compare it with two widely different alternatives: (*a*) a gold standard and (*b*) a pure fiat standard combined with a stabilizing budget policy.

A. THE GOLD STANDARD

Among commodity standards, the gold standard is by all odds the most attractive alternative to the commodity-reserve standard. It has a long history as a monetary standard; many countries profess to be on a gold standard or to intend to return to or adopt a gold standard. Gold is widely used as a circulating medium, and tens of millions of people all over the world regard gold as "money," if not the only "true" money.

The chief technical difference between the gold standard and the commodity-reserve standard is that the base of the gold standard is much narrower, in the sense that the normal nonmonetary production of gold is a much smaller fraction of aggregate output than the normal nonmonetary production of the commodities that might be included in the commodity-reserve bundle. Offhand, one would expect the broader base of the commodity-reserve standard to mean a more stable price level. It is not clear, however, that this expectation would be realized. The prices of commodities in general would have fluctuated at least as much over the last century and a half if they had been expressed in terms of a currency unit consisting of metals and metal products—which would be the major components of the commodity-reserve bundle—as they did in terms of gold.

The wider base of the commodity-reserve currency would probably make it a more effective countercyclical instrument than the gold standard. This is almost certain to be true of the direct income flows created by expansion and contraction of the industries producing the currency commodity or commodities and hence of the associated expansion or contraction of the money supply. It may not, however, be true of the indirect effect of shifts between monetary and nonmonetary stocks.

In other relevant aspects, the gold standard and the commodity-reserve standard would be essentially identical if one were starting from scratch. Both provide the possibility of essentially complete automaticity and freedom from political control if all changes in the money supply are in the form of the currency commodities themselves or literal warehouse certificates for them. Under either standard this would require the use of substantial resources to provide for secular growth in the money supply. If the community were unwilling to devote the required resources to this purpose, both would tend to become partial commodity standards, probably of a fractional reserve variety. Both would then become subject to political intervention and be part of an inherently unstable monetary system. Both can be international currencies and give fixed exchange rates among countries if the appropriate internal policies are adopted by the countries involved.

Though the two standards would be identical in these respects if one were starting completely from scratch, the gold standard is clearly vastly superior if account is taken of the existing situation. The commodity-reserve standard has no strong emotional appeal, no widespread popular support. No myths have grown about it. Support for it would have to be built from practically nothing. Once adopted, it would be on trial for a considerable period, and there would be little hesitancy in dropping or changing it. It could easily become a political football rather than a safeguard against political intervention. The gold standard, on the other hand, already has widespread support and emotional appeal. Diluted though it has become, it has unquestionably served to inhibit "tinkering" with the currency. One can conceive—though, I admit, only with some difficulty—of nations again submitting themselves to its stern discipline. I find it hard to conceive of nations submitting themselves to even mild discipline from commodity-reserve currency.

There already exist monetary stocks of gold, so the initiation of a strict gold standard—say, with a fixed fiduciary issue to avoid an enormous increase in the nominal price of gold—would be easier than the institution of a commodity-reserve currency. The business of digging up gold in one part of the world to bury it in another, though occasionally the butt of jokes or the occasion for sarcastic comment, is fairly widely accepted, though by no means understood. The production of a wide variety of obviously useful goods for permanent retention in warehouses, though neither more nor less foolish, is neither accepted nor understood. The chance that a strict gold standard would be allowed to operate, however negligible, is many times the chance that a strict commodity-reserve standard would.

Finally, nominal international free trade in gold already exists, and actual free trade could more readily be obtained than in the commodities it would be desirable to include in the commodity-reserve currency. Agreement on gold would be simpler to achieve than agreement on the contents of the commodity-reserve bundle. On both scores, gold offers more hope of being a feasible international currency.

B. PURE FIAT CURRENCY

The particular variant of a fiat currency with which I propose to compare the commodity-reserve currency is one embodied in a monetary and fiscal framework that I have described and analyzed in some detail elsewhere.[24] This proposal calls for a pure fiat currency issued by the government, combined with 100 per cent reserve banking and the elimination of all discretionary control of the quantity of money by central bank or other monetary authorities. Changes in the quantity of money would be produced entirely through the government budget. Deficits would be financed by issuing additional fiat currency, and surpluses would be used to retire the currency. The quantity of money would therefore expand by the amount of any

24. "A Monetary and Fiscal Framework for Economic Stability," *supra,* pp. 133–56.

deficit and contract by the amount of any surplus. Deficits and surpluses themselves would be generated automatically by changes in business conditions. The level of government expenditures, the program of transfer payments, and the tax structure would be held cyclically stable. They would be changed only in response to changes in the range of activities that the community desires to have the government undertake; they would not be changed in response to cyclical fluctuations in business. In consequence, with a progressive tax system and program of transfer payments, cyclical increases in income would tend to generate surpluses, and cyclical decreases to generate deficits.

Under the proposal, changes in the level of public services or transfer payments that the community chooses to have would call for corresponding changes in the tax structure. The change required would be calculated on the basis of a hypothetical level of income corresponding to reasonably full employment at a predetermined price level rather than on the basis of actual income. The principle of balancing outlays and receipts at a hypothetical stable income level would be substituted for the principle of balancing actual outlays and receipts. To provide for a secular increase in the quantity of money, the budget could include an allowance for a regular annual revenue to be derived from an addition to the supply of circulating medium.

This proposal furnishes a national currency standard designed to promote domestic stability. The currencies of different countries would be connected through flexible exchange rates, freely determined in foreign-exchange markets, preferably entirely by private dealings.

This proposal starts with one great advantage over the commodity-reserve standard: it is essentially costless, requiring neither the maintenance of a stock of useful goods destined never to be used nor the diversion of current resources to the production of additional goods to be added to stockpiles.

On the other hand, there are two immediate potential advantages of the commodity-reserve standard. First, because a strict commodity-reserve standard would be completely separate from the government budget and would require no further legislative action, once it was set up, it could be less subject to impairment or destruction through unwise government action and offer less temptation to use currency expansion as a means of financing government expenditures. Second, the commodity-reserve standard could provide an international currency with fixed exchange rates.

Both these potential advantages seem to me largely, if not wholly, illusory. As already noted, the cost of a strict commodity-reserve standard is almost certain to lead to the adoption of devices designed to provide without cost at least some part of the annual addition to the circulating medium required to provide for secular growth. The most desirable arrangement would be a regular annual addition to an initial fiduciary issue, the addition being used to finance government expenditures. But this would link the commodity-reserve currency with the government budget in the same way as the proposed fiat currency, would raise the same necessity for periodic revisions, and would offer the same temptation to overdo the financing of expenditures by currency issue. Of course, overissue of currency would sooner or later undermine the commodity-reserve standard, just as it would undermine the proposed fiat standard. In either case the defense would have to be a willingness to abide by previously accepted rules, and this could be based only on a wholehearted acceptance of the rules and development of a tradition favoring adherence to them. The problem of getting acceptance and developing such a tradition is much the same for the two standards. I do not see that either is obviously simpler or easier to sell.[25]

In order to present the most favorable case for the commodity-reserve currency, I shall assume that only the device of a fixed annual addition to the fiduciary issue is used. But it should be noted that the use of fractional reserves is perhaps a more likely, and far less satisfactory, outcome of the attempt to avoid the costs of a strict commodity-reserve standard. It would mean government intervention into lending and borrowing and inherent instability in the monetary system. Fractional reserve banking might not be eliminated under the fiat standard either. Its re-

25. In this respect, of course, the gold standard has a head start on either of the other two standards.

tention would not, however, be fostered by pressure to create more than one kind of circulating medium to reduce the costs of providing for secular additions to the money supply.

As to international arrangements, the desideratum is not fixed and rigid exchange rates but stable exchange rates. If a number of countries adopted the proposed fiat standard and adhered to it, the resulting stability in internal prices and business conditions would automatically produce reasonably stable exchange rates, just as would adoption of the commodity-reserve standard and adherence to it. The failure of any country that adopted the fiat standard to follow stable internal policies would be reflected primarily in exchange rates and would have only secondary effects on international trade and on other countries. On the other hand, the failure of a country that adopted the commodity-reserve standard to follow stable internal policies would be the source of internal difficulties for other countries on the same standard and would threaten the maintenance of the standard. The country following the unstable policies would probably be forced off the standard ultimately; in the meantime, however, international trade might have been seriously disturbed and pressures for interferences with free trade created. Thus on this score, too, the advantage seems to be with the flexibility of the fiat standard rather than with the rigidity of the commodity-reserve standard, entirely aside from the difficulties enumerated above of getting effective international adoption of the commodity-reserve standard.

The two other respects in which it is important to compare the commodity-reserve and fiat standards are the behavior of the price level and the effectiveness of countercyclical reactions.

The "absolute" element in the fiat standard that makes the level of prices determinate is the fixed tax structure, with its exemptions, tax rates, and so on expressed in nominal currency units and the fixed transfer program similarly expressed in nominal currency units. The relation between the yield of this tax system minus payments under the transfer program and the cost of the fixed government services determines whether the government budget exerts an influence toward higher or lower prices. This means that the standard will itself be a source of instability if there are changes in either the yield of the fixed tax and transfer structure for a given per capita income[26] or in the relative price of government services. Changes in yield would arise primarily because of changes in the inequality of the distribution of income, and these have historically been extremely small. The bundle of goods and services bought by government is highly varied; therefore, its relative price should not fluctuate greatly. Put differently, the "base" of the fiat standard is, as it were, a complex weighted average of incomes subject to tax or to supplementation through transfer payments and of prices of goods and services purchased by government. This is currently wider and more representative than the base of a commodity-reserve standard. The fiat standard could therefore be expected to be the source of less price instability than the commodity-reserve standard.

The secular behavior of the price level of final products to be expected under the fiat standard depends on the precise details of the arrangements made to provide for secular growth and is more difficult to predict.[27] But there is even greater uncertainty about the secular behavior of the price level under the commodity-reserve standard, since this depends on the future behavior of relative costs of production.

Under the fiat standard there is no possibility of changes in the supply of money via shifts from monetary to nonmonetary stocks; hence this possible countercyclical reaction is absent. Although small under the commodity-reserve standard, this reaction is present. Under both standards, however, the dominant countercyclical reaction is produced by offsetting changes in the flow of income and the associated creation or destruction of money. Under the commodity-reserve standard the offsetting flows of income occur in the industries producing the commodities in the currency bundle. Under the fiat standard they occur through changes in the government budget—the government is, as it were, producing the commodities in the fiat currency bundle. As we have seen, the induced flow of income under

26. Changes in population might be expected to affect both tax receipts and expenditure in much the same proportion.

27. See *supra*, pp. 154–55 and n. 25; Mints, *op. cit.*, pp. 215–19.

the commodity-reserve standard might, at most, offset 10-20 per cent of the initiating change in income. Various estimates suggest that in the United States the induced flow of income under the fiat standard would currently offset at least a quarter and possibly more than a third of the initiating change in income.[28] So both the direct countercyclical income effect and the associated indirect effect through the change in the community's stock of assets and of money would be something like two to three times as large under the fiat standard as under the commodity-reserve standard.[29]

The transitional problems associated with the introduction of the two standards would in many respects be the same. Both would call for the same banking reforms, for the same surrender of present discretionary authority, and for the adoption of similar fiscal rules. The commodity-reserve scheme would, in addition, require agreement on the composition and price of the commodity bundle, the accumulation of an initial reserve, and the provision of storage facilities. The fiat standard would require the selection of a hypothetical level of income and budget principle. It would require no change in the fiscal structure, since a large degree of built-in flexibility already exists in the government budget. On the whole, these transitional problems seem somewhat less serious for the fiat standard.

IV. Conclusion

The commodity-reserve scheme can be carried only a small way toward the symmetallic ideal of universal coverage of an economy's output. The necessity for the commodities in the currency unit to be standardized, traded in broadly based mar-

28. This is based on R. A. Musgrave and M. H. Miller, "Built-in Flexibility," *American Economic Review,* XXXVIII (March, 1948), 122–28, and other scattered bits of evidence.

29. A larger effect is not necessarily conducive to greater stability. There is some optimum beyond which supposedly greater anticyclical reactions may increase rather than decrease instability. I doubt that the fiat standard does go beyond this optimum, but I can offer little support for this. See Milton Friedman, "Rejoinder to Philip Neff," *American Economic Review,* XXXIX (September, 1949), 950–51 and n. 2; "The Effects of a Full-Employment Policy on Economic Stability: A Formal Analysis," *supra,* pp. 117–32.

kets, supplied under reasonably competitive conditions, and physically and economically storable limits the commodities eligible for inclusion largely to agricultural field crops, metallic mineral products, and highly standardized manufactured products. The impossibility of controlling the output of agricultural crops over short periods and the dependence of agricultural output on the erratic forces determining growing conditions make them undesirable components of the bundle. The remaining products—metals, some metal products, and some other standardized manufactured goods—would probably not account for more than 3–6 per cent of the normal output of a nation like the United States.

This narrowness of coverage means that the commodity-reserve standard could not be expected to yield reasonably stable prices either secularly or over fairly short periods. Changes in the relative cost of production of the currency commodities would themselves be a potent source of price instability.

The normal nonmonetary stocks available for conversion to monetary stocks would be small, so that the quantity of money would change primarily through additions from current output or subtractions for current use. The countercyclical reactions of a commodity-reserve scheme would therefore operate primarily through variations in the rate of output of commodity-reserve industries. Since these have a fairly elastic current output, any decline in other prices would lead to a substantial increase in their output, thereby adding both to the stock of money and to the flow of current income; any rise in other prices would have the opposite effects. The offsetting flow of income might be as much as 10–20 per cent of the initiating change. The associated changes in the quantity of money would affect both the total volume of real assets held by the community and the fraction of total assets in the form of money, and these, in turn, would have additional countercyclical effects on expenditures and income. Commodity-reserve currency would therefore have substantial potency as a countercyclical instrument.

The commodity-reserve scheme would have the virtue of almost complete automaticity and freedom from political control if it were made the only means of changing the supply of circulating medium, i.e., if it were combined with 100 per cent reserve banking and all other means of issuing currency were eliminated. But in that case a steady accumulation of commodity stocks would be required to provide secular growth in the stock of money, and this would mean the use of very substantial amounts of resources for this purpose. Devices for reducing this cost would undoubtedly be adopted at the sacrifice of the freedom from political control and intervention.

The commodity-reserve scheme could operate internationally and produce stable exchange rates if, and only if, the various countries were willing to permit complete free trade in the commodities in the bundle and to submit their internal monetary and economic policies to its discipline.

Compared with a gold standard, commodity-reserve currency has one significant technical advantage—its greater potential capacity for offsetting cyclical movements in income, production, and employment. For the rest, the two standards are technically nearly equivalent. Both rest on a relatively narrow and unrepresentative base and so could themselves be the source of fluctuations in the price level. Despite its somewhat broader base, available evidence suggests that a commodity-reserve standard would be at least as unsatisfactory in this respect as a gold standard. Both require the use of resources to provide for secular growth in the stock of money and so give an incentive for the introduction of fiat money. Both could be international standards with fixed exchange rates between countries.

The possible technical advantage of the commodity-reserve currency is, in my view, more than outweighed by its tremendous inferiority to gold in the ability to command unthinking support and reverence. The only basically attractive features of any commodity standard are the restraints it can impose on unwise political intervention and the possibilities it offers of an international currency. If political intervention is not to be feared either because it is universally wise or because other restraints exist, there is no reason to waste resources in piling up monetary stocks instead of adopting the essentially costless alternative of a fiat standard. But a commodity currency can be a bulwark against political intervention and attain acceptance by many countries only if the popular support for it is sufficiently strong and widespread to make "tinkering" with it politically dangerous and to overcome differences in national interests and attitudes. Gold has had, and may still have, this kind of support. Commodity-reserve currency does not.

Widespread support for commodity-reserve currency cannot be expected to develop in the same way that the present support for gold arose—through its acceptance as a standard by accident and historical evolution rather than by design, through long experience with its use and relative stability in value during repeated collapses of fiat currency, through the benefits derived by persons who held the actual currency commodity instead of other forms of money, and through the rest of the long historical process responsible for the mythology of gold.

Support for commodity-reserve currency would have to come through persuasion; the community would have to be convinced that it was the best available currency standard. It is, of course, not impossible that the community could be so convinced. But our comparison of the commodity-reserve standard with a strict fiat standard linked to an automatically stabilizing government budget indicates that conviction could not be based on the technical superiority of the commodity-reserve currency; it would have to be based on essentially nonrational grounds. In every important respect the commodity-reserve currency is technically inferior to the fiat currency. It involves substantial costs of accumulating reserves of commodities, whereas the fiat currency would be essentially costless; it would, in consequence, give a greater incentive for the retention or extension of inherently unstable monetary arrangements and of unnecessary government intervention into lending and investment activities; it would itself be the source of greater instability in prices and economic conditions than the fiat standard; it would probably be less effective in countering any instability arising from other sources; it would not promote international trade any more effectively than the fiat currency if a group of countries submitted themselves fully to the discipline of the one or the other; and it would cause greater disturbances to international trade if any countries departed from the one or the other standard.

In seeking to gain the countercyclical advantages of a fiat standard while retaining the physical base of the gold standard, commodity-reserve currency seems to me to fall between two stools and, like so many compromises, to be worse than either extreme. It cannot match the nonrational, emotional appeal of the gold standard, on the one hand, or the technical efficiency of the fiat currency, on the other.

Discussion of the Inflationary Gap*

DRIVING along the beautiful Skyline Drive in Virginia recently, we passed Lands Run Gap and then Compton Gap. A bit later another sign came into view. I expected it to read "Inflationary Gap," but it was only Jenkins Gap. Again and again I was disappointed. Inflationary Gap never appeared. And this was entirely appropriate: Inflationary Gap is never of the past or the present; it is always in the future.

The inflationary gap is one of those *ex ante* concepts with which recent theory has made us all familiar. Double-entry books always balance, aside from numerical errors. Expenditures by consumers must always equal receipts of sellers. But expected expenditures by consumers during some future period need not equal the value at some specified price level of commodities and services that will be available for sale. It is this difference between expected expenditures and the value of goods expected to be available that constitutes the inflationary gap—at least, in one of its variants.

When the future has become the past, the books will still balance; expenditures will equal receipts; and the inflationary gap for that period will be no more. How does the gap between expected expenditures and expected value of goods available work itself out? How does it lead to the particular level of expenditures and receipts that is realized? Speaking loosely, how is the gap closed?

The adjective "inflationary" implies one method whereby the gap may be closed; namely, through a price rise. But this implication is in many ways misleading. The mere revaluation of the goods available for sale does not by itself close the gap; it

* Reprinted from *American Economic Review*, XXXII (June, 1942), 314–20, with indicated additions to correct a serious error of omission in the original version. The article was a comment on the subject matter of an article by Walter Salant, "The Inflationary Gap: Meaning and Significance for Policy Making," *American Economic Review*, XXXII (June, 1942), 308–14.

is the redistribution of income and the change in spending-saving habits accompanying a price rise that closes the gap. And a price rise is not the only way in which the gap may be closed.

Suppose that, at some specified price level, the value of resources (including, of course, enterprise) expected to be employed in the forthcoming period is $100; that half of these are expected to be utilized, directly or indirectly, by government in producing goods that will not be available for sale, and the other half by industries producing consumer goods; that no consumer goods are available for purchase except from current production; that there are no taxes; and that all payments for resources constitute individual income (i.e., in the terminology of national income, that there are no "business savings"). Under these assumptions the aggregate income of individuals would be $100, and the aggregate value of goods available for purchase (at the assumed price level) would be $50. Suppose, further, that at the assumed price level and with an income of $100, individuals would *want* to spend $70 on consumer goods. The inflationary gap—or that variant of it designated by Mr. Salant as the primary consumer expenditure gap—would be $20.

With $70 trying to buy goods, and $50 worth of goods available, at the assumed price level, it may seem that a 40 per cent price rise would close the gap by making the aggregate value of the goods equal to $70. But, if this were to happen, aggregate income would no longer be $100. If, for the moment, we assume other things unchanged, government would be spending $50, consumers would be spending $70, and aggregate income would be $120. The increase in the price of consumer goods means an increase in payments to some resources and, hence, in their price. If government, to compete, should have to raise the price paid to comparable resources, total income would rise even more— at this stage to $140. But, with a higher price level and a higher income, consumers will want to spend more than $70. Indeed, if the aggregate spending-saving pattern were unchanged, they would want to spend 70 per cent of their unchanged real income, or $98. At the new, higher price level, then, there is a gap of $28, replacing the initial gap of $20. In short, if consumers were to insist on spending 70 per cent of income, and government were to insist on employing half the resources, the immovable object would be meeting the irresistible force.

The answer to this dilemma is, of course, that a price change does not involve merely a revaluation of goods and of incomes. Because of frictions and lags, price changes lead to a redistribution of incomes and to a change in spending-saving relationships. The initial increase in income from a price rise is likely to be concentrated in the hands of recipients of profits, a group that tends to receive fluctuating incomes and accordingly to save a disproportionately large part of any increase in income. Moreover, the receipt and the spending of incomes are not simultaneous. All along the line it takes time for recipients of higher incomes to readjust their spending patterns. Finally, competitive readjustments of resource prices take time. While employing, in some sense, half the real resources, government may not disburse half the money income. Under conditions like the present, of course, this last adjustment is likely to be concealed. The initiating impulse is arising from the government, not the private, sector. Government, in bidding away resources from the private sector, is raising the prices of resources. The share of money income it is disbursing may well be larger than the share of resources it is employing.[1] The point is that the secondary changes in the private sector make this difference less than it would otherwise be.[2]

The change in spending-saving relationships produced by the redistribution of income and lags in adjustment ordinarily associated with inflation plays an important role in determining the pace and pattern of inflation. Nonetheless, it cannot be regarded as the only or even the most fundamental factor that closes the gap. These concomitants of inflation would disappear if the inflation were fully anticipated or if prices reacted instantaneously and consumers instantaneously adapted their con-

1. These are inexact statements, touching on the extremely troublesome problem of defining the volume of real resources in other than monetary terms.

2. The next seven paragraphs and the subsequent material inclosed in brackets are additions to the article as originally published. As I trust the new material makes clear, the omission from that version of monetary effects is a serious error which is not excused but may perhaps be explained by the prevailing Keynesian temper of the times.

sumption patterns to any change in their circumstances. Yet, in either of these cases, there would remain a force tending to close the gap, namely, the effect of the price rise on the real value of those net obligations of government that are expressed in nominal monetary units. The price rise imposes, as it were, a tax on the holding of such obligations. The proceeds of this tax can be garnered by the government, either directly, through the creation of money, or indirectly, through a reduction in the real value of outstanding government obligations. The payment of this tax, as of any other, reduces the income available to consumers for spending or saving and so tends to reduce the fraction of their income, measured before payment of the tax, that they want to spend on consumer goods.

To see how this monetary effect operates, let us make explicit assumptions about monetary conditions for the simple example we have been using. Suppose that the assets of individuals consist exclusively of two kinds of government obligations: noninterest-bearing obligations stated in nominal units ("money") and interest-bearing obligations ("bonds"). For simplicity, suppose further that both the principal and the interest of the bonds are stated in real rather than monetary units—that the bonds are "purchasing-power bonds"—so that the price rise operates entirely through its effect on the real value of the stock of money; and that, if prices are stable, individuals spend on such bonds whatever part of their income they do not spend on consumer goods. The earlier assumption that this amount is $30 out of an income of $100 then implicitly assumes some given interest rate on these bonds, since the amount individuals want to spend on bonds is a function, though perhaps a relatively inelastic function, of the interest rate they offer. Finally, suppose that any excess of government expenditures over the amount of bonds individuals are willing to buy at the given interest rate is financed by money creation.

Let government now proceed to spend at a rate in excess of $30. Given our assumptions, this will tend to produce a price rise, since individuals are not willing to hold the additional money created to finance such expenditures at an unchanged price level. This price rise reduces the real value of the initial stock of money. Individuals can keep their *real* cash balances at the initial level only by using some of their income to add to their nominal balances, in the process absorbing the additional currency issued by the government. But if they stubbornly insist on keeping their real cash balances unchanged, they cannot also spend 70 per cent of their income on consumer goods and 30 per cent on bonds; one or the other must give, and presumably both will. This force therefore tends to reduce the fraction of income individuals want to spend on consumer goods and tends to bring it into equality with the fraction of resources available to produce consumer goods.

Of course, individuals will not stubbornly insist on maintaining their real cash balances at the same level when prices are rising as when they are stable. When prices are stable, the (real) cost of holding a dollar in the form of money instead of a purchasing-power bond is the interest foregone on the bond; when prices are rising, it is this interest plus the rate at which the real value of the dollar is declining, that is, plus the rate at which prices are rising. A price rise of 10 per cent per year is precisely equivalent, in this respect, to a stable price level plus a tax of 10 per cent per year on the average amount of cash balances, or plus an increase of 10 percentage points in the annual interest rate on bonds. Other things the same, therefore, individuals want to hold smaller real cash balances when prices are rising than when they are stable, and when prices are rising rapidly than when they are rising slowly. Corresponding to each (expected) rate of rise in prices, there is some level of real balances individuals want to hold, and this level may be expected to be constant, other things the same, so long as prices continue to rise at the same rate. The preceding paragraph is, therefore, fully applicable to an inflation proceeding at a constant rate, though not to the transition from price stability to inflation. In such a transition period the attempt by individuals to reduce the level of real balances would make prices rise more rapidly than otherwise, though this effect might of course be offset for a time at least by a sluggish reaction to the price rise.

Given instantaneous adjustments, and an inflation proceeding at a constant rate, how large a price rise will be required, or is there any that will be sufficient, to enable the government to get control of half the real resources in our simplified example? The answer clearly depends on the size of the real cash balances individuals want to hold at various costs of holding such balances and on the effect on their spending-saving pattern of using some of their income to add to their nominal cash balances. For example, suppose they continue to divide any income not so used between spending on consumer goods and spending on bonds in the proportions of 70 to 30 and suppose they want to hold, in the form of money, assets equal in value to $4/7$ of a year's income when prices are rising at the rate of 50 per cent a year. The required price rise will then be at the rate of 50 per cent a year. For, at this rate of price rise, individuals would have to use $2/7$ of their income to acquire the additional nominal cash balances needed to keep their real balances unchanged and would spend $3/10$ of the remaining $5/7$ or $3/14$ of their income on bonds and $7/10$ of the remaining $5/7$ or $1/2$ of their income on consumer goods. The final result is precisely the same as if an explicit tax of 50 per cent per annum had been imposed on cash balances, the revenue from which amounted to $2/7$ of a year's income; the additional nominal units of money individuals acquire can, indeed, be regarded as receipts certifying the payment of taxes.

More generally, in order for the government to acquire half the total resources, the 70 per cent that individuals spend on consumer goods out of the income not used to acquire nominal cash balances must amount to 50 per cent of their total income, since this is the fraction of resources available to produce consumer goods. It will amount to 50 per cent of total income if $2/7$ of total income is used to acquire additional nominal cash balances ($7/10$ of $5/7$ equals $1/2$). Now there may be no price rise that will induce individuals to use $2/7$ of their income to acquire additional nominal cash balances, in which case the gap cannot be closed by this route, and hyperinflation and a collapse of the currency would result from any attempt to do so. Once again, translation into an explicit tax on cash balances may help. As for any other tax, there is some rate of tax that will give the maximum yield, the rate and maximum yield depending on the conditions of demand and supply for the product taxed. In this case the product taxed is real cash balances, and the supply is, or can be, perfectly elastic at essentially zero cost, so the maximum yield is at a point on the demand curve of unitary elasticity. In our example, if this maximum yield is less than 2/7 of total income before tax, the gap cannot be closed by currency issue alone, given instantaneous reactions and our other assumptions.

How should we classify income used to add to nominal cash balances in order to keep real cash balances at the initial level? If we keep our books in nominal monetary units, it will show up as "savings," since our books will record an increase in an asset, namely, nominal cash balances, corresponding to it. But, clearly, it is savings only in a bookkeeping sense; no matter how long or how much the individual "saves" in this form alone, there is no increase in the volume of goods and services he can command by liquidating his assets. There is at least as much justification for classifying it as "consumption"—if we consider individuals only in their capacity as consumers—by analogy with our treatment of excise taxes. The consumer pays this sum in order to have the services yielded by possession of the real cash balances. Finally, and perhaps best of all, we can classify it as a tax payment. This has one disadvantage: in our actual society, by contrast with our hypothetical example, fiduciary money is issued not only by government but also by private banks, and so we must either draw an artificial distinction between money issued by the one or the other or regard the "tax" proceeds as going partly to private individuals. But this terminology has the great advantage of emphasizing the important truth that there are only two fundamental ways in which government can acquire real resources from individuals: either it can induce the individuals to lend the resources by paying them enough to make it worth their while to do so or it can take the resources by using its taxing power. The power to issue money does not, in any meaningful sense, add a third way.

A price rise will close the gap, therefore, by changing the ratio of saving to spending and by changing the ratio of the value of goods available for sale to the total value of goods produced [and by imposing an implicit tax on the holding of government obligations expressed in nominal monetary units]. At the end of the period the balanced books will show a percentage of income saved exactly equal to the percentage of income disbursed in the production of goods not available for sale. In our simplified example, if we assume that government throughout disburses half the income, the balanced books will show that individuals have saved [or used to acquire additional nominal cash balances] half their income.

How large a price rise will be required depends on the speed with which readjustments take place, [on the habits of the community with respect to holding government obligations, and on the institutional arrangements for issuing money]. If, for example, labor is quick in demanding and successful in obtaining higher wages when profits rise, and consumers are quick in interpreting rising prices as a forerunner of further price rises and hence in increasing their expenditures, a very large price rise may be required, and conversely. [However, these factors are important primarily in the early stages of an inflation and in determining the time pattern of inflation. In any extended inflation the amount of money created by government and private institutions and the size and elasticity of the demand for real cash balances and other government obligations will play a more important role in determining the size of the price rise.] The same primary gap may, therefore, be associated with a wide range of price changes.

Even in the absence of direct government intervention, a price rise and the attendant redistribution of income [and implicit tax on government obligations expressed in nominal monetary units] is not the only way in which the gap might be closed. For example, to take a highly unreal extreme, sellers of consumers' goods might simply refuse to raise prices despite the high level of demand, permitting, instead, their shelves to empty and bare-shelves rationing to replace price rationing. Consumers would then be forced to save $20 more than they wanted to. This type of behavior by sellers would, in practice, be rare; but, to whatever extent it occurred, it would help to close the gap.

Again, aside from the increase in savings as a result of the redistribution of income, savings might increase because of a "buyers' strike"—unable to obtain the desired goods at accustomed prices, buyers might simply refuse to purchase at higher prices. This type of behavior is contrary to experience, which reveals a higher percentage of income spent on consumption goods the lower the real income. But it is not entirely inconceivable under wartime conditions and psychology.

Finally, the gap might be closed by changes arbitrarily ruled out in our simplified example. [An increase in the interest rate paid on government bonds might increase the fraction of their income individuals want to save.] As Mr. Salant quite properly points out, aggregate output—at least "economic" output—is not unique. A price rise might mean a larger output than the $100 assumed in our example and, hence, more goods available for sale. And goods can be made available for sale not only from current production but also from capital. Such an increase in goods sold does not increase *incomes;* it merely substitutes one form of asset for another—money for goods.

Under these conditions it may well be asked what significance can be attached to the number describing the primary expenditure gap—in our example, $20. The primary expenditure gap— the concept most frequently used in measurements of *the* gap— is significant in only two ways: (1) It measures the amount by which the estimate of voluntary savings at the assumed income level would have to be in error in order that the gap should be the product of statistical error rather than of economic reality. If the statistician had underestimated voluntary saving by $20, there would in reality be no gap. (2) It measures the task of one of the many public policies that might be used to close the gap; namely, a campaign to stimulate "voluntary" savings. In terms of our example such a policy, in order to succeed, would have to induce consumers with an income of $100 to save $20 more than they would want to save in the absence of such a campaign.

The $20 that measures the primary expenditure gap does not, as is often mistakenly supposed, measure the amount that would have to be raised in taxes to close the gap. If, in our example, $20 were withdrawn in taxes, consumers would have available $80 for saving and spending—at the assumed price level. Out of $80 of income, they would presumably want to spend less than $70 but more than $50, since a reduction in income ordinarily reduces both saving and spending. In order to eliminate the gap, enough would have to be withdrawn in taxes to reduce disposable income to a level at which consumers would want to spend $50. This would clearly require more than $20, how much more depending not only on saving-spending habits but also, as Mr. Salant has pointed out, on the kinds of taxes imposed.

An analysis directed toward policy should not, therefore, stop with an estimate of the primary expenditure gap. It should take as its function the evaluation of the quantitative aspects of the alternative measures that might be taken to close the gap. Such an evaluation is essential to an intelligent choice among measures or an intelligent combination of measures. It is not enough to list the various measures that might be employed: direct stimulation of savings; reduction of consumer income through taxation or compulsory savings; indirect stimulation of savings by [raising the interest rate paid on such savings, or by] rationing some goods and thereby narrowing the range of goods freely available for purchase, or by imposing restrictions on consumer credit; rationing of over-all purchasing power; reduction of expenditures by industry on nonwar capital formation and by state, local, and federal governments on nonwar activities; prevention of wage rises; elimination of overtime payments; etc. There is needed, in addition, quantitative estimates of the contribution that would be made by each possible variant of each measure and by combinations of different measures. The ideal would be a series of indifference surfaces, so to speak; that is, a list of the alternative combinations of policies that would serve to close gaps, however defined, of alternative sizes.

The analyses that have so far been made fall far short of this ideal. In the main they have been directed at measuring either the primary expenditure gap, the measure appropriate for a policy of direct stimulation of savings, or the tax gap, the measure appropriate for a policy of reducing consumers' disposable incomes through taxation. True, these studies have attempted to take into account the effect of other policies, in so far as these policies could be foreseen. But only to a minor extent have they attempted to state the consequences of extensions of the other policies—to say, for example, that this and this extension of rationing would change the amount of taxes needed by this and this amount.

Mr. Salant stresses the importance of a somewhat different elaboration of the estimates—a breakdown of the gap among broad classes of output. He considers such a breakdown vital for policy purposes because, in his view, "general measures of the income tax variety are appropriate" primarily "if demand is generally excessive in terms of potential output at the desired prices." This apparently innocent statement conceals a joker— "at the desired prices." The composition of the gap is determinate only at specified relative prices for different classes of goods.[3] It can be anything at all if relative prices are permitted to vary. Mr. Salant's policy conclusion is valid only if (1) stabilization of particular prices as well as of the general level of prices is desired or (2) relative prices are generally and necessarily rigid. Neither point seems to me to be acceptable. General measures of the income-tax variety seem appropriate under almost any circumstances—certainly any that are at all probable in the United States. The price system seems the least undesirable method of allocating the limited resources that will be available for the production of civilian goods. If they could be constructed, breakdowns of the type suggested by Mr. Salant would be desirable under alternative relative prices, not for determining basic policy, but rather for estimating the relative price changes that would be likely to occur.

The present state of gap analysis is unsatisfactory not only because it does not go far enough but also because the estimates that are made are subject to such wide margins of error. At the present stage of our knowledge of the functioning of the economic system, estimating the gap is a presumptuous undertaking. One of the main by-products of attempting to do so is a keener realization of how little we know about the quantitative

3. It should be noted that the aggregate amount consumers will want to spend out of a given income may also be affected by the relative prices of different classes of goods even if the general level of prices is, in some sense, fixed. But this effect would presumably be of secondary importance.

interrelationships of the economic system and how much there is to know. To estimate the gap, and the consequences that will flow from it, requires precise and quantitative knowledge of the process of economic change—of how impulses are transmitted throughout the economic system, of lags in adjustment, technical possibilities, and human reactions.

Useful estimates are possible at all only because of the special circumstances of the moment. The necessities of war require an ever increasing stream of expenditures whose desirability is unquestioned. These expenditures constitute the dominant factor making for expansion of money incomes. The direction of the change in expenditures is known: so long as war continues, expenditures will increase and not diminish. The magnitude of the change can be forecast with reasonable accuracy for short periods. Many factors that would be important to the estimator in ordinary times have no independent influence in wartime. For example, nonwar capital formation is subject to direct control and is determined by availability of materials rather than profit possibilities. The factors that determine capital formation in peacetime can be almost entirely neglected and attention concentrated on productive potentialities. Finally, possible discrepancies between the amount consumers want to spend and the value, at specified prices, of the goods available for purchase are so large that even substantial errors of estimate will not alter major policy implications.

The development of methods for estimating the gap and the apparent usefulness of the resulting estimates for public policy during wartime have led many to suppose that a new technique has been developed for guiding public policy in peacetime. As the preceding paragraph indicates, this is an illusion. Gap analysis has added nothing to our understanding of economic change. We know no more now about how the business cycle runs its course than we did before. The special circumstances of a war period make it possible to use this imperfect knowledge to construct quantitative estimates that are useful for policy purposes. When these special circumstances have passed, the problems that plagued us before will plague us again.

Comments on Monetary Policy*

I

"THE Federal Reserve," Professor Harris writes near the beginning of his paper, "is surely in a position to deny the economy the money without which a large inflation could not be carried out. . . . In fact, the Federal Reserve even today could impose a drastic deflation on the country. . . . Monetary restraints are the easiest approach to inflation control—much less painful than more taxes or less public expenditures, or than wage or price control, or than control of supply and demand of commodities."

"We are not optimistic," he writes at the end of his paper, "concerning the contribution *likely* to be had from monetary policy. In the present (Spring, 1951) state of the world crisis, we *should* depend primarily on fiscal policy and secondarily on limited income and other controls" (italics added).

The reader will search in vain the pages that intervene for a demonstration that the prescription in the second quotation is a valid inference from the diagnosis in the first. But he will find an explanation of how one man could make both statements —an explanation that is suggested by two words I have italicized in the second quotation: "likely" and "should." For Harris mixes prediction and prescription so thoroughly that it is difficult to tell when he is recording what is going to be done and when recommending what should be done. His "recommendations" sometimes seem to be simply a confusion of the indicative and imperative moods; and his "predictions" sometimes seem to be an indirect means of supporting recommendations held for other reasons.

* Reprinted from a symposium on "The Controversy over Monetary Policy," *Review of Economics and Statistics,* XXXIII (August, 1951), 179–200, this comment, pp. 186–91. Seymour E. Harris' "Introductory Remarks" served as the text for the subsequent comments.

II

The role of the economist in discussions of public policy seems to me to be to prescribe what should be done in the light of what can be done, politics aside, and not to predict what is "politically feasible" and then to recommend it. Accordingly, I shall not attempt a detailed criticism of Harris' comment. Instead I shall state positively and dogmatically my own conclusions about the appropriate role of monetary policy at the present time and then consider some of the objections to this position. Since monetary policy cannot be considered in isolation, the initial statement of my position will necessarily range rather widely.

1. Monetary and fiscal measures are the only appropriate means of controlling inflation. Direct controls—price and wage ceilings, the rationing or allocation of goods, qualitative credit controls—are not appropriate means of controlling inflation. This is true for total war as well as for a period of mobilization like the present. At best, such controls repress rather than remove inflationary pressure, and their capacity even for repressing pressure is severely limited. Besides being weak instruments for controlling inflation, direct controls hinder production and distribution and threaten the foundations of a free society.

2. Monetary and fiscal measures are substitutes within a wide range. A large budget surplus would mean that *relatively* easy money would be consistent with no (or any given degree of) inflation. A balanced budget would require tighter money to prevent inflation; a budget deficit, still tighter money. Similarly, inflation is a substitute for either a tighter fiscal or a tighter monetary policy. The possibilities of substitution may, however, be limited; there may be no monetary policy sufficiently "easy" to prevent deflation with a sufficiently large surplus or no monetary policy sufficiently "tight" to prevent inflation with a sufficiently large deficit.

It is not clear that there is a single "best" combination of monetary and fiscal measures and degree of inflation. A good combination, however, would be a roughly balanced budget together with whatever associated monetary policy would prevent inflation. No policy very far from this combination is likely to be appropriate. However, when the fraction of aggregate resources to be used by government is very—and abnormally—large, it may be desirable to depart from this combination in the direction of a budget deficit, to rely more heavily on monetary policy, and perhaps even to permit some inflation. The main reason is that beyond some point the release of resources from other uses produced by the incentive of high interest rates will be better adapted to individual capacities than that produced by higher taxes levied on necessarily crude tax bases, and hence will be both more equitable and less injurious to incentive. Similarly, beyond some point the tax implicit in mild inflation may be as equitable as *additional* taxes and less injurious to incentive. At the moment, however, we are far from the point at which inflation could be justified on these grounds.

3. At the present time and under existing conditions, monetary policy should be directed exclusively toward the prevention of inflation and must take the form primarily of open-market operations in government securities, conducted at the discretion of the Open Market Committee of the Federal Reserve System. These should be conducted solely to prevent inflation, and no consideration *at all* should be paid to their effect on the rate of interest on government securities. If the budget were roughly balanced, I would guess that a successful anti-inflationary monetary policy would not involve much of a rise in the rate of interest on government bonds; but this is a guess and has no bearing on the desirable policy. A large rise would simply mean that there was more pressure for inflation to be counteracted.

4. The belief that discretionary open-market operations are the best monetary instrument available for the current emergency does *not* imply its indorsement as a permanent instrument of stabilization policy. Under more usual circumstances such a policy is likely to be undesirable; it may well increase rather than decrease instability. As a matter of long-run reform, I would like to see the Federal Reserve System in its present form abolished and replaced by a 100 per cent reserve deposit banking system in which there was no monetary authority possessing

discretionary powers over the quantity of money.[1] I am convinced by the evidence Harris alludes to that the establishment of the Federal Reserve System was a mistake and that the system has failed to promote the objectives for which it was established. While this is as good a time as any to begin this long-run institutional reform, it cannot be accomplished overnight. We must, willy-nilly, meet the present emergency with present institutions. Moreover, the very nature of the emergency and the associated danger of inflation enormously simplify the technical (as opposed to political) problem of discretionary monetary policy by making prediction relatively easy.

III

It is obviously impossible to defend this position in detail here. I shall therefore concentrate on one component of it: the recommendation that control of the quantity of money through open-market operations can and should be a major instrument for controlling inflation. This is, I believe, the key proposition, in the sense that its rejection implicitly or explicitly accounts for failure to accept other components of the position just stated. In discussing this proposition, I shall, for simplicity, assume a roughly balanced budget at constant prices.

The objection likely to be raised in the first instance to my position is that monetary policy *cannot* perform the task assigned to it; that it is ineffective. But I submit that this is not the real objection—that on consideration practically everyone will agree with Harris that "the Federal Reserve even today could impose a drastic deflation on the country." Suppose the Federal Reserve were to sell $10 billion worth of government securities and thereby roughly halve the reserve balances of member-banks. Could inflation nonetheless proceed? If so, then what if it sold $15 billion? $20 billion? Clearly, a sufficiently drastic reduction in the supply of money could bring economic activity almost to a halt. If it is answered that such amounts could not be sold (at any price?), it will be found on examination that this is equiv-

1. See "A Monetary and Fiscal Framework for Economic Stability," *supra,* pp. 133–56.

alent to saying that such amounts would not have to be sold to produce a deflation.

If the analysis is pushed further, I think it will be found that the real objections to the use of monetary policy take one of two forms: first, that monetary policy can be effective only if it is "extreme" and in that case must go "too" far and produce a deflation; second, that monetary policy can be effective in preventing inflation but only at the cost of undesirable consequences in other directions.

The essence of the first objection is that there is some kind of discontinuity in the effects of monetary policy—mild measures are not enough, extreme measures are too much, and there is nothing in between. What is this discontinuity? If sales of $10 billion of securities by the Federal Reserve are too much, is there not some smaller figure that is just right? I think one must grant that there is. But this by no means disposes of the argument. For how can we be sure that it will be found? May the important discontinuity not be in the *effect* of a mistake? If, in the inevitable process of trial and error, too much were done, might this not give rise to expectations capable of producing sharp cumulative movements that could in turn be counteracted only by "extreme" actions in the opposite direction liable to the same kind of error? I have a great deal of sympathy with this kind of argument; indeed, it is part of the reason I am extremely critical of *discretionary* monetary (and equally fiscal) policy for "ordinary" times. But it does not seem to me a valid objection under existing conditions. For these are precisely the conditions when a "mistake" is least likely to give rise to strongly destabilizing expectations. The practical certainty that larger government expenditures will be made in the future and the widespread knowledge that all past large-scale government expenditure programs have been associated with inflation seem to me ample insurance against deflationary expectations. Is it really conceivable that overvigorous Federal Reserve sales of government securities on the outbreak of the Korean war could have created a widespread expectation of deflation incapable of being overcome by subsequent purchases? Furthermore, this objection is equally applicable to any effective means of combating inflation, including fiscal measures or direct controls. For the objection depends on the irreversibility not of *policy* but of *expectations*.

The second argument, that monetary policy can prevent inflation but only at the cost of undesirable consequences, varies according to the consequences that are considered undesirable. One set of such consequences can be disposed of out of hand; namely, those which are inherent in the prevention of inflation. If their occurrence is considered undesirable, the valid conclusion is that inflation should be permitted, not that monetary policy is an undesirable means of preventing inflation. For example, Harris says, "The use of the monetary axe may interfere with this growth" in output, in a context in which he is implicitly attributing the growth to inflation itself. To whatever extent his argument is valid, it is equally applicable to any other method of preventing inflation. If taken seriously, it argues for permitting some limited amount of inflation. The question still remains by what means the inflation should be kept within these bounds.

More generally, an inflationary situation is one in which consumers, firms, and governmental bodies are trying to buy a larger real volume of goods than is available for sale. Some prospective purchasers will have to be frustrated, if in no other way, then by inflation itself. It is therefore no objection to a means of preventing inflation that it will frustrate some economic units; it must do so. A valid objection is either that the wrong units (or more precisely, real expenditures) are frustrated or that units are frustrated in unnecessary ways.

I think we can best isolate the valid elements of this objection by tracing the channels through which monetary policy can frustrate expenditures and thereby prevent inflation. This process can be described in either of two alternative languages—that of the quantity theory or that of Keynesian analysis. Since there is a high correlation between those who object to assigning monetary policy a major role and those who prefer to use Keynesian language, I shall myself use that language despite some doubts whether it is the more fruitful for this problem.

An open-market sale of government securities by the Federal Reserve System under conditions like the present when banks have little excess reserves tends to reduce the aggregate quantity of money in the hands of the public. This in turn will tend to raise "the" rate of interest. The quantitative effect on the rate of interest will depend on the willingness of holders of money to substitute bonds for money, that is, on liquidity preference. The more elastic the liquidity preference schedule with respect to the rate of interest, the less the rise produced in the rate of interest by any given sale of government bonds. But clearly there will be some rise; or, stated differently, however elastic the liquidity preference function at the existing position, it is not infinitely elastic everywhere so there will be some amount of sales which will raise the interest rate.

The mere substitution of bonds for money is of no importance per se: it makes no difference which asset people hold except as their (spending) behavior, or the behavior of someone else, is influenced by their asset holdings. If they were willing to exchange the one asset for the other at no change in the price of securities, this would be a clear indication that they were indifferent which they held; the fact that the price of securities must be reduced to make them willing to hold more means that they are not indifferent. Hence an open-market sale can be said to prevent inflation only in so far as it affects "the" rate of interest.

Of course, "the" rate of interest is a complex notion, and full analysis would require elaboration of the concept. Here it will be enough to point out that it stands for anything that makes it more costly or difficult to get control over capital. The nominal rate charged by banks or other lenders may not change, but the "quality" of loans they will make may rise; there may be what has, somewhat unfortunately, been called "capital rationing." Thus I shall regard the lesser availability of loans at the former rate of interest as equivalent to a rise in "the" rate of interest.

The rise in the rate of interest will tend to reduce attempted "investment"; that is, it will reduce the quantity of goods that individuals or firms seek to buy to add to their stock of capital goods or to replace items used up or sold. "Investment" in this context includes not only expenditures on plant and equipment but also business expenditures on inventories and goods in process and consumer expenditures on durable goods and houses. How much investment will be reduced depends of course on the interest elasticity of the demand for investment. The rise in the rate of interest will tend also to reduce the fraction of income devoted to consumption (the propensity to consume) in two ways. First, it will make "savings" more attractive. Second, the rise in the rate of interest tends to reduce the capital value of existing streams of income and hence to reduce the ratio of wealth to income, which in turn may be expected to make people more desirous of adding to wealth.

The rise in the rate of interest thus tends to reduce attempted expenditures on both investment and consumption and thereby to eliminate the "inflationary gap." How much will the rate of interest have to rise at a time of inflationary pressure? This depends, first, on the magnitude of pressure, that is, the volume of attempted expenditures that must be frustrated; second, on the elasticities of the relevant investment and consumption schedules with respect to the rate of interest, that is, the ease with which the expenditures can be frustrated. Note that it does not depend at all on the elasticity of the liquidity preference function per se; this only determines the amount by which the stock of money will have to be reduced to produce the necessary rise in the rate of interest. Note also that to assert that the relevant schedules are completely inelastic with respect to the rate of interest and so there exists no rise in the rate of interest that will eliminate the inflationary pressure is equivalent to saying that there is no reduction in the quantity of money by means of open-market operations, however large, which will prevent the inflationary price rise. Note, finally, that the circumstances under which a large rise in the rate of interest is required are circumstances under which any other means of preventing inflation will also have to be pressed far, for it will be necessary to frustrate a relatively large volume of attempted spending, and the resistance to frustrating those expenditures will be great.

What now are the "unnecessary" and "undesirable" consequences of this process that might constitute objections to its use?

1. Even if the capital market were "perfect," the necessary reductions in attempted expenditures would be according to

private interests; but private interests may not coincide with public. This is a specific form of a general objection to the price system that obviously cannot be dealt with here. So I pass it by with simply an expression of disagreement and a reminder that public interests, like private, can be expressed in the prices offered for goods.

2. The capital market is in fact imperfect. The reductions in attempted expenditures will thus be inappropriately distributed. There will be a bias in favor of persons or units with large liquid resources, good connections with banks, etc. This objection must be granted. In so far as the market is imperfect, there is nothing to be said in favor of the resulting distribution of resources. My own judgment is, however, that market imperfections are not very significant. Perhaps more important, the imperfections here must be compared with the imperfections in alternative methods of frustrating attempted expenditures. I submit that the alternative methods so far suggested are vastly more imperfect and would lead to even wider deviations from the optimum distribution of resources.

3. The higher rate of interest imposes a budgetary burden on the "Treasury." This has been the most important explicit argument cited as preventing effective monetary action; otherwise it would hardly deserve mention, since its actual importance is negligible. Clearly the rate of interest paid on government debt is not an objective in its own right. It must be judged by its consequences. A lower rate of interest can be obtained by permitting inflation or by levying heavier taxes. But, surely, the level of government interest payments is one of the least important considerations in choosing either the desired degree of inflation or the desired fiscal policy.

4. A rise in the rate of interest "now" will make it difficult to lower interest rates later, and "low" interest rates are likely to be needed later to prevent "stagnation." Entirely aside from the meaning of "stagnation" or the likelihood that it will be a danger, it should be noted that this argument is unsatisfactory. Given a free investment market throughout, what would be required when stagnation threatened is not a "low" interest rate but a "lower" interest rate. Thus, the stimulation later would come not from

a "low" interest rate but from the elimination of deterrents to investment or consumption used as a substitute for a "high" interest rate.

5. The open-market operations required to produce a rise in the interest rate will "disorganize" the securities market; it will produce "chaos," or have an "unstabilizing effect," etc. I must confess that I do not understand this argument except as another version of the discontinuity argument cited earlier. It seems to me that a "disorganized" market is precisely what we want, that is, a market in which people cannot get capital with which to try to make expenditures that cannot be matched by physical goods.

6. Finally, the rise in the rate of interest changes the relations between wealth and income. Attempted expenditures of perhaps $10 billion have to be discouraged, it is said; total national wealth is of the order of $1,000 billion. Why disturb this enormous sum to achieve the paltry reduction required? But it has been pointed out that one channel whereby expenditures are discouraged is precisely through altering the ratio of wealth to income. Consequently, the disturbance in wealth-income ratios is proportioned to the magnitude of expenditures that must be discouraged. If these were considered small, then only a small disturbance in the wealth-income ratios will be required.

Perhaps there are other consequences of monetary restraints that are regarded as undesirable and unnecessary and that can be avoided by alternative economic policies. If so, the opponents of monetary policy have an obligation to point out precisely what they are and how they can be avoided. To the best of my knowledge they have not done so to date; they have rather tended to take refuge in vague phrases denoting alarm. Such content as I have been able to give these phrases in the six points just listed seems no very serious objection to the vigorous use of monetary policy.

IV

An appropriate combination of monetary and fiscal policy can and should be used to prevent inflation. Such a combination would consist of a roughly balanced budget and whatever level of monetary ease or tightness is required to prevent civilian expenditures from producing inflation. Pending long-run reform of our monetary and banking structure, monetary control should be exercised through open-market purchases or sales of government securities directed solely to the prevention of inflation. Such open-market operations should be persevered in regardless of their effect on the rate of interest on government or other securities. Such a policy could have prevented the inflation that we have experienced since the outbreak of the Korean war; it can prevent any further inflation.

An excellent summary of the effects of the post–World War I inflations comments: "A host of popular remedies vainly attempted to cure the evils of the day; which remedies themselves —subsidies, price and rent fixing, profiteer hunting, and excess profits duties—eventually become not the least part of the evils."[2] And the avoidance of these "remedies" now is not the least part of the case for monetary policy.

2. J. M. Keynes, *Monetary Reform* (New York, 1924), p. 30.

PART IV
Comments on Method

Lange on Price Flexibility and Employment
A Methodological Criticism[*]

THIS article, initially undertaken as a conventional review of Oscar Lange's *Price Flexibility and Employment*,[1] has, in process, turned into a lengthy critique of the methodology used by Lange to evaluate the effects of price flexibility. This shift reflects contradictory impressions derived from a first reading of the book—impressions that paralleled and reinforced those derived from reading other work of the same kind. Here is an obviously first-class intellect at work; yet the analysis seems unreal and artificial. Here is a brilliant display of formal logic, abstract thinking, complicated chains of deduction; yet the analysis seems more nearly a rationalization of policy conclusions previously reached than a basis for them. What is there about the type of theorizing employed that makes it sterile even in the hands of so competent a practitioner as Lange?

Lange's book is an excellent example to use in examining this question, precisely because it is, within its own frame of reference, so good. There is no magic formula for wringing knowledge about complicated problems from stubborn facts. No method is proof against incompetent application. The merits of a method of analysis can be judged only when it is carefully used by a master of it. Lange is clearly a master of what we shall later term "taxonomic theorizing," and he has used it in this book to examine carefully an important problem. The book is, therefore, a good text for a methodological sermon.

I. Summary of Lange's Analysis

Lange seeks to answer the following question: Granted that the direct effect of a fall in the price of an underemployed factor

* Reprinted from *American Economic Review*, XXXVI (September, 1946), 613–31.

1. Bloomington, Ind.: Principia Press, 1944. Pp. ix+140.

of production is to increase the employment of that factor, what indirect effects may frustrate or reinforce this direct effect? There are, of course, an indefinitely large number of possible sources of indirect effects. Lange analyzes five: (1) changes in the demand for and supply of money (chap. iv); (2) changes in expected future prices (chap. v); (3) uncertainty (chap. vi); (4) imperfect competition (chap. vii); and (5) international trade (chap. viii). The chapters dealing with these effects follow three chapters setting forth the problem and are followed by five chapters that seek to apply the analysis to an examination of (1) the "orthodox" theory which "denies that oversaving and limitation of investment opportunities can take place in an economy with flexible prices of factors of production and flexible interest rates" (p. 51); (2) the effects of "innovations"; and (3) "the problem of policy," that is, the economic policy that ought currently to be adopted by society.

The analysis is consistently abstract; the style is perhaps best described as verbal mathematics; and the text is followed by a formal mathematical appendix analyzing the mathematical conditions for the stability of economic equilibrium. "Facts" are introduced to limit somewhat the range of possibilities considered but, except for the final chapter, play no other role in the analysis. In the final chapter, which deals with "The Problem of Policy," facts are used to select from the bewildering variety of theoretical possibilities those that, in Lange's view, correspond most closely with the economic world prior to the first World War and subsequent to the second. As would be expected, the abstract reasoning is of a high order; Lange's past work has adequately demonstrated his mastery of formal logic and his ability to manipulate symbols and concepts and to lead the reader astutely through a lengthy and abstruse theoretical argument.

The full detail of Lange's analysis of indirect effects cannot be reproduced here; a brief summary may indicate the kinds of indirect effects treated.

A. MONETARY EFFECTS

Suppose that an initial equilibrium position is disturbed by the appearance of an additional supply of some factor of production and that in consequence its price falls. This fall in price will stimulate the substitution of this factor for others (the intratemporal substitution effect), and the associated fall in the price of products produced primarily with this factor will stimulate the substitution of these products for products produced primarily with other factors (the expansion effect). These substitutions will in turn cause the prices of other factors and of other products to fall. Where and how will the process end?

This depends, in the first instance, on the monetary effect of these price changes. The initial and induced price declines increase the real value of the cash balances previously held by the community. If there is no change in either the real quantity of cash balances the community desires to hold or the nominal quantity of money, there is an excess supply of cash balances. The inflationary influence of this excess supply of cash balances prevents the prices of other factors and other products from falling as much as the price of the factor initially underemployed and the prices of the products produced primarily with that factor and thereby permits the initial price decline to be effective in producing a new equilibrium with full employment of the initially underemployed factor.

There is, in Lange's terminology, a positive monetary effect. But suppose the price declines lead to a reduction in the real quantity of cash balances available relative to the real quantity desired—for example, because the nominal quantity of money is reduced by a larger fraction than prices fall. This negative monetary effect is a deflationary influence that forces all prices down, leads to more unemployment than there was initially, and causes a cumulative decline in prices. Why should the nominal quantity of money remain constant, increase, or decrease? What is the mechanism or process whereby this occurs? Lange is not interested in such questions. He is enumerating theoretical possibilities, not describing the real world.

B. PRICE EXPECTATIONS

Expectations about future prices constitute one important factor, so far neglected, that may cause a change in the real quantity of cash balances the community desires to hold. Suppose the fall in the price of the underemployed factor leads to a general expectation of a larger (percentage) fall in the price expected to prevail at a later date and that the associated declines in prices of products and other factors lead to similar expectations about their future prices (elastic price expectations). It will then be advantageous to shift purchases from the present to the future. In so far as this shift affects the underemployed factor, it may partly, fully, or more than offset the direct increase in employment. In so far as it affects products and other factors, it is equivalent to a general desire to hold a larger real quantity of cash balances—to substitute money for goods. Unless the real quantity of money available increases at least proportionately, there will be a negative monetary effect. Similarly, if future prices are expected to fall by a smaller percentage than present prices (inelastic price expectations), it will be advantageous to shift purchases from the future to the present, the real quantity of cash balances that the community desires to hold will decrease, and the monetary effect will be positive unless the real quantity of money available decreases at least proportionately.

C. UNCERTAINTY

The strength of the intertemporal substitution effects engendered by changes in expected future prices depends on the degree of uncertainty that attaches to these expectations. The periods of time for which men will plan—their economic horizons—will be shortened by an increase in the uncertainty they attach to their expectations and lengthened by a decrease in uncertainty. "An economy with flexible factor and product prices is likely to involve greater uncertainty of price expectations than one in which some prices are rigid" (p. 34). In consequence, intertemporal substitution effects will tend to be smaller in the former than in the latter economy.

D. IMPERFECT COMPETITION

Imperfections of competition arising from monopolies and monopsonies, or monopolistic competition and monopsonistic competition, add nothing new to the analysis; they necessitate

TABCO 5081

solely a change in the form of statement. Oligopolies and oligopsonies are another matter. Lange regards a "kink" in the demand schedule as the essential feature of oligopoly and in the supply schedule as the essential feature of oligopsony. These "kinks" imply discontinuities in the corresponding marginal revenue or marginal cost curves. In consequence, the marginal cost curve can shift without giving an oligopolist an incentive to change the output or price of his product, and the marginal-value-productivity curve of a factor can shift without giving an oligopsonist an incentive to change the quantity purchased or the price of the factor. Oligopoly and oligopsony may, therefore, thwart both intratemporal and intertemporal substitution, the incentive to a change in output or in the employment of factors being lost in the discontinuities. Indeed, if the underemployed factor is purchased solely by oligopolists, even the direct effect of a reduction in its price may be simply an increase in the oligopolist's profit and no increase in employment.

E. INTERNATIONAL TRADE

The final source of indirect effects, international trade, hardly deserves separate consideration. The direct effect of a reduction in the price of an underemployed factor is likely to be concentrated mainly in the country in which the factor is located, whereas the indirect effects spread through the world. Consequently, if the country in question is a small part of a world in which trade is tolerably free, most of the indirect effects are experienced elsewhere, and international trade is a stabilizing influence. If the country is a large part of the world economy, the indirect effects will have important reactions on it, and "the result depends on the net effect upon the real quantity of money in the country under consideration" (p. 50).

II. CRITICISM OF LANGE'S ANALYSIS

"We have found," says Lange in summarizing some of his results at the beginning of the chapter on "The Problem of Policy," "that only under very special conditions does price flexibility result in the automatic maintenance or restoration of equilibrium of demand for and supply of factors of production.

These conditions require a combination of such a responsiveness of the monetary system and such elasticities of price expectations as produce a positive monetary effect, sensitivity of intertemporal substitution to changes in interest rates (if the positive monetary effect leads to a change in the demand for securities rather than to a direct change in the demand for commodities), absence of highly specialized factors with demand or supply dependent on strongly elastic price expectations, and, finally, absence of oligopolistic or oligopsonistic rigidities of output and input. To a certain extent, the absence of a positive monetary effect may be replaced by the stabilizing influence of foreign trade in an atomistic international market (among the different countries)" (p. 83).

The implication might be thought to be that these "very special conditions" for full employment will seldom or never be fulfilled. But such an implication is contradicted by Lange's next sentence: "There are good reasons to believe that these conditions were approximately realized in the long run during a period which extended from the 1840's until 1914" (p. 83).

This apparent contrast between "very special conditions" and their satisfaction for some seventy years emphasizes what seems to the reviewer the fundamental weakness of the kind of theorizing incorporated in this book—a weakness of the species, not of this example, since the book is perhaps as ably constructed an example of the species as one could hope to find.

A. ALTERNATIVE THEORETICAL APPROACHES

Theory can be used in two very different ways in the development of a science. The approach that is standard in the physical sciences is to use theory to derive generalizations about the real world. The theorist starts with some set of observed and related facts, as full and comprehensive as possible. He seeks a generalization that will explain these facts; he can always succeed; indeed, he can always find an indefinitely large number of generalizations. The number of observed facts is finite, and the number of possible theories is infinite; infinitely many theories can therefore be found that are consistent with the observed facts. The theorist therefore calls in some arbitrary principle such as "Occam's razor" and settles on a particular generalization or theory. He tests this theory to make sure that it is logically consistent, that its elements are susceptible of empirical determination, and that it will explain adequately the facts he started with. He then seeks to deduce from his theory facts other than those he used to derive it and to check these deductions against reality. Typically some deduced "facts" check and others do not; so he revises his theory to take account of the additional facts.

The ultimate check of deduced against observed facts is essential in this process. A theory that has no implications that facts, potentially capable of being observed, can contradict is useless for prediction: if all possible occurrences are consistent with it, it cannot furnish a basis for selecting those that are likely.

The approach used by Lange, and all too common in economics, is very different. Lange largely dispenses with the initial step—a full and comprehensive set of observed and related facts to be generalized—and in the main reaches conclusions no observed facts can contradict. His emphasis is on the formal structure of the theory, the logical interrelations of the parts. He considers it largely unnecessary to test the validity of his theoretical structure except for conformity to the canons of formal logic. His categories are selected primarily to facilitate logical analysis, not empirical application or test. For the most part, the crucial question, "What observed facts would contradict the generalization suggested, and what operations could be followed to observe such critical facts?" is never asked; and the theory is so set up that it could seldom be answered if it were asked. The theory provides formal models of imaginary worlds, not generalizations about the real world.

This formal approach takes a rather special cast in this book—a cast that tends, on the one hand, to conceal somewhat the formal and artificial character of the analysis, while, on the other, it gives special play to many of the weaknesses of formal theorizing in general. Theory is here used largely as a taxonomic device. Lange starts with a number of abstract functions whose relevance—though not their form or content—is suggested by casual observation of the world—excess demand functions (the orthodox demand schedule minus the orthodox supply schedule) for goods and money, the variables including present and future (expected) prices. He then largely leaves the real world and, in effect, seeks to enumerate all possible economic systems to which these functions could give rise. The kind of economic system and the results in that system will depend on the specific character of the functions and their interrelations, and there clearly are a very large number of permutations and combinations.

Having completed his enumeration, or gone as far as he can or thinks desirable, Lange then seeks to relate his theoretical structure to the real world by judging to which of his alternative possibilities the real world corresponds. Is it any wonder that "very special conditions" will have to be satisfied to explain the real world? If a physicist or astronomer were to explore all possible interrelations among a variable number of planets, each of which could be of any size, density, or configuration, and possess any possible gravitational properties, he would surely find that only very special conditions would explain the existing universe. There are an infinite number of theoretical systems; there are only a few real worlds.[2]

Wherein is the procedure attributed to the natural sciences superior to the formal theorizing, and its taxonomic variant,

2. Cf. A. C. Pigou, *The Economics of Welfare* (4th ed.; London: Macmillan & Co., 1932), pp. 6–7: "It is open to us to construct an economic science either of the pure type represented by pure mathematics or of the realistic type represented by experimental physics. Pure economics in this sense—an unaccustomed sense, no doubt —would study equilibria and disturbances of equilibria among groups of persons actuated by any set of motives x. Under it, among innumerable other subdivisions would be included at once an Adam-Smithian political economy, in which x is given the value of the motives assigned to the economic man—or to the normal man— and a non-Adam-Smithian political economy, corresponding to the geometry of Lobatschewsky, under which x consists of love of work and hatred of earnings. For pure economics both these political economies would be equally true; it would not be relevant to inquire what the value of x is among the actual men who are living in the world now. Contrasted with this pure science stands realistic economics, the interest of which is concentrated upon the world known in experience, and in nowise extends to the commercial doings of a community of angels. Now, if our end is practice, it is obvious that a political economy that did so extend would be for us merely an amusing toy. Hence it must be the realistic, and not the pure, type of science that constitutes the object of our search. We shall endeavour to elucidate, not any generalised system of possible worlds, but the actual world of men and women as they are found in experience to be."

adopted by Lange? Is it not preferable to derive all possible theories rather than a single theory? The reason this question cannot be answered with the affirmative it seems superficially to invite is that each theory included in the set of possible theories derived by the Lange approach is of necessity very different from, and much inferior to, the single theory devised to explain a full and comprehensive set of related facts. The attempt to construct a system of models leads the theorist to make each a formal entity. And this, in turn, leads him to consider an enormously oversimplified universe and to make classifications within that universe that have no direct empirical counterpart. The complexity of the approach, the limited range of factors it can comprehend, and the urge to have the results bear on pressing current problems are likely to, though they need not, lead him into positive error. The resulting system of formal models has no solid basis in observed facts and yields few if any conclusions susceptible of empirical contradiction. Lange's book offers apt illustrations of each of these points, and we shall consider them in order.

B. STRUCTURAL WEAKNESSES OF LANGE'S APPROACH

1. *Oversimplification.*—To make the search for all possible theories at all feasible, the theorist must start with but a few kinds of functions. If he insists on making his analysis specific, he will have to use only a few functions of each kind and introduce only a few separate variables. (This approach is exemplified by much of what is termed "Keynesian" economics.) If he is willing, as Lange is, to keep his analysis exceedingly abstract, he can consider an indefinitely large number of variables and of functions of each kind, since, on the abstract level on which he has chosen to operate, multiplication of variables and functions of the same kind is likely to mean simply the insertion of appropriate "etc.'s" into the argument; it is not likely to add any essential complication.

The theorist thereby gains the appearance of generality without the substance. For example, Lange deals at most with four kinds of functions: they are the excess demand functions for (1) commodities (factors of production and products); (2) stocks (securities promising an indefinite income); (3) bonds (fixed-income securities); and (4) money.[3] There may be an indefinitely large number of functions of each of the first three kinds, since there may be many commodities, stocks, and bonds. And each function may have an indefinitely large number of independent variables, since excess demand is taken to be a function of all present and future (expected) prices. Further, other functions (cost functions, supply functions, etc.) are sometimes introduced. But the only purpose they serve is to provide a basis for imposing restrictions on the shape or structure of the excess demand functions.

The basic fact is that Lange's system—his abstract economic world—contains only four kinds of things and four kinds of functional relations. There is no room in his theoretical system (as contrasted with his digressions—see the discussion in Sec. II, C, 3, below, of friction) for such obviously important factors as lags in response, discontinuities in feasible investment undertakings, and physical limitations on the time that it takes for economic activities to be initiated and conducted or for differentiation in the structural role of different kinds of products or factors of production, different kinds of securities or bonds, or even different kinds of money. There is no room for any mechanism of response, except as the mechanism is incorporated in the abstract functions, or, in any fundamental sense, for uncertainty—probability distributions rather than single-valued expectations (see the discussion in Sec. II, C, 4, below, of uncertainty). And even the functions considered are far from general; they are, for example, implicitly assumed to be single-valued.

The theorist who seeks to devise a generalization from observed facts will also have to simplify and abstract from reality. But it is clear that he need not limit himself to anything like so simple a system as Lange uses.

2. *Use of classifications that have no direct empirical counterpart.*—A second weakness of formal theorizing, and especially the taxonomic variant adopted by Lange, is the kind of classifications

3. A minor qualification is necessary when imperfect competition is introduced. This requires a change in the name of the excess demand function but not in its abstract character or role.

to which it leads. The theorist starts with a simplified system, either specific and containing only a few functions and variables or, as in Lange's work, highly abstract and nonspecific and containing many functions and many variables. He seeks to determine all results that can flow from the assumed system. The number of results, of possible interrelations among the elements of his system, is bound to be very large. Only a few of the combinations and permutations correspond with real worlds, since there are only a few real worlds. His desire to be realistic motivates him to classify his theories, results, or concepts along lines that have a direct empirical counterpart. But such classifications will not fit the greater part of his theoretical structure, since only by chance would a classification suited to the small part of his analysis that corresponds with reality also be suited to the larger part that does not.

The theorist's urge to be realistic therefore almost inevitably conflicts with his urge to be theoretically comprehensive. The result is likely to be a compromise. He uses classifications (and especially names) that appear to have empirical meaning; but, in order to apply them to his entire analysis, he is forced to define them in a way that eliminates their direct empirical content. The end result is likely to be classifications that do not satisfy the initial empirical motivation and yet are not those best suited to the theoretical analysis.

An example of a classification that has no direct empirical counterpart is Lange's classification of monetary changes as having positive, neutral, or negative effects. Lange considers that an initial decline in the price of an underemployed factor may have one of three ultimate results on its employment: (1) a new equilibrium at full employment of that factor; (2) continued underemployment of that factor of the same magnitude as the initial underemployment; or (3) a cumulative increase in the underemployment of that factor.[4] In discussing the effect of changes

---

4. Lange recognizes the existence of two other possibilities: continued noncumulative underemployment (4) less than the initial underemployment, or (5) more than the initial underemployment. He disregards these because they imply multiple positions of equilibrium and "the possibility of multiple equilibrium . . . seems to be very unlikely in practice." The adequacy of this justification is discussed below (see

in price expectations and in the monetary system on the ultimate result, he is naturally led to classify different kinds of changes in price expectations and the monetary system according as they lead to one or another result. If they result in full employment of the initially underemployed factor, the monetary effect is said to be positive; if they result in continued underemployment at the initial level, the monetary effect is said to be neutral; if they result in a cumulative increase in underemployment, the monetary effect is said to be negative.[5]

The words used lead one to expect that a neutral monetary effect, for example, would be produced by some kind of neutral monetary policy—a policy that in some way would involve setting up a monetary framework and then not manipulating it in response to detailed economic changes. Nothing like this is the case. An explicit monetary policy aimed at achieving a neutral (or positive or negative) monetary effect would be exceedingly complicated, would involve action especially adapted to the particular disequilibrium to be corrected, and would involve knowledge, particularly about price expectations, that even in principle, let alone in practice, would be utterly unattainable.

Similarly, suppose one could observe in isolation the reaction of an economic system to the initial underemployment of a single factor of production. Would it be possible to tell whether the monetary effect was positive, neutral, or negative? One could observe the result and then say that the monetary effect was of the kind stated as necessary to produce that result. But this would, of course, be pure tautology. One could not, by any reasonable stretch of the imagination, obtain and combine the information about monetary action, price expectations, and the shape of the relevant functions that would be necessary to determine what the monetary effect would be and thereby to predict the ultimate

---

Sec. II, C, 1, below). In principle there are still other possibilities involving one or more changes in direction.

5. This definition is, in part, read into Lange. His explicit definition is in terms of the relative changes in the demand for and supply of money; as he uses it, this definition reduces to that stated above.

result. Lange's classification is designed to classify theoretical possibilities; it has no direct counterpart in the real world.[6]

C. ERRORS OF EXECUTION FOSTERED BY LANGE'S APPROACH

The weaknesses of oversimplification and unsatisfactory classification so far considered are implicit in the logic of the formal theorizing, and its taxonomic variant, adopted by Lange. The errors of execution to be considered now are not. Psychological, not logical, considerations make them likely. It is obviously impossible to make a comprehensive list of possible errors; there is no limit to the kinds of errors mortal man may commit. We shall, therefore, restrict the discussion to the following, which are exemplified in Lange's book: (1) casual empiricism; (2) invalid use of inverse probability; (3) introduction of factors not included in the fundamental theoretical system, exemplified by the introduction of "friction"; and (4) unwillingness to accept logical but unrealistic implications of the system, exemplified by the treatment of "uncertainty." The first two are fostered by the complexity induced by the taxonomic approach and the resultant desire to limit the number of possibilities considered; the second two, by the urge to be realistic.

The number of permutations and combinations of even a small number of elements each of which can have several forms or values is so large that there is a strong incentive to limit the number of possibilities considered in detail. One obviously attractive method, though one that is really inconsistent with the basic theoretical approach, is to rule out possibilities that on one ground or another can be judged "unrealistic" or "extreme." There is nothing wrong with this procedure if the evidence on which the possibilities are judged to be unrealistic is convincing. The danger is that the urge to simplify and the preoccupation with abstract logic will lead to the ruling-out of possibilities on grounds that are either unconvincing or wrong. Lange does not

---

6. Two other examples of classifications that have no direct empirical counterpart are the classification of claims into stocks, bonds, and money (p. 15) and the classification of the set of elasticities of price expectations as prevailingly elastic, inelastic, or of unit elasticity (p. 22).

avoid this danger. He rules out many possibilities simply by asserting that they are unrealistic, without presenting any empirical evidence (causal empiricism), and others because they are special theoretical cases (invalid use of inverse probability).

1. *Casual empiricism.*—The example of casual empiricism that shows the motivation best is Lange's statement: "These complications are disregarded in the text in order to simplify the argument and also because they do not seem to be very important in practice" (p. 57 n.). The complications in question are certain possibilities that arise when, contrary to the assumption made in the text, the "amount of real excess cash balances available . . . [enters] as an independent variable in the function expressing the propensity to consume" (p. 57 n.). The statement does not, therefore, refer to facts of immediate experience; yet no evidence is given for the validity of the empirical conclusion.

The example that perhaps shows best why no confidence can be placed in such statements and how difficult it would be to test them is a statement cited in footnote 4: "We disregard, however, the possibility of multiple equilibrium because it seems to be very unlikely in practice" (p. 10, n. 13). How could this empirical statement be tested? One way would be to evaluate explicitly from empirical evidence, or, at least, discover the form of, each of Lange's indefinitely numerous equations, and determine mathematically whether, and, if so, under what conditions, the resultant system of equations has one or more solutions for a relevant range of values of the independent variables.

Another way would be to specify some criterion for determining when an empirical situation is an equilibrium position in Lange's system and when it is a disequilibrium position in the process of being corrected; secure data on both the dependent and the independent variables for a large number of empirically realized equilibrium positions; classify these positions into sets for which the values of the independent variables are the same; and for those sets (if any) containing more than one position compare the dependent variables to determine whether they are the same.

Lange, of course, presents no evidence along either of these lines; it seems exceedingly doubtful that it would be feasible to do so; and there appears to be no other method of judging from empirical evidence the likelihood of multiple positions of equilibrium.

Another example of casual empiricism is Lange's statement that "empirically it seems highly unlikely that there is any decrease at all in the rate of increase of uncertainty" (p. 33, n. 12). The only definition of uncertainty Lange gives leaves at least one numerical parameter unspecified.[7] Even if specific values were given to the unspecified parameters, it is exceedingly doubtful that it would be possible, even in principle, to measure the degree of uncertainty attached to a man's expectations about future prices, as Lange defines that term. Yet he finds it possible to make an empirical statement about not only the first derivative of uncertainty but even the second derivative.[8]

The kind of casual empiricism exemplified by the statements quoted and cited is bad empiricism not because these statements are wrong but because there is no way of telling whether they are right or wrong. None of them refers to a fact of immediate experience about which the reader can be expected to be an expert,[9] or a fact about which Lange can be expected to be an expert, or a fact that thorough and widely known empirical research has so firmly established that it can be taken as demonstrated without citation. Yet they are simply asserted to be true, and not a shred of evidence is offered for them. The reader must take them or leave them; he cannot judge them. If this is good practice for empirical work, it is equally good for theoretical. Lange might as well simply assert his theoretical conclusions without giving the

7. Lange defines the degree of uncertainty of price expectations as the difference between two extreme expected prices, the higher being attributed a probability x of being exceeded, and the lower a probability y of not being exceeded (Lange does not introduce these symbols but gives a numerical example in which both x and y are .05). x and y are the unspecified parameters referred to above. A single parameter would suffice if x were always required to be equal (or bear any other fixed relation) to y or if the degree of uncertainty were defined as the width of the narrowest price band (or set of price bands) within which the entrepreneur feels z per cent confident $[z=100(1-x-y)]$ that the future price will be.

8. Other examples of what I have called "casual empiricism" appear on pp. 9, 29, 40, 53, 59, 61, 65, 67, 74. This list is not intended to be exhaustive.

9. Lange makes a few empirical statements that might be interpreted as referring to facts of immediate experience. These have been excluded from the list given in the preceding footnote.

basis for them; and no empirical worker need hesitate to assert: "It is obvious on theoretical grounds that . . . ."

In the absence of the empirical evidence, no one of Lange's empirical statements can be considered more than a conjecture, and his theoretical analysis must be considered incomplete and fragmentary, since he uses these empirical statements to limit the number of possibilities analyzed.

2. *Invalid use of inverse probability.*—A second method which Lange uses to reduce the number of possibilities he considers is to rule out certain possibilities because they are "special cases." The quotation cited earlier from the beginning of Lange's chapter entitled "The Problem of Policy" demonstrates that Lange realizes that "very special" theoretical conditions may well be empirically realistic. Yet elsewhere he writes as if this were impossible. For example, Lange asserts that "the marginal-revenue schedule [of a monopolist] is negatively sloped . . . as a rule, because the demand schedules are assumed in the text to be negatively sloped. Exceptions are possible when the demand schedule has a strong curvature which is convex toward the axis of abscissae" (p. 37).

But how does he know that what he calls "exceptions" are not the rule in experience? The only justification he gives for regarding them as exceptions is the sentence just quoted. The implication of this sentence presumably is that "a strong curvature which is convex toward the axis of abscissae" is mathematically a special case; that, if all possible negatively sloping curves were enumerated, only a small fraction would have this property. The conclusion that only a small fraction of real marginal revenue schedules have this property follows only if certain assumptions are made about the probability of the various mathematical possibilities. But there is no basis for assigning such probabilities; the conclusion therefore represents an invalid use of inverse probability reasoning.[10]

10. None of the examples in Lange of what seems to be invalid use of inverse probability is as explicit as the hypothetical example given in the next paragraph of the text. The attribution of this fallacy to him, though it involves some measure of interpretation, seems justified both by the general phrasing and by the absence of any other possible basis for statements he makes. The justification is clearest for the example cited above and the parallel example on the same page dealing with the

The essence of the fallacy can be more simply indicated by an example that is faithful to Lange's logic but refers to immediately observable facts. We start with the proposition that the price of a single newspaper will be a whole number of cents. The price of a newspaper could be 1 cent, 2 cents, 3 cents. . . . We conclude that, as a rule, the price will be more than 10 cents, since there are only 10 possible prices equal to or less than 10 cents, but an indefinitely large number more than 10 cents, and a price of 10 cents or less is therefore a "very special" case. The conclusion is of course false, yet the reasoning by which it was reached does not differ from that implied by Lange at many points.

If this kind of reasoning is to lead to valid conclusions, there must be some basis for judging the probability of the various theoretical possibilities. A classical example where this is possible is the reasoning underlying the conclusion that, under essentially static conditions, demand curves are, as a rule, negatively sloped. The exception, Giffen's paradox of a positively sloped demand curve, corresponds to conditions (inferior good, large income effect relative to substitution effect) that are not only theoretically special but also appear empirically special, as judged by everyday observation of the world.

3. *Introduction of friction.*—We turn now to a pair of errors that derive less from the urge to simplify than from the urge to be realistic. As said above, the urge to be realistic is likely to conflict with the urge to simplify. When it does, one way to attain both objectives is to be illogical. Lange's book provides examples of two quite different devices whereby realism can be gained by the sacrifice of logic: the introduction of "friction" and the treatment of uncertainty.

Despite the numerous possible results that can flow from Lange's simplified theoretical system, there are realistic possibilities left out. As mentioned earlier, there is no place in Lange's system for lags in response, for delayed reactions, for the manifold hindrances to change we are wont to refer to as "friction." Accordingly, to make the possibilities he considers more compre-

---

marginal expenditure schedule of a monopsonist. For other, somewhat less clear, examples see pp. 51, 53, 65, 68, 69, 80.

hensive, Lange introduces friction. For example, "with some friction present, the effects of changes in factor prices may become too weak to be of great practical significance" (p. 34).[11] Despite Lange's care to define such terms as "securities," "bonds," "money," and "products," he nowhere defines "friction." There is a very good reason for this. Lange's "friction" is a *deus ex machina;* it has no place in his theoretical system; he cannot really define it without going outside his system and, indeed, contradicting it.

His system contains equations purporting to show the excess demand for commodities, stocks, bonds, and money as a single-valued function of all present and future (expected) prices. What can friction mean in terms of this system? It might be interpreted as meaning that the excess demand is not always that shown by the equations; but that would simply mean that the equations were wrong. Either a different system of equations is required (e.g., one containing stochastic elements) or no system of equations exists that describes the economy about which Lange is talking. It might be interpreted as meaning that excess demand is a function not only of present and future prices but also of past prices and quantities. (This seems the interpretation that accords best with common-sense notions about friction.) But then the equations should be rewritten and the system expanded to include these additional variables; if this were done, friction would disappear as a separate entity.

There are presumably other possible interpretations, but those I have been able to think of are either inconsistent with Lange's theoretical system or require a thorough revision of the system; none gives "friction" a separate existence as a supplement to Lange's theoretical system. Those of Lange's conclusions that rely on the introduction of friction are therefore different in kind from the rest of his conclusions. They are not the logical implications of a consistent theoretical system but simply obiter dicta

11. Friction is introduced on pp. 18, 19, 34, 47, 51, and 61. On p. 51 it is used in describing an "orthodox" position. The other five uses are all in connection with Lange's own analysis. It is interesting that, in each of these cases, friction is introduced to minimize the possible favorable influence of flexible prices on employment; at no point is it introduced as a factor that might offset unfavorable influences.

whose acceptance involves implicit expression of skepticism about the rest of the analysis.

4. *Treatment of uncertainty.*—Lange's treatment of uncertainty exemplifies an unwillingness to carry his theoretical reasoning to its logical conclusion if that conclusion is clearly unrealistic. The phase of uncertainty with which he deals is the uncertainty attaching to men's expectations about future prices. "At best, the entrepreneur or consumer expects that a given future price can have *a set of possible values,* some probability corresponding to each of these values" (p. 29; italics in original). To deal with these stochastic phenomena in full generality would enormously complicate the analysis. Lange avoids this by arguing that "we can substitute for the most probable prices expected with uncertainty equivalent prices expected with certainty. Let us call them the *effective* expected prices. . . . By means of this device, uncertain price expectations can be reduced to certain ones. In consequence, an increase in sellers' uncertainty acts in the same way as a reduction of their expected future selling prices, while an increase in buyers' uncertainty acts in the same way as an increase in their expected future prices of purchase" (pp. 31–32).

The substitution of a single "effective expected price" for a probability distribution of expected prices is a definite departure from the taxonomic approach followed in most of the book. The taxonomic approach would require consideration of all possibilities—those in which a single price cannot be substituted for a probability distribution of expected prices, as well as those in which it can. Such generality could have been attained by treating the entire probability distribution, rather than a single "effective expected price," as an independent variable in the appropriate excess demand function. The resulting model would, formally at least, have been consistent with any observable phenomenon and hence, like most of Lange's theoretical system, incapable of empirical contradiction.

This is not true of the partial model that results from Lange's departure from his usual procedure. Since it is only a partial model, its implications need not include all possible observable behavior; hence it is susceptible of empirical contradiction. Lange does not test his model by deducing all its implications and comparing them with actual behavior. He states some of the implications of his model, and these are all consistent with actual behavior. He does not, however, state all the implications of his model. Had he done so, he would have found, as we shall show, that some of them are contradicted by the actual behavior of men in the presence of uncertainty. His model must therefore be rejected.

Lange uses his model

to determine the length of the period of time over which individuals plan their purchases and sales. This period has been called very aptly the *economic horizon* of the individual. As long as price expectations are *subjectively* certain, the economic horizon is indeterminate. This indeterminateness disappears when uncertainty is allowed for.

As a rule, the uncertainty of price expectations is the greater the more distant the planned purchase or sale is (at least from a given date on). . . . Consequently, the effective expected prices of goods to be sold at various future dates decrease, while the effective prices of goods to be bought at various future dates increase. This imposes a limit upon the dates for which any sales or purchases are planned at all. Firms (entrepreneurs) find that, beyond a certain date, the effective expected prices of their products are less than the effective expected marginal costs and that the effective expected marginal value productivities of the factors they plan to employ are less than the effective expected prices of these factors. In a similar way, households (consumers) find that beyond a certain date the effective prices of goods they plan to buy are higher than the effective marginal rates of substitution of the respective goods for money. Thus beyond a certain date the effective expected prices of goods to be sold are too low to induce the planning of sales, while the effective expected prices of the goods to be bought are too high to induce the planning of purchases. No sales or purchases are planned beyond this date. In this way the length of the economic horizon of each individual and corporation is determined [pp. 32–33].

Now this conclusion, which is as far as Lange goes, sounds eminently reasonable. No man plans specific purchases or sales extending into the indefinite future. It does not pay to do so when the future is uncertain. And if this were (*a*) a necessary implication and (*b*) the only logical implication of Lange's theoretical model, no fault could be found with the model. But neither condition is satisfied. It is not a necessary implication because the effective expected selling prices could fall at a rapidly decreasing rate, the effective expected buying prices (for comparable units) could rise at a rapidly decreasing rate, both could approach asymptotes, and the asymptote of the selling prices could be above the asymptote of the buying prices. In this case there would be no finite economic horizon.[12]

Suppose effective expected selling prices decline and buying prices rise at rates that make the economic horizon finite. Lange's conclusion is then a necessary implication of his model, but by no means the only implication, and some of the other implications are far less reasonable. Consider again his model in terms of an individual family. According to the model, the head of the family can be supposed to behave in the real and uncertain world as he would in a fictitious world in which he expected with certainty that his income would decline steadily over time and that the prices of the things he buys would increase steadily over time.

In the fictitious world these are not conjectures; they are expectations held with certainty. He is certain that ultimately his current income will be so small relative to the prices of the things he wishes to buy that starvation will be inevitable for his family unless he can command resources other than his current income. (This follows from the conditions imposed on the rates of rise and decline in order to assure a finite economic horizon.) His first impulse will be to save and thereby provide additional resources. But it will do him no good to save in the form of money, since the certain rise in prices will wipe out the real value of the savings. Nor will it do him any good to save in the form of securities, since these will then become something he wants to sell, and Lange tells us that he must be assumed to behave as if he expected with certainty that the prices of goods to be sold will decline. It will therefore be even worse to put his sav-

12. In a footnote attached to the passage quoted above, Lange states: "There is good reason to believe that the risk premium increases at an increasing rate as the date of the planned purchase or sale extends farther into the future. . . . Our conclusion in the text is quite independent of the fact that the increase in the risk premium takes place at an increasing rate." The condition in the first of these sentences would be sufficient to guarantee a finite economic horizon, though it is more stringent than is necessary. The second of the sentences is therefore wrong or misleading. If the risk premium is not assumed to increase at an increasing rate, some other condition must be imposed to guarantee a finite economic horizon.

ings in securities than to keep them in cash. How can he escape this dilemma, since everything he touches turns to ashes?

One escape is to convert his savings into physical stocks of foodstuffs and other necessities and store them in storage space he purchases outright. (If he were to rent storage space, he would expect with certainty that the rent would rise so high that at his economic horizon he could not meet it.)[13] If he were fortunate, that is, if the expected future prices of goods to be bought did not rise too rapidly or of goods to be sold fall too rapidly, and if the expected life of his family (also converted presumably into an equivalent single value expected with certainty) were not too long, he and his family might be able so to contrive their affairs as to die natural deaths. The only other alternative to letting nature take its course at the appointed time is definitely to plan to commit suicide at a definitely specified future date. If the pincers of falling selling prices and rising buying prices is expected with certainty to close so fast that no possible skimping can yield a stockpile sufficient to last until natural death ends all planning, what else is there to do but plan for suicide?

Whichever alternative the man adopts, if we assume him to behave as if he expected with certainty falling income and rising prices, his actions will be affected immediately, and not only when the economic horizon arrives (as of course it never would, since he would soon find out that he was wrong to hold expectations with certainty). He will immediately curtail his standard of living below the one he would adopt if his expectations were rosier and immediately start accumulating physical stockpiles and buying storage space. And, similarly, businessmen, acting in accordance with Lange's model, would immediately start planning the liquidation of their enterprises.

This is, of course, a fantastic picture. It certainly does not correspond to the way men behave when faced with uncertainty.

13. If we were to extend Lange's model to uncertainty about things other than prices, even stockpiling would be no solution. There is some uncertainty about the future safety of goods in the stockpile; they might deteriorate or be destroyed by disaster. Following Lange, we may substitute for the actual expectations the certain expectation that a specified fraction of the stockpile, and no more, will be usable. This fraction will decline with time. Ultimately, therefore, even the stockpile will not suffice.

Yet it is a logical consequence of Lange's model, arrived at simply by filling in the gaps in Lange's deductions from the model.[14] Either the model must be discarded or all its implications, and not merely those that seem realistic, must be accepted. The device Lange adopts to simplify his analysis apparently also makes it a false image of reality. His model does not allow, in any fundamental sense, for stochastic variation.

III. CONCLUSION

We have not considered Lange's application of his theoretical analysis to "The Problem of Policy," as he entitles the last chapter of his book, nor do we intend to do so. This chapter represents the combination of unsupported empirical statements and theoretical conclusions that, as we have seen, neither deserve any particular confidence nor bear very directly on the real world. The lack of relevance of most of the theoretical analysis to the real world that derives from oversimplification and formal classification is concealed by the errors of execution enumerated above—casual empiricism, invalid use of inverse probability, introduction of factors external to the theoretical system, and the use of only some of the implications of a formal model that has others that are unrealistic.

Correction of these errors would make the analysis formally correct; it would also make it abundantly clear that the analysis has only the remotest bearing on problems of policy. The analysis would then assume the cast of Lange's mathematical appendix— which no one would be likely to consider directly applicable to problems of policy. Indeed, the analysis purged of the fallacies might best be formulated mathematically, since this would be

---

14. The point can be put more nearly in Lange's own terminology. Lange draws the conclusion from his model that "no sales or purchases are planned beyond this date [the economic horizon]" (p. 33). The argument above is that his model justifies the broader conclusion: "It is planned to make no sales or purchases beyond this date." This broader conclusion implies the conclusion Lange states but is not implied by it. The fact that this broader conclusion is an implication of Lange's model means that Lange's footnote 15 on p. 33, in which he argues that "the economic horizon, as here defined, does *not* limit the time over which provisions for the future are made," is inconsistent with his model, though reasonable as a description of human behavior.

more likely to assure logical rigor and, in addition, would avoid a tendency, almost unavoidable in verbal mathematics, to state conclusions that flow from special assumptions as if they had wider relevance and to stress special cases that lead to conclusions of particular interest.

The basic sources of the defects in Lange's theoretical analysis are the emphasis on formal structure, the attempt to generalize without first specifying in detail the facts to be generalized, and the failure to recognize that the ultimate test of the validity of a theory is not conformity to the canons of formal logic but the ability to deduce facts that have not yet been observed, that are capable of being contradicted by observation, and that subsequent observation does not contradict. In consequence, these defects are found in much economic theorizing that is not taxonomic in character. They are, however, especially likely to arise when the taxonomic approach is adopted, as their presence in the writings of so able and careful a theorist as Lange testifies.

A man who has a burning interest in pressing issues of public policy, who has a strong desire to learn how the economic system really works in order that that knowledge may be used, is not likely to stay within the bounds of a method of analysis that denies him the knowledge he seeks. He will escape the shackles of formalism, even if he has to resort to illogical devices and specious reasoning to do so. This is, of course, a poor way to escape the shackles of formalism. A far better way is to try to devise theoretical generalizations to fit as full and comprehensive a set of related facts about the real world as it is possible to get.

Lerner on the Economics of Control*

THE recent book by A. P. Lerner, *The Economics of Control,* is an analysis of the problem of maximizing economic welfare.[1] It deals with a wide range of the substantive topics requiring attention: the organization of production and allocation of resources under given conditions; the distribution of income; the role of investment and the adaptation of society to investment; unemployment and the business cycle; and foreign trade. On each topic it seeks to derive the formal conditions for an optimum and to propose institutional arrangements adapted to achieving these conditions.

Most of the book is devoted to the formal analysis of the conditions for an optimum. The institutional problems are largely neglected and, where introduced, treated by assertion rather than analysis. This disparity in the attention devoted to the formal and institutional problems is, however, obscured by an intermingling of the formal and institutional analysis. Formal analysis takes on the cast of institutional proposals, and conclusions about institutional arrangements seem to be derived from the formal analysis and supported by it, though, in fact, the formal analysis is almost entirely irrelevant to the institutional problem.

The result is that not only the title and the Introduction but even a first reading somehow generate the expectation and the illusion that the book contains a concrete program for economic reform. "In this way we shall be able to concentrate on what would be the best thing that the government can do in the social interest—what institutions would most effectively induce the individual members of society, while seeking to accomplish their own ends, to act in the way which is most beneficial for society as a whole" (p. 6). An attempt to set down the explicit details of the program dispels the illusion. Much of what at first reading

* Reprinted from *Journal of Political Economy,* LV (October, 1947), 405–16.

1. Abba P. Lerner, *The Economics of Control.* New York: Macmillan Co., 1944. Pp. xxii+428.

sounds like a concrete proposal, particularly about the general structure of society, turns out to be simply an admonition to the state that it behave correctly and intelligently.

The hortatory character of the proposals is foreshadowed in Lerner's initial discussion of "the rationally organized democratic state," which he names "the controlled economy":

> The fundamental point of the controlled economy is that it denies both collectivism and private enterprise as *principles* for the organization of society, but recognizes both of them as perfectly legitimate *means*. Its fundamental principle of organization is that in any particular instance the means that serves society best should be the one that prevails [p. 5].

Now surely it is no principle of organization that society do what is best for society. At most, it is an objective of society, though even as an objective it is obviously question-begging.

To illustrate more fully the difference between Lerner's formal analysis and his institutional proposals, we turn to his discussion of some of the major problems facing the "controlled economy." Three such problems occupy a central place in Lerner's analysis: (1) the optimum organization of resources under given conditions, (2) the optimum division of income, and (3) the dynamic problem of unemployment and fluctuations in economic activity.

I. THE ORGANIZATION OF RESOURCES UNDER GIVEN CONDITIONS

A. THE FORMAL CONDITIONS FOR AN OPTIMUM

Practically all economists, Lerner included, who have worked on the static problem of the organization of resources and who have regarded the welfare of the individual (rather than that of the "state" or some special class of individuals) as dominant and his ends as supreme have started with much the same assumptions and therefore reached much the same conclusions about the appropriate utilization with given techniques of given resources for given ends. Certain special problems have received rather more attention from some than from others (e.g., Lerner is especially attracted by problems associated with "indivisibilities" and neglects almost entirely problems raised by "unpaid costs" and "inappropriable services"). These special problems aside, the major and well-known result is that, given the distribution of the available resources among individuals, an optimum exists when any small change in the application of resources leads to a combination of decrements and increments in the output of various goods such that there is no system of barter exchanges whereby individuals would voluntarily accept the increments as compensation for the decrements.

Much of *The Economics of Control* is devoted to presenting the formal reasoning underlying this broad result and to developing in detail its implications for various sectors of the economy— the allocation of goods among consumers, the allocation of resources among industries, the utilization of resources within industries, foreign trade, and so on. Early in the analysis Lerner demonstrates the advantage of using a monetary system in place of barter, and thereafter the discussion is in money terms rather than in the physical terms in which the basic result is stated above. This enables him to give a fairly thorough exposition of current price theory along with his analysis of the optimum utilization of resources.

This part of the book is novel in exposition, though not in substance. Motivated by the question how society ought to work rather than how it does work, Lerner puts primary emphasis on the human wants and technical possibilities to which society must adjust rather than on the market expression of these wants and possibilities. The result is a highly unusual organization of topics. For example, demand and supply curves are first introduced on page 151 and then only in a footnote explaining that the elasticities of demand and supply are concepts analogous to the elasticity of substitution.

The exposition is novel not only in organization but also in style. Most of it is entirely abstract, yet Lerner uses graphs sparingly and mathematics not at all. He uses words, abbreviated substitutes for words, and simple arithmetical examples. The resulting exposition seems to the reviewer to have most of the disadvantages of a strictly mathematical exposition (it is abstract and artificial and requires sustained attention and retention of symbols) and none of the advantages (it is neither brief nor rigorous).[2]

B. INSTITUTIONAL ARRANGEMENTS TO ACHIEVE AN OPTIMUM

Granted that the optimum allocation of resources requires that marginal social benefit equal marginal social cost, to use Lerner's terms, what institutional arrangements will lead to the closest possible satisfaction of this condition? Lerner's answer to this question is imbedded in his analysis of the meaning and implications of the formal conditions, and some measure of exegesis is therefore required to extract it.

The one common principle of economic organization underlying his answer seems to be the use of the price mechanism for organizing economic activity. Lerner's acceptance of the price mechanism does not, however, mean acceptance of the particular institutional arrangements with which the price system is historically associated, namely, a free-enterprise exchange economy characterized by private ownership of the means of production. In such an economy prices perform five related but distinguishable functions: (1) they are a means of transmitting information about changes in the relative importance of different end-products and factors of production; (2) they provide an incentive to enterprises (*a*) to produce those products valued most highly by the market and (*b*) to use methods of production that economize relatively scarce factors of production; (3) they provide an incentive to owners of resources to direct them into the most highly remunerated uses. Prices are enabled to perform functions (2) and (3) because they are also used (4) to distribute output among the owners of resources. And, finally, prices serve (5) to ration fixed supplies of goods among consumers.[3]

2. Lerner's discussion on pp. 81–82 of the relation between marginal and average measurements is a simple illustration of what is meant by the statement that his exposition is not rigorous. He gives a numerical example, states "irrespective of the figures in any particular example we can see," and then indicates the general relationship. He does, of course, state the relationship correctly; but the intuitive leap from example to general result is an unsatisfactory substitute for rigorous derivation.

3. See F. H. Knight, *The Economic Organization* (University of Chicago, 1933), pp. 6–13, 31–35.

Lerner places major emphasis on the first function. He recognizes clearly, and states effectively, the enormous difficulty that would be involved in any attempt to control directly the allocation of resources.

In a collectivist economy this [the allocation of resources] might be attempted directly by the Ministry of Economic Planning, and many writers have proposed that it be done this way, even claiming that such centralization would be very efficient in planning everything to fit into everything else. This would require a centralized knowledge of what is going on in every factory, what are the changes from day to day in the demands and supplies at all possible prices of all goods and services and factors of production at all places in the economy, as well as the latest changes in technical knowledge in all branches of production. Obviously this calls for the Universal Mind of LaPlace, as Trotsky has suggested, and this is not practical. . . . Again the solution is to call in the price mechanism [p. 119].

Lerner recognizes, of course, both the interdependence of the various functions of the price mechanism and the efficiency and desirability of the price mechanism in providing incentives to individuals to adjust to the information transmitted by the price mechanism. "In private enterprise under conditions of perfect competition . . . the incentive is of exactly the right intensity" (p. 84). The reason he rejects exclusive reliance on price incentives is that individuals, in seeking to maximize their own incomes, will make the adjustments that are socially desirable (i.e., will bring about the satisfaction of the formal conditions for an optimum discussed above) only if they have no appreciable influence on the prices they pay or receive, that is, are operating under competitive conditions. The presence of monopoly power means that private and social interests diverge.

Lerner would therefore use the private-enterprise exchange system only for the competitive sector of the economy. For another sector he would use a device he entitles "counterspeculation" to eliminate any influence of sellers or buyers on price. By "counterspeculation," Lerner means a government guaranty to purchase an unlimited amount at a fixed price from sellers who would otherwise be monopolists or to sell an unlimited amount at a fixed price to buyers who would otherwise be monopsonists. The effect would be to replace a sloping segment of the demand curve for the monopolist's product (or of the supply curve facing the monopsonist) by a horizontal segment. If the price guaranteed by the government were equal to the competitive price, it could sell what it purchased (or buy what it sold) in the open market without loss.[4] Despite such comments as that cited above about the difficulties of centralized organization of economic activity, Lerner is quite sanguine about the ability of the Board of Counterspeculation to estimate what the competitive price would be. Counterspeculation will not, however, work if the monopoly arises from indivisibilities sufficient to lead to declining costs throughout the relevant range of output, since a price equal to marginal cost would mean that firms would go bankrupt. For such monopolies Lerner would use government ownership and operation. Lerner would also include in the collectivist sector some industries for which he regards counterspeculation as feasible, though he nowhere specifies the principles on the basis of which he would choose between counterspeculation and government ownership when both are feasible. Similarly, he nowhere discusses how to distinguish in practice between those industries that are sufficiently competitive to be left alone and those that are not.

For the collectivist sector it is obviously necessary to provide a substitute for the price (i.e., profit) incentives operative in the private sector. Two things are required: (1) instructions to managers how to use the information transmitted by prices and (2) means of assuring that the instructions are followed. Lerner would instruct the managers to pretend that they are operating under conditions of perfect competition and to play at private enterprise. His instructions would take the form of the *Rule:*

If the value of the marginal (physical) product of any factor is greater than the price of the factor, increase output. If it is less, decrease output. If it is equal to the price of the factor, continue producing at the same rate. (For then the right output has been reached.) [P. 64.]

This sounds simple enough. The simplicity is, however, deceptive. The rule is a purely formal statement that conceals all the diffi-

4. To be effective, the government would not only have to guarantee to purchase an unlimited amount from putative monopolists at a specified price, but it would also have to make its price the price ceiling for private sales; and, similarly, it would have to make its price the price floor on private purchases by monopsonists.

culties. Casual observation of the divergent fate of entrepreneurs in a highly competitive industry (like agriculture, retail trade, or manufacturing of furniture or clothing) is enough to indicate the difficulty of the problem, since they are trying to follow the rule and have an incentive "of exactly the right intensity" to do so.

It is therefore important not only to formulate instructions but also to specify effective means of assuring that they are followed. Lerner hardly discusses this problem at all. About all he says is that

some incentives in the form of rewards (and punishment too perhaps) will have to be developed for the manager who is subjected to the Rule, and there will be a delicate problem of making them neither too weak nor too strong. . . . It may seem strange to some that incentives to efficiency could be too strong, but this can be very serious. It can lead to a tyrannous disregard for the welfare of the workers and an inhuman red-tapism that would ultimately mean less and not more efficiency [p. 84].

But this is only part, and probably the least difficult part, of the problem, as the example of competitive entrepreneurs indicates. The manager's intentions must not only be good; he must be able to translate his intentions into practice. The higher administrators (who themselves need both incentives and tests of performance) must have some means of determining the extent to which the manager has been successful in his attempt to follow the rule. Under private enterprise profits are not only an incentive but also a criterion of performance and determine the entrepreneur's ability to get command over resources. They cannot serve these other functions in the collectivist sector, since Lerner seeks to collectivize precisely those industries for which he regards private profits as an inadequate test of social performance.

II. The Division of Income

A. FORMAL CONDITIONS

The distribution of resources among individuals, which is taken as one of the given conditions in analyzing the organization of resources, cannot, of course, be taken as given in fact, since the distribution can be modified by appropriate collective action.

Lerner does not consider directly the distribution of resources among individuals, but rather the associated problem of the distribution of income. The brief chapter dealing with this problem is extremely interesting. It presents a formal analysis leading to the conclusion that "if it is desired to maximize the total satisfaction in a society, the rational procedure is to divide income on an equalitarian basis" (p. 32). The analysis as given is not rigorous, primarily because of appeal to "equal ignorance."[5] It requires only a slight modification of the argument, however, to eliminate this appeal and to make Lerner's conclusion a rigorous implication of his assumptions, of which the following five are essential: (1) "It is not meaningless to say that a satisfaction one individual gets is greater or less than a satisfaction enjoyed by somebody else" (p. 25). This is taken to mean that numerical utilities can be assigned to the satisfactions enjoyed by individuals; and the values assigned to different individuals can appropriately be added. (2) "Each individual's satisfaction is derived only from his own income and not from the income of others" (p. 36). This means that the utility to an individual of any given income is not a function of the income of other individuals. (3) When incomes are unequal, the amount of income an individual receives is statistically independent of his capacity for enjoying it; that is, if individuals were classified by capacity to enjoy income, the probability distribution of income would be the same for all such classes. (4) The marginal utility of money income to an individual diminishes as income increases. (5) The total amount of income is unrelated to its distribution.[6]

5. E.g.: "The possibility of an increase in gain offsets the possibility of the diminution of gain since they are *equally likely to occur* in any particular case. There remains the net gain that is seen by itself in the case of equal capacities but which becomes only a *probable* gain on account of the possible increase or diminution of the gain which arises with unequal capacities" (pp. 29–30). (First italics mine.) "Such a blind shift from an equal division of income is *just as likely,* then, to increase as to diminish total satisfaction. . . . This would leave us indifferent as to the distribution of income . . . but for one other thing that tips the scale. Although the probability of a loss is *equal* to the probability of a gain, every time a movement is made away from an equalitarian division the *probable size* of the loss is greater than the *probable* size of the gain" (pp. 31–32). (All italics mine except *size.*)

6. Lerner's problem is closely analogous to a rather common problem in the theory of statistical inference, and his reasoning to the inverse probability reasoning that was initially used in statistics. The revolution in statistics during the last few decades has been associated with a replacement of the loose and inexact inverse probability reasoning by an exact, operationally defined, reasoning that makes no appeal to

Lerner recognizes, of course, that the fifth assumption is invalid and therefore concludes that "the principle of equality would have to compromise with the principle of providing such incentives as would increase the total of income available to be divided" (p. 36). The difficulty here is that the distribution of income is itself in considerable measure a resultant of the process of satisfying the mathematical conditions for an optimum utilization of given resources. Analytically, therefore, the distribution of income is not an independent "given" that can be manipulated without affecting the rest of the analysis. This difficulty could have been largely avoided by considering instead the distribution of resources. This point is of more than formal interest, since it suggests that measures to reduce inequality by altering the distribution of resources (such as social investment in the training of individuals, inheritance taxation, etc.) may interfere less with the optimum utilization of resources than measures that seek to redistribute income directly.

Lerner uses his analysis of the optimum distribution of income

---

"equal ignorance." Precisely the same substitution will make Lerner's argument rigorous.

The problem is to determine the distribution of income that will maximize the arithmetic sum of the utilities received by the individuals in the society subject to the assumptions listed in the text.

Consider any initial unequal distribution of income. Conceptually classify the individuals by their (unknown) capacities for satisfaction. Each such "satisfaction class" will contain only individuals who have identical capacities, i.e., have identical utility functions. By assumption (3) the average income of the persons in each such class is the same for every class. Furthermore, any redistribution of income among classes would invalidate assumption (3), so only redistributions within these classes will be consistent with the assumptions. Moreover, by assumption (2), changes in any one class will not affect any other class, so the problem reduces to the simpler problem of maximizing the aggregate utility of each satisfaction class separately.

For a particular satisfaction class, it is clear, given assumptions (1), (2), (4), and (5), that an equal distribution will maximize aggregate utility. If a dollar is taken from an individual with a larger income and given to an individual with a smaller income, the former loses less utility than the latter gains, by assumption (4); the aggregate income to be distributed is unaffected, by assumption (5), and the utility schedules of the two individuals, which were the same before the transfer, remain the same after, by assumption (2). This completes the proof, since equal distribution within each class, given equal mean incomes of different classes, implies equal income throughout the society.

to convert equality from an end in itself to a means to a more fundamental and presumably more obviously desirable end—namely, the maximization of total satisfaction in a society. For reasons stated in the next two paragraphs, Lerner's analysis seems to the reviewer rather to discredit the maximization of total satisfaction as a desirable end and to suggest that equality is much the more fundamental of the two.

An essential step in Lerner's analysis is the introduction of ignorance. Granted, says Lerner, that individuals differ in their capacities to enjoy satisfaction, that they are not equally efficient pleasure machines, there is no method of determining how efficient they are as pleasure machines and therefore no hope of adjusting the amount of income to the individual's efficiency. Any actual unequal division of income must therefore involve a random association of income with innate efficiency as a pleasure machine (assumption [3] above). Since the mistake of giving too much to an individual is more serious (because of the assumed diminishing marginal utility of income) than the mistake of giving too little, an unequal division of income yields a smaller total satisfaction than an equal division.

Eliminate the assumption of ignorance, and the same analysis immediately yields a justification of inequality if individuals do differ in capacity to enjoy satisfaction. And we must clearly be prepared to eliminate the assumption of ignorance. The talk about capacity to enjoy satisfaction is just empty talk unless there is at least a conceptual possibility of determining the relative efficiency of individuals as pleasure machines. One could hardly take the position that an analysis based on the capacity to enjoy satisfaction is relevant if it is impossible to determine an individual's capacity but irrelevant if it is possible to do so. Suppose, then, that a feasible technique is devised to determine each individual's capacity to enjoy satisfaction. Suppose, further, that it is discovered by this technique that a hundred persons in the United States are enormously more efficient pleasure machines than any others, so that each of these would have to be given an income ten thousand times as large as the income of the next most efficient pleasure machine in order to maximize aggregate utility. Would Lerner be willing to accept the resulting division of income as optimum even though it were entirely consistent with all other objectives (such as maximization of the total to be divided)?[7]

B. INSTITUTIONAL ARRANGEMENTS

There is little discussion, and that not systematic, of techniques for achieving the equalization of income that Lerner takes as the relevant formal condition for an optimum. Though Lerner does not explicitly say so, it is a reasonable inference that he would, in the main, retain the existing techniques for distributing income via payments to owners of resources for the services of those resources. The only basic change would be that ownership of capital resources employed in the collectivist sector would be transferred to the government, and returns to these, as well as the corresponding entrepreneurial income (positive or negative), would accrue to the government. The primary distribution to individuals for the use of their resources might be modified by a "social dividend" and by a personal income tax, which Lerner looks on with favor "where taxation is necessary" (p. 234), though even the income tax "can interfere with the use of resources" (p. 235). "If it is desired to take measures for the equalization of income, it might be better to deal with that through an inheritance and gift tax" (p. 236).

III. UNEMPLOYMENT AND FLUCTUATIONS IN ECONOMIC ACTIVITY

A. FORMAL CONDITIONS

The possibility of changing the amount of resources available to society by investment raises directly the problem of the appropriate amount of investment; indirectly it leads into the dynamic problem of maintaining a stable high level of output in a world in which technological development requires continual change in the method of utilizing resources. Lerner dismisses the problem of the appropriate amount of investment as a "political" problem. He devotes considerable attention to the dynamic problem of fluctuations in output and investment. The analysis is strictly Keynesian and entirely concerned with the danger of general

7. This argument is essentially taken from Henry C. Simons, *Personal Income Taxation* (Chicago: University of Chicago Press, 1938), pp. 5–15.

equilibrium at a low level of output and employment. Though much of it is worded in terms of the "trade cycle" or "business cycle," there is no real discussion of the business cycle. The explanation of "the fundamental cause of the business cycle" on pages 296 and 297 is a masterful evasion of the problem. The "fundamental cause" turns out to be (1) the possibility of a stable long-run level of low output and employment and (2) the fact that there is a business cycle.[8]

Lerner therefore states the formal condition for maintaining a stable high level of output and employment as the maintenance of adequate aggregate demand. This is nowhere spelled out in fuller detail, nor is there any systematic discussion of the criteria in terms of which "adequacy" is to be judged. It is implied that the level of employment is the primary general criterion and "full" employment the chief objective. It is implied also, however,

---

8. "The fundamental cause of the business cycle is the inadequacy of demand" (p. 296). "At an income corresponding to full employment the gap between income and equilibrium consumption is very large. . . . This level of income can be maintained only if there is sufficient investment to fill the gap. But this tremendous level of investment is very much more than it is profitable to maintain for very long. *If such a position of full employment should be reached,* the opportunities of investment would soon begin to be used up and investment would decline. This sets in motion the cumulative processes of crisis and depression. . . . With little investment going on for a long time, *opportunities for investment accumulate* that are profitable even at the very low income level. *When some investment starts,* this raises income and so . . . we now have a cumulative movement upward. . . . The impetus of the expansion may carry it up to full employment or it may stop before that level is reached" (p. 297). (Italics mine.) The inadequacy of demand alone would explain a continued low level of income; the italicized statements are clearly crucial to the conversion of the low level of income into cyclical fluctuations. The first simply starts the analysis going; the other two do no more than to assert that there is a cycle. In terms of Lerner's analysis alone, one would expect the "crisis and depression" to stop at the low level of employment that can be permanently maintained in light of the inadequacy of demand. If this occurred, no opportunities for investment would accumulate, since current investment would exploit all the limited opportunities for investment currently becoming available. In order to get a cycle it is essential that the decline be "cumulative" and go further than the low level of employment that the inadequate demand would permanently support. But clearly the inadequacy of demand is no explanation why this should occur. Note that even the "inadequacy of demand" is supported only by adjectives—"very large," "tremendous." The numerical example Lerner gives—which presumably suggests what these adjectives mean to him—indicates very much larger savings than statistical evidence suggests as reasonable in peacetime.

that there is little or no danger of rising prices or inflation so long as full employment has not been attained, giving the impression that Lerner considers stability of prices an equally good criterion of the adequacy of aggregate demand.

B. INSTITUTIONAL ARRANGEMENTS

Lerner would handle the problem of maintaining adequate aggregate demand through "functional finance," which is defined as "the principle of . . . judging fiscal measures only by their effects or the way they *function* in society" (p. 302 n.). Lerner's discussion of functional finance is a brilliant exercise in logic. It strips governmental fiscal instruments to their essentials: taxing and spending, borrowing and lending, and buying and selling; and throws into sharp relief the function of each. In the process it throws into discard conventional patterns of expression, verbal clichés which at times embody valid implications of more subtle reasoning but which, taken by themselves, muddle analysis of the effect of governmental actions. Reading Lerner's discussion of functional finance is almost sure to induce a much-required reorganization of the mental filing case that one has been using to classify the factors involved in governmental fiscal operations. But for our present purpose the relevant question is whether the discussion of "functional finance," besides being a logical exercise, is also a prescription for public policy. The answer, it seems to this reviewer, is clearly negative. Once again, what looks like a prescription evaporates into an expression of good intentions:

> The government decides on the buying and selling that is socially desirable for all sorts of particular reasons. Then it undertakes such taxation and pays out such bonuses as are justified by special particular circumstances. . . . If there is insufficient total demand, so that there is unemployment, the government will lend money (or repay debt) to lower the rate of interest until the rate of investment is at the level it considers proper, and it will reduce taxes or increase bonuses until the level of consumption is enough, together with the investment, to produce full employment [pp. 314–15].

To make this into a prescription to "produce full employment," Lerner must tell us how to know when there is "insufficient total demand," whether this insufficiency is a temporary deficiency in the process of being corrected or the beginning of an increasing deficiency that, if left alone, will lead to drastic deflation. He must tell us how to know what medicine to use when a diagnosis has been made, how large a dose to give, and how long we may expect it to take for the medicine to be effective. The casual reader of Lerner's book—or, for that matter, of the majority of works on the control of the business cycle—might suppose that these are simple questions. A glance at a few monthly time series depicting the movement of important economic magnitudes, preferably subdivided regionally and by industries, and a brief review of attempts at restrospective identification, current diagnosis, and forecasting suggest that they are anything but simple.

As Burns and Mitchell say:

> Our examination of business indexes, and less definitely of business annals, forbade us to think of business cycles "as sweeping smoothly upward from depressions to a single peak of prosperity and then declining steadily to a new trough." On the contrary, the expansion and contraction of many cycles seem to be interrupted by movements in the opposite direction, and some cycles apparently have double or triple peaks or troughs.[9]

Not all economic activities participate in what, after the event, may be judged a cyclical expansion or contraction, and those that do, participate in uneven measure and with variable timing. Serious investigators seeking to establish a chronology of business cycles from past records agree in the main about the movements they regard as cyclical but differ in not unimportant detail in the dates they set for peaks and troughs.[10] Contemporary interpreters of the course of business have notoriously failed not only to predict the course of business but even to identify the current state of affairs. It is not at all abnormal for some to assert that we are in the early stages of deflation and others that we are entering into an inflation.[11]

9. Arthur F. Burns and Wesley C. Mitchell, *Measuring Business Cycles* (New York: National Bureau of Economic Research, 1946), p. 7. Quotation within quotation from Mitchell, *Business Cycles: The Problem and Its Setting* (New York: National Bureau of Economic Research, 1927), p. 329.

10. See Burns and Mitchell, *op. cit.*, chap. iv, esp. pp. 91–114.

11. This has clearly been true during much of 1946 and 1947. An interesting earlier case, called to my attention by Arthur F. Burns, is the 1920–21 contraction. The National Bureau of Economic Research sets January, 1920, as the peak of the cycle and September, 1921, as the succeeding trough (Burns and Mitchell, *op. cit.*,

 An easy answer to these difficulties is to say that they are ir-relevant; that the government should act on its best estimate of the state of affairs and should take measures of whatever magni-tude seems appropriate; and that errors in these actions are unim-portant, since they can be corrected quickly. If deflationary ac-tion is taken, and turns out to have been unnecessary, the govern-ment can simply reverse itself and turn on the inflationary spigot; if the action was too drastic or not drastic enough, the government can then turn down or up the appropriate spigot. This answer is, of course, too easy. It conflicts with the hard fact that neither government action nor the effect of that action is instantaneous. There is likely to be a lag between the need for action and govern-ment recognition of this need; a further lag between recognition of the need for action and the taking of action; and a still further lag between the action and its effects. If these time lags were short relative to the duration of the cyclical movements government is

---

p. 78). Yet in May, 1920, the National City Bank said in its monthly letter on *Economic Conditions, Governmental Finance, United States Securities:* "General trade is good in all parts of the country," and in June: "It would be a mistake to assume that we are on the eve of immediate deflation on a large scale." As late as September, 1920, the letter reported: "The general business situation in our opinion has been developing in a satisfactory manner during the past month. . . . The general trend is toward normal and permanent conditions. . . . The recession of industrial activity which is under way is not severe enough to be alarming." In October: "General business is moving along in a reasonably satisfactory manner. . . . There is good reason to think that in the industries that have been most disturbed the price reductions have gone about as far as they will in the near future." Not until the November, 1920, letter was there explicit recognition of the existence of a serious recession. That letter reported: "The expectations indulged in during the summer that the state of depression which was affecting certain of the industries would disappear with the opening of the fall season has not been realized; on the contrary, business is generally receding and there is no longer room for doubt that the country has passed the crest of the post-war boom." The December, 1920, letter said: "The downward movement of prices of which the first signs appeared last May, and which became quite evident in October, has become more general and precipitate in the last month. The hopes that had been entertained that the descent to a lower level would be accomplished . . . gradually . . . have proven illusory. Rarely, if ever, has there been so great a decline in commodity prices in so short a time."

One of the leading and best-informed observers of current business conditions thus failed to recognize the existence of one of the sharpest contractions on record until it was almost half over.

trying to counteract, they would be of little importance. Unfortunately, it is likely that the time lags are a substantial fraction of the duration of the cyclical movements. In the absence, therefore, of a high degree of ability to predict correctly both the direction and the magnitude of required action, governmental attempts at counteracting cyclical fluctuations through "functional finance" may easily intensify the fluctuations rather than mitigate them. By the time an error is recognized and corrective action taken, the damage may be done, and the corrective action may itself turn into a further error.[12] This prescription of Lerner's, like others, thus turns into an exhortation to do the right thing with no advice how to know what is the right thing to do.

IV. The Relation between the Formal Conditions for an Optimum and Institutional Arrangements

The chief general criticism implicit in the preceding sections is that Lerner writes as if it were possible to base conclusions about appropriate institutional arrangements almost exclusively on analysis of the formal conditions for an optimum. Unfortunately, this cannot be done. It has been long known that there are alternative institutional arrangements that would enable the formal conditions for an optimum to be attained. Furthermore, the institutional arrangements adopted are likely to have important non-

12. There is much confusion on this point, largely because of an erroneous application of the statistical "law of large numbers" which leads to the belief that government needs to guess right only a little more than half the time to achieve some success in mitigating cyclical fluctuations. This is incorrect. If a number of random disturbances, each varying by about the same amount, are added, their mean tends to fluctuate less than any one of the disturbances, and in this sense, the errors tend to cancel out; but their sum tends to fluctuate more than any one of the disturbances, and the larger the number of disturbances added, the larger the fluctuations in the sum. The effects of countercyclical actions of government are added to, not averaged with, the economic movements that would otherwise take place. If the countercyclical actions of government were entirely random disturbances, unrelated in any systematic fashion to the other movements, they would tend to increase the amplitude of cyclical movements. A slight ability to guess correctly would, therefore, serve only to mitigate or eradicate this undesirable effect, and a considerable ability to guess correctly would be required to convert government action into a stabilizing influence. See "The Effects of a Full-Employment Policy on Economic Stability: A Formal Analysis," *supra,* pp. 117–32.

economic implications. So it is necessary both to make a choice and to introduce additional criteria in making the choice.

Some fifty years ago Pareto pointed out that the equilibrium allocation of resources in a freely competitive society based on private property is identical with the allocation that should be sought by a socialist state striving to achieve a maximum of "ophelimity" and that, on the formal level alone, totalitarian direction might achieve the same allocation of resources as a free price system (i.e., both might solve the same equations).[13] More recently, Taylor, Lange, Lerner, and others have outlined the form of organization for a socialist society, discussed briefly above, in which the individual productive units would "play" at competition and thereby reproduce the results of a competitive-enterprise economy.[14] Another arrangement that would accomplish the same end, given sufficient information, is to impose taxes and grant bounties so devised as to induce monopolists to set prices at the levels that would prevail under competition. Lerner in this book adds yet another device, counterspeculation, and it would doubtless be possible to construct still other institutional arrangements that, judged solely on a formal level, would permit the conditions for an optimum to be satisfied.

None of these arrangements will, of course, operate perfectly in practice. The most that can be expected is a reasonable approximation to the economic optimum. They must, therefore, be judged in part by (1) the practical administrative problems entailed in so operating them as to approximate the economic optimum and (2) as a corollary, the extent to which they lend themselves to abuse, that is, the ease with which they can be used for objectives other than the general welfare. Economic institutions do not operate in a vacuum. They form part, and an extremely important part, of the social structure within which individuals live. They must also be judged by (3) their noneconomic implications, of which the political implications—the implications for

13. Vilfredo Pareto, *Cours d'économie politique* (Lausanne, 1897), Vol. II, Book II, chap. ii, pars. 717–24, pp. 84–95. Pareto, of course, went further and discussed also some of the nonformal considerations appropriate to the choice.

14. Oscar Lange and Fred M. Taylor, *On the Economic Theory of Socialism,* ed. Benjamin E. Lippincott (Minneapolis: University of Minnesota Press, 1938).

individual liberty—are probably of the most interest and the ethical implications the most fundamental.

As already noted, Lerner neither discusses nor even appears to recognize the first two bases for judging the appropriateness of economic institutions. He clearly recognizes the importance of the third—indeed, he states in the Preface that recognition of the importance of political implications was largely responsible for leading him to alter the character of the book from a discussion of a completely collectivist society to a discussion of a society which retains large elements of private property and free enterprise—but he explicitly rules out systematic discussion of political implications. "In this study we shall not go into the merits of this political issue. We shall assume a government that wishes to run society in the general social interest and is strong enough to override the opposition afforded by any sectional interest" (p. 6). The only other comment of any substance on this issue is a brief discussion of "the significance of private enterprise as one of the guarantees of the freedom of the individual." There is a sound basis, he says,

for this argument even if it is often distorted by fanatical capitalists who identify the freedom of the individual with the license of the capitalist millionaire or even with the economic powers of giant corporations. . . . The liberty of the individual obtained its first start in modern times with the freeing of private enterprise and . . . the possibility for the individual of finding a means of livelihood outside of employment by the state can be a check on undue subservience to the employers who represent the state. Of course this is one only of many forces that must be developed and maintained if democracy is to be preserved and by itself it can not guarantee democracy, but anything that may contribute to the safeguarding of democracy is of great value.

The controlled economy may consider that even some sacrifice of efficiency in the allocation of resources is worth while as a contribution to the safeguard of democracy, though the kind of government that would take this into account could put up adequate safeguards even if it were 100 per cent collectivist [pp. 84–85].

(But would it or could it stay the same government if it became 100 per cent collectivist?)

It would be unfair to Lerner to end without stressing again that the distribution of space in this review is very different from the distribution of space in the book. The book is at one and the same time (1) an elementary text in economic principles written from a novel point of view and emphasizing formal analysis rather than descriptive material and (2) a tract for the times advocating a "controlled economy." Most of the book is devoted to teaching principles, though the tone of a tract permeates it all. Most of this review is devoted to the tract.

The proposals in the book have considerable suggestive value and may stimulate others to useful and important work in developing them. The book throughout reveals Lerner's very considerable gifts—his acuteness as a theorist and dialectician, his skill and patience in exposition, his flexibility of mind, his profound interest in social welfare, and his willingness to accept and courage to state what seems to him right social policy, regardless of precedent or accepted opinion. In the reviewer's judgment, however, these gifts have been imperfectly realized because they have been employed in a vacuum and have not been combined with a realistic appraisal of the administrative problems of economic institutions or of their social and political implications.

Index

Index

Alchian, Armen A., 19 n., 21 n.
Alexander, Sidney S., 33 n.
Allen, Edward D., 101 n.
Allen, R. G. D., 64 n.
Allocation of resources; *see* Resources, allocation of
Andrews, P. W. S., 31 n.
Assets, 147, 150, 155, 208, 211, 246, 254, 269
Assumptions, 69, 70, 71, 72, 79, 81, 119, 302, 308; methodological role of, 14–16, 23–24, 26, 28, 40
Average cost pricing, 33

Bach, G. L., 131 and n.
Bacon, Nathaniel, 81 n.
Bagehot, Walter, 218
Balance of payments: methods of adjusting, 159–73; timing of adjustment, 182–87
Banking Act of 1844; *see* English Banking Act of 1844
Banks, 135, 136, 139, 150, 217, 218, 219, 220, 222, 241, 257, 265, 266, 267, 268, 269, 273
Basing-point pricing, 27
Beale, W. T. M., Jr., 220 n.
Bennett, M. K., 205 n., 221 n., 222 n., 224 n., 227 n.
Bernstein, Joel, 157 n.
Berry, D., 101 n.
Bishop, R. L., 39 n.
Borgatta, Gino, 101 n.
Boulding, K. E., 50 n., 68 n., 73 n., 101 n.
Brady, Dorothy S., 3 n.
Break, George F., 102 n.
Bricks, as monetary commodity, 212–13
Brown, E. Cary, 119 n.
Brownlee, O. H., 101 n.
Budget, government; *see* Government budget
Burns, Arthur F., 3 n., 47 n., 133 n., 314 and n.
Business cycle: control of, 117–32, 133–56, 265, 311–16; effects of monetary standards on, 207–9, 211, 233–35, 242, 244; theory of, 42, 262, 312

Cambridge School, 42
Capital flight, 175, 189
Cash balances, 66, 67, 78, 225–58, 279–80
Casual empiricism, 279–80, 289–92, 299
Ceteris paribus, 47, 48–49, 58, 74, 79, 80
Chamberlin, E. H., 38 and n., 39
Chang, Ching-Gwan, 119 n.
Clark, J. B., 88 n., 90
Clark, John M., 119 n.
Collectivist sector, 305, 306–7
Committee for Economic Development, 138 n.
Commodities: in commodity reserve currency, 223–29, 246; in demand analysis, 36, 51, 57–59, 77, 79, 80
Commodity-reserve currency, 204–50; commodities to be included under, 223–29; compared with fiat currency, 249–50; compared with gold standard, 239–41, 248; countercyclical effects of, 233–35; and international trade, 237–39; price behavior under, 229–32; provision for secular growth of, 235–37
Commodity standard: countercyclical effects of, 207–9, 211, 233–35; defined, 205; partial, 206, 214–20; strict, 206–14
Compensating variations: in income, 52, 54; in other prices, 51, 53, 55
Competition: imperfect, 15, 37, 38–39, 280–81; perfect, 15, 34, 37, 305, 306, 317
Competitive firm, definition of, 35–36
Competitive order, 134
Consumer's rent, 95
Consumer's surplus, 65, 68–72, 73, 81, 87, 96
Controls, 6, 161, 203, 204; over allocation of resources, 305; as anti-inflation device, 260, 263, 264, 273; over foreign trade, 167–70, 172, 186, 197, 201, 202, 203
Cooper, Gershon, 13 n.

323